DARING TO FIND
OUR NAMES

**Recent Titles in
the Beta Phi Mu Monograph Series**

"An Active Instrument for Propaganda": The American Library During World War I
Wayne A. Wiegand

Libraries and Scholarly Communication in the United States: The Historical Dimension
Phyllis Dain and John Y. Cole, editors

Carnegie Denied: Communities Rejecting Carnegie Library Construction Grants, 1898–
1925
Robert Sidney Martin, editor

Publishing and Readership in Revolutionary France and America: A Symposium at the
Library of Congress, Sponsored by the Center for the Book and the European Division
Carol Armbruster, editor

DARING TO FIND OUR NAMES

The Search for Lesbigay Library History

EDITED BY
JAMES V. CARMICHAEL, JR.

Beta Phi Mu Monograph Series, Number 5

GREENWOOD PRESS
Westport, Connecticut • London

Library of Congress Cataloging-in-Publication Data

Daring to find our names : the search for lesbigay library history /
  edited by James V. Carmichael, Jr.
        p.   cm.—(Beta Phi Mu monograph series, ISSN 1041–2751 ; no. 5)
    Includes bibliographical references and index.
    ISBN 0–313–29963–3 (alk. paper)
    1. Gay librarians—History.   2. Lesbian librarians—History.
  3. Gay librarians—United States—History.   4. Lesbian librarians—
  United States—History.   5. Libraries and gays—History.
  6. Libraries and lesbians—History.   7. Libraries and gays—United
  States—History.   8. Libraries and lesbians—United States—History.
  I. Carmichael, James Vinson, Jr.   II. Series.
  Z682.4.G39D37   1998
  020′.86′63—dc21   97–48579

British Library Cataloguing in Publication Data is available.

Library of Congress Catalog Card Number: 97–48579
ISBN: 0–313–29963–3
ISSN: 1041–2751

First published in 1998

Greenwood Press, 88 Post Road West, Westport, CT 06881
An imprint of Greenwood Publishing Group, Inc.

Printed in the United States of America

The paper used in this book complies with the
Permanent Paper Standard issued by the National
Information Standards Organization (Z39.48–1984).

10 9 8 7 6 5 4 3 2 1

By viewing the past from the present, historians know full well (or they should) the risks they run of distorting the vision of what they describe. The greater the contrast between the present and past, the greater the risks of distortion. The dangers are further intensified when the moral foundations of the present order rest, even remotely, on the ruins of the old order being described.

— C. Vann Woodward, "The Primal Code"

Out there, in America, our faces are withdrawn and remote, made eccentric by isolation. On Columbus Avenue, collective loneliness is a stable element. It has culture-making properties.

—Vivian Gornick, *Approaching Eye Level*

In memory of John Richard Noonan (1957–1994)

Contents

Acknowledgments

This collection grew from three papers presented at the Summer 1995 conference of the American Library Association (ALA) in Chicago. The session, entitled "The Importance of Lesbigay Library History," represented a joint venture on the part of ALA's Library History Round Table and the Social Responsibilities Round Table of which the Gay, Lesbian and Bisexual Task Force is a part, and as such, it was the first general ALA session on lesbigay issues in the Task Force's twenty-five-year history. After the conference, at the suggestion of noted library historian Wayne A. Wiegand, I approached the librarians' honorary association, Beta Phi Mu, about the possibility of publishing a collection on lesbigay library history, and received unqualified support from that organization's president, Dr. Mary Biggs of the College of New Jersey. Greenwood Press, which carries the Beta Phi Mu monographic series, gave similar immediate support in the person of Dr. George Butler. It was proposed that proceeds of the book could, contrary to the usual practice, be divided equally among the Justin Winsor Scholarship Fund of the Library History Round Table, The Gay Book Award Fund of the Task Force, and Beta Phi Mu. The Board of Beta Phi Mu graciously consented to this proposal, and the Task Force's then-co-chair, Roland Hansen, counseled me about proper ALA procedures for making these arrangements. All of the authors, without exception, gave immediate backing to this plan, and I hope it may inspire similar agreements in the future from other academic authors and editors, whose personal benefit from such ventures are small enough, but who may make a significant difference in establishing and maintaining funds from which future scholars may draw.

I owe much to my close association with superlative professional and personal models: historian Wayne A. Wiegand of the School of Information and Library Studies at the University of Wisconsin-Madison, who first encouraged my own closeted research agenda; Marilyn Miller, Professor Emeritus and Former Chair, the Department of Library and Information Studies, the University of North Carolina at Greensboro, the first American Library Association President to defend the rights of lesbians and gays in the profession; Edward G. Holley, Kenan Professor Emeritus and Former Dean, School of Information and Library Studies, the University of North Carolina at Chapel Hill, friend, mentor, and surrogate father, whose faith in me has never failed; library historians Pam Richards, Suzanne Hildenbrand, Peggy Sullivan, Laurel Grotzinger, Mark Tucker, and Lee Shiflett, whose perceptiveness, enthusiasm and friendship for far longer than the course of this project has meant more than they probably realize; gay activists Barbara Gittings and Louie Crew, who have served as ideological touchstones and unstintingly generous friends since I discovered them in 1978; contributor Israel Fishman, who bared his soul; and Janet Cooper, whose thoughtful analysis of political power and gay activism she has shared generously over the past several years; the late Lester E. Asheim, Kenan Professor Emeritus, the University of North Carolina at Chapel Hill, whose endless curiosity and disdain for academic snobbery never stood in the way of his "accurate naming of the things of God"; James T. Sears, whose invaluable work on southern gay history has opened up my own regional heritage to me; my sisters Mary Emma Stewart and Elizabeth Oliver, who have never allowed me to feel unloved; my feline family—Babette, Nanette, Cosima, and Doolah—who have been forgiving about my absences and editorial preoccupations; Jim Marks, a gay man who for more than twenty years has inspired in me the courage to equal my bravado; and Nick Woods, a straight man from Haywards Heath, UK, to whom I owe a sustaining friendship that has endured for over thirty-three years. I should also mention the incomparable value of friends in my current life: Marilyn Shontz and Kathy Franks; Nancy Busch and Virginia Nelson; Ranny Umberger and Benjamin Keaton; Jim Holt and Michael Randall; and Debra Wagner White. As Emily Dickinson wrote, "My friends are my estate."

I also am deeply grateful to all of the contributors to this volume who have become close as well as "family." In the process of compiling these essays, James D. Woods of New York, who originally was to have been a contributor to this volume, died, and I will always remember his gracious enthusiasm for the project. Jim Kepner, whose chapter appears herein, died on November 15, 1997, just as the manuscript was entering the final phase of assemblage; I feel privileged indeed to have known him. Finally, I am especially grateful to my fellow historian and friend, Dr. Plummer Alston Jones, Jr., who volunteered to prepare the index for this volume "for the good of the order."

I wish to acknowledge the significant contributions of personnel at Greenwood Press for their comments, suggestions, and superb editorial work, notably by my production editor, Betty Pessagno. Any remaining errors in the resulting volume are my own.

Finally, I thank all of my students for letting me be a part of their lives, and letting me share my emerging ideas with them in class. I particularly want to thank Betty Moore and Ben Lea, who helped me with transcriptions, Michael Norman, who checked my facts, and Katie Schlee, who proofed the final copy.

There are many other people, some deceased, to whom I owe more than passing thanks for helping to make me the person that I am. I accept that debt willingly, and trust that the present volume justifies at least a part of their faith.

DARING TO FIND
OUR NAMES

Introduction:
Makeover Without a Mirror—
A Face for Lesbigay Library History

James V. Carmichael, Jr.

FACELESSNESS, IMAGE AND FEAR IN LIBRARIANSHIP

A central tenet of professional library rhetoric holds that "libraries change lives." Certainly in the case of the lesbigay population, the meaning of that statement is literally true, for through reading, many lesbigays first find confirmation of their identity and learn that they are not alone. Gay actor Stephen Fry writes of the importance of "slim volume after slim volume cataloguing the pansy path to freedom" (Fry 1997, 86), whether that freedom lies solely in alternative sexuality, or indeed in "freedom of the mind" (87). Given the minority "identity wars" of the 1990s, such a distinction as Fry makes may indeed be critical, for it is not inconceivable that lesbigays may find confirmation of their individual identity not in the lesbigay section of the library collection, but in another section of the library, or in another realm entirely.

In a repressive social climate, responsibility for serving the lesbigay population may carry more weight than many librarians wish to bear. After all, librarians have not always been defined as guardians of the freedom to read; early leaders "avoided controversial literature and endorsed the librarian as moral censor" (Geller 1984 [xv]). Sexology texts such as Havelock Ellis's *Studies in the Psychology of Sex* and Alfred Kinsey's *Sexual Behavior of the Human Male,* as well as novels with a homoerotic theme, such as Radclyffe Hall's *The Well of Loneliness* (1928), were usually available only upon request from the public librarian. Library catalog subject headings and classification schemes placed homosexuality with "sexual perversions" or "criminal behavior," or for more progressive and sympathetic titles, "mental illness" and its analogs, and broad-minded nonfiction generally concerned the psychosocial causes of this "disease" (Streitmayer 1995, 45).

The revolution in personal sexual mores in the 1960s and 1970s was accompanied by a broader judicial distinction between erotica and pornography and more liberal publishing practices, although some of the titles that came under review might seem extremely tame in the present climate: D.H. Lawrence's *Lady Chatterley's Lover*, Henry Miller's *Tropic of Cancer*, William H. Burroughs's *The Naked Lunch,* Ralph Ginsberg's avant-garde magazine *Evergreen Review* (Carmichael 1995a). Not until 1970, however, when the first dissertation on gay behavior was published (Humphreys 1970), was the stage set for changing research conventions concerning homosexuality (Desroches 1990; Murden 1993; Nardi 1995). Since that time, and particularly in the 1990s, lesbigay studies and queer theory have become prolific academic specialties (Taylor 1993), not to mention a profitable publishing venue. The unspeakable has become speakable, even if the hysterical tone of talk-show debate seems to dominate much of the dialogue, and the lingering specters of antigay violence, harassment, and discrimination, some of them egged on by federal law and mandate, serve to remind the lesbigay community of the illusory nature of their achievements. Homosexual "identities"—never mind the definition of that term, sexual act or lifestyle or unfortunate mannerism or eccentricity—can rob their holders instantly of their jobs or even their lives. Without a history, the very "identity" of lesbigays becomes tenuous, an easy picking for the "ism" of the moment, and the gay self gazes into a mirror without reflections. Part of the greater purpose of this volume is to clarify some of the illusions, emotional detritus, and light-barriers that obscure that reflection, using librarianship as a focus.

Since the library, or at least the literature that it housed, was historically paramount to the coming-out process of many lesbigays, it is perhaps not surprising that gays and lesbians in the American Library Association (ALA) formed the first gay professional association in the world in 1970. Since that time, the energies of ALA's Gay, Lesbian and Bisexual Task Force (GLBTF) have been devoted largely to service concerns for lesbigay patrons (Gough and Greenblatt 1990), the development of nonpejorative subject headings and classification schemes (Berman 1981), the bibliographic control (Ridinger 1997) and promotion (Gittings 1978) of lesbigay literature, both through the annual programs of the GLBTF and its annual Gay Book Awards. The ALA has practiced nondiscrimination against lesbigays through its own employment policies since 1974, although it has no jurisdiction over individual libraries. Librarianship generally has acted only as *de facto* midwife to the lesbigay movement, often unwittingly and sometimes unwillingly. Moreover, the ideology of American librarianship as it has evolved historically and the customs of individual practice in different library environments contain elements uncongenial to lesbigay collections, and therefore to research on lesbigay librarians. In the public library, this fact strikes home to the core value of freedom of inquiry expressed in ALA's "The Freedom to Read" Statement (Broderick 1993).

PROFESSIONAL/SOCIOLOGICAL CONTEXT

The characteristics of the classic professions, with which for several decades at least, sociologists seemed secure, traditionally excluded librarianship, teaching, nursing, and social work as "feminized" "semi-professions" (Simpson and Simpson 1969). The niceties of this distinction have been discredited in recent years by economic and social changes beyond the predictive power of the social sciences: the rise of qualitative research, narrative analysis, and meta-analysis (Reissman 1993); the information revolution; increased specialization, the birth of new disciplines, and the realignment of academic departments; and the democratization and "dumbing-down" of professionalization.   Cosmetologists, acupuncturists, massage therapists, domestic engineers (not to mention butlers and well-heeled prostitutes) all have professional associations and meetings, standards for certification, licensure or practice, and codes of ethics.   In an age highly critical of "the arrogance of [traditional] professional expertise," evolving discourse has grown to exalt "the virtues of dispossession" in some quarters (Casey 1996). Structuralists will agree that not all workers deserve to be called professional simply because they are organized, or can limit entree into their ranks, but it is fair to admit that in late twentieth-century American enterprise, "seeming" is more than half of "being."

IMAGE AND THE GENDER PERPLEX

Librarianship suffers an image problem (Wilson 1982), although many of the ramifications of the librarian image are not without humor. Research studies find the public surprisingly supportive and appreciative of librarians (Stevens 1988), even if their social values are middling (Bryan 1952). On an international ranking scale, the library profession's prestige seems stable if somewhat average, but certainly not marginal or imperiled (Treiman 1977). Librarians nevertheless remain inordinately sensitive about their professional image, and at times have monitored it closely in an "image" column in *American Libraries,* the national professional association journal.

All "feminized" professions experience image problems and low self-esteem, and practitioners traditionally lay the blame for this problem at the feet of a benign if repugnant female stereotype (in librarianship, the bespectacled and sexless dotty old maid in bun and sneakers who shushes the smallest titters) and the feminine image of the profession (Newmyer 1976). Practitioners blame everything from low salaries to low morale on the prevalence of females in the profession—an ingenuous argument that denies the more serious charge of the poor treatment that women actually receive in these professions and others (Schiller 1974). More recent research questions the identity of men in feminized professions, the majority of whom identify a feminine or gay *male* stereotype (although many homosexual men are not effeminate at all, and some heterosexual men are), and employ compensating strategies to disassociate themselves from more "feminine" tasks in favor of "masculine" corporate or managerial work (Williams 1989; Carmichael 1992; Williams 1995). Ironically, because men occupy a disproportionate number of administrative positions in teaching, nursing, and librarianship, they may in effect exert an influence on the future direction of their professions that is inimical to feminist interests (Harris 1992).

SEX AND LIBRARIANS

The struggle for lesbigay rights obscures an underlying characteristic of American character that has an impact on gay librarianship: obsession with sex, either what one has to do to attain it (for example, consumer and youth culture) or control it (for example, "family values" rhetoric) (see Cornog and Pepper 1996; Geller 1984). That Americans are both puritanical and hypocritical about sex (D'Emilio and Freedman 1988) can be seen in the recent military don't-ask-don't-tell recruitment initiative toward homosexuals,[1] Penisgate at The White House, and ambivalence about the culpability of heterosexual adulterers in the service. The judicial climate also makes clear that sex in the workplace is taboo, and that the workplace is in many cases more sacrosanct than the home. Professional ethics require that impersonal probity should govern all professional relationships, but, at least since the Industrial Revolution, the home has been the place where official codes of behavior could be dropped (Dubbert 1979). While it is true that the courts have become choked with sexual discrimination and harassment suits, it is less clear who is the oppressor and who is the oppressed. It is tempting but probably foolish to assume that gender parity of a sort is in process of being achieved in the workplace, in the home, or in the courts.

PROFESSIONAL CULTURE

Library conferences and literature of the 1990s challenge readers and listeners to "reinvent the librarian," although advertisements, rhetoric, and letters in *Library Journal* and *American Libraries* suggest that the makeover is more cosmetic than curative, a generic and ironically antiquated adaptation of corporate manner, dress, and style, which along with the technological gospel of the 1990s, promises more professional status than it delivers (Special Libraries Association 1990; Stevens 1988). At the same time that industry has adapted the dressed-down workaholism/creativity of Microsoft Corporation as a model of productivity, many librarians are still wandering through the maze of "quality circles" only to learn that not much has really changed. The big-business alliance between librarianship and computer software vendors seems to echo the traditional relationship between librarian and publishers, but the stakes are higher during a period when many jobs are being outsourced, de-professionalized, or downgraded to part-time specialties. Librarians are not connected to the computer industry and the creators of its software in the same way they are related to publishers because libraries constitute a smaller market share of the computer business than they do the book and journal business. Moreover, the volume of computer rhetoric in journals, speeches, and products outstrips the ability of some librarians to absorb any but a small part of it; technologically literate teenaged patrons can now outperform librarians who are employed to help them. Meanwhile, the increase in customer demand sparked by Internet searching and database use leaves little room for speculation about the future of professional enrichment in terms of badly-needed staff training.

There are numerous voices of dissent, some protesting the denigration of the humanities (Broderick 1997), others the loss of integrity in professional roles (Harris 1992), but relatively few librarians heed substantive philosophical conflicts as the profession strives to keep abreast with innovation. In this environment of technological crisis, the historical identity, role, and future of lesbigay librarians may seem to strike an insignificant, possibly even a dangerously narcissistic note indeed (Cronin 1995, for example, is a critic).[2]

PUBLIC LIBRARIANSHIP

American librarianship, with its unique emphasis on tax-supported free public library service, embodies its own historical contradictions. Libraries, after all, mirror the societies in which they are situated. From the inception in 1854 of America's first tax-supported library in Boston, theories of social utility were always near at hand, no doubt in part because of the peculiar brand of Christianity embraced by the New England divines. Admittedly, Calvinism, with its emphasis on worldly success as a sign of divine favor, embodied a rigid illogic and dualism at odds with the holistic and unitary message of the Gospels. That education was central to the colony of Massachusetts as early as 1647 when the "Satan Deluder" Law was passed, making education compulsory, reflected the view that education was the only weapon against the wickedness bred by ignorance. Americans were not predisposed to value the intellectual pursuits of "effeminate gownsmen" for their own sake (Dubbert 1979, 57; Hofstadter 1963, 188), so that Gilded Age library advocates often questioned the value of literature that did not seek to instruct as "pernicious trash" (Carmichael 1995a). It did not strain this philosophical foundation to fashion library collections that would instruct immigrants in the prevailing value system while at the same time supporting a lucrative publishing market, especially in the years when Literary Culture held full sway (c.1880 to c.1930, for example, until at least the birth of "talkies"). The unreckoned costs of inherent contradictions in this utilitarian approach became evident in the post-Warhol era when funding for the arts and humanities was threatened at the national and at the local level, and public library service in several states was relegated to the level of popular entertainments—to the Parks and Recreation budget line in California, for example. At the same time, recent surveys fault many public libraries' gay collections as inadequate, if they exist at all (Murden 1993; Bryant 1995), and even in some large urban public libraries, homosexual users and their informational needs seem to be only dimly understood (Joyce and Schrader 1997).

ACADEMIC LIBRARIANSHIP

The great diversity in regional variation, institution type, funding base, and mission among the 2,800 or so institutions of higher education makes any generalization about them difficult to sustain. Censorship incidents are not unknown in college libraries, and are not necessarily confined to institutions with denominational ties (Schrader et al. 1989; Bukoff 1992). One of the most famous academic freedom cases involved the librarian of Montana State University who had been fired for protesting the efforts of the Board of Trustees to remove a questionable title (McReynolds 1997).   During the student revolutions of the 1960s, libraries were the object of vandalism and takeover—a symbol of authority. It is ironic, then, that libraries and the university campuses that housed them came to be associated with left-wing politics and liberality in the 1980s, although in the politically correct 1990s, the left has become increasingly doctrinaire and liberality is therefore harder to define. In Canada, censorship incidents occur mainly in denominational colleges, and lesbigay titles are among those challenged (Schrader et al. 1989; Kinsman 1996, 361, 390–93). Approximately one-twelfth of U.S. colleges and universities operate under policies or guidelines that prohibit antigay discrimination and harassment, and only fifteen campuses had a Lesbigay Task Force as of 1992 (*The Gay Almanac* 1996, 152).   Generally, however, in nondenominational colleges and universities, campus sexual taboos are confined to student-professor misconduct (Blythe et al. 1993). Increasing numbers of campus lesbigay organizations, lesbigay listservs, and gay studies programs presage a more open climate, one favorable to lesbigay research. But no such research has been forthcoming from lesbigay academic librarians, although they have contributed refinements to classification and subject heading schemes.

Logically, academic librarians are well suited to perform research because many professional positions call for multiple masters' degrees and specialties in their job announcements. Academic librarians are more in the habit of doing research, and their normal career expectations include the possibility of publication, which in fact, many of them do (Steuart 156–57). Yet the rewards for research are not always equal for academic librarians and faculty.   Although the library is touted as the "heart of the university," the academic librarian in many environments works under a different reward system than does the professorate. Academic librarians have deliberated the dubious benefits of faculty status for academic librarians *ad nauseam* (see Johnson 1992, for example, for a partial inventory of the ongoing debate), particularly if attendant tenure-track duties require research and publication efforts beyond the forty- to sixty-hour work week. Attempts to upgrade bibliographic instruction courses to required or even elective curricular status have in most cases proven futile, and in understaffed libraries, such programs overtax already overworked librarians. What research does emanate from the academic library sector usually is managerial or technical in nature, perhaps because the role of the librarian essentially supports or supplements the central teaching and research functions of full-time faculty and has no apparent importance in and of itself to many faculty observers.

SPECIAL LIBRARIES

Libraries in the corporate, private, and government sectors also serve a supportive role, although librarians in this environment also exert more autonomy. Special librarians generally receive the highest salaries but are under the most pressure to prove the existence of their work to the parent organization by the addition of value-added features, especially when the business cycle is in retrograde. Special libraries range from one-person operations to massive information centers, and comprise such types as business, hospital, law, and government agency libraries.

Over half of Fortune 1000 companies have employment policies that contain nondiscrimination clauses for lesbigays, as do over twenty federal agencies. There are over sixty lesbigay employee groups (*The Gay Almanac* 1996, 153). Progressive companies exert considerable pressure in the forty-one states that do not prohibit antigay discrimination through relocation decisions and negotiations. Moreover, the lesbigay market niche has become an important factor in market considerations.

While corporate policies may create an ideal climate for lesbigay research, special librarians have little incentive to produce such studies unless they bear directly upon the parent organization's research and development priorities, case law, or health issues.[3] In competitive corporate settings, special librarians also operate under constraints of confidentiality; freedom of access to information applies only to authorized employees. In other words, studies dealing solely with professional library issues are not appropriate in such an environment, because the librarian's role is essentially supportive, and often, economically unstable.

SCHOOL MEDIA CENTERS AND SERVICES FOR CHILDREN AND YOUTH

By far the most hostile environments for lesbigay librarians, both school media centers (SMCs) and children's and youth departments in public libraries have come under attack for holding controversial titles in their collections dealing with adult themes, but no subject area receives as many challenges as does homosexuality. Although exploratory essays indicate that some lesbigay teachers are more vocal than previously (e.g., Harbeck 1992),[4] conditions throughout portions of the United States do not favor lesbigay activism of any sort in schools.

The school media specialist may be subject to pressure from parents, teachers, and school boards to justify the content of the SMC collection in terms of state-mandated curricula, and usually, the school budget leaves little room for experimentation in recreational reading matter. Within the education field, school media services are considered ancillary to the teaching function, because use of school media is not required in teacher education programs. Much of the effort expended by the American Association of School Librarians over the past several decades concerns making the SMC more central to curricular decisions and teaching.

Right-wing attacks on children's and youth services collections in public libraries take the form of theft, mutilation, and challenges to selection decisions. These actions frequently target books dealing with homosexual themes, although other subjects, such as the supernatural (Halloween), horror (the Goosebump Series), or themes dealing with conflict with authority also may arouse community sentiment. In the past several years, however, *Daddy's Roommate* and *Heather Has Two Mommies*, which deal with same-sex parents, top the chart of censorship incidents ("Gay Publications Under Fire" 1994; "OIF Says Gay Titles Top" 1994) and indicate "fundamental" dis-ease with the subject of homosexuality generally, and confusion between explication of gay issues on one hand and gay advocacy on the other, in particular.

Moreover, children's and youth services librarianship are considered, along with school media services, the most feminized and low prestige subfields within librarianship. Work with children generally is denigrated in the U.S. marketplace, whatever rhetoric government officials lend to the importance of adult role modeling, reading programs, and literacy (Miller and Shontz 1995). Librarians follow suit, as they did in 1993 when the Directors of the Public Library Association nixed ALA President Marilyn Miller's initiative of "Billions of Bucks for Books for Kids." Children's librarians have received little support for research, as have school media specialists, and they have developed their own professional ideology, value systems, and literature (Lord 1968).

A 1993 survey found that 52 percent of Americans were against teaching about lesbian or gay orientation. A South Carolina study reported that eight out of ten prospective teachers and two-thirds of school counselors had negative feelings about homosexuality, lesbians, and gay men (*The Gay Almanac* 1996, 182) in spite of the fact that lesbigay teens are two to three times as likely to commit suicide. Moreover, 26 percent of lesbigay teenagers are forced to leave home over complications resulting from their homosexuality (246). Thus, even though the discussion of homosexuality has become banal in mainstream media, it is not likely to surface in the literature of the school media specialist or children's librarians, except in urban centers where experimentation with large and diverse populations is encouraged (e.g., Herdt 1993). Nor are gay activists likely to step forward in the schools, because the threat to their jobs is quite real, and the conditions for fostering research of any kind are practically nil.

LIBRARY EDUCATION

Professional service schools have never fit comfortably in the university structure, and the less prestigious among them have been particularly hard-pressed to justify their existence in a period of oversupply and downsizing. Not only do credos of professional service and graduate scholarship frequently clash with university priorities (Division I sports status; corporate or government interests; and the inflexibility of university protocols, admission, and retention criteria, plus emphasis on quantitative evaluative criteria for students *and faculty*), but special professional initiatives (for example, practicums and independent studies) or needs (distance education, minority enrollments, or evening classes) may or may not be equally well accommodated by local conditions. In universities, small or middling programs are discounted in favor of high-prestige specialties like law and medicine, not to mention the undergraduate cash cow, and may face a very imperiled existence indeed except in extraordinary circumstances. Alumni of professional service programs generally do not bring great sums to the university in terms of endowments, scholarships, or grants, and, because enrollments are small, the cost per pupil ratio is higher than average.

Particularly since the Great Society years, library schools have come under more scrutiny from university officials, and some of the most venerated library education programs—among them, Case Western University, Emory University, Peabody School of Education (Vanderbilt University), The University of Chicago, Columbia University, and Brigham Young University—abandoned library education programs during a period of supposedly unparalleled prosperity—The Reagan ·Years. In at least a few of these cases, strong leadership was indeed lacking, although financial exigencies were used to excuse the closures (Paris 1988). Whatever the reasons, these universities saw little future in the low-profile labor-intensity and high cost of library education, never mind its benefits to society.

Library schools represent the logical point of origin from which should issue studies of lesbigay librarianship, yet a national survey of library school graduates in 1995 found that nearly half of them had not received any information about lesbigay issues in their library education programs (Carmichael and Shontz 1996, 43). To date, only the Carmichael and Shontz study, plus one other study of gender attitudes among a gay sub-sample of male librarians (Carmichael 1995a) have appeared in the literature as research studies. Another article addresses the information needs of lesbians (Whitt 1993); and one unpublished dissertation concerns the treatment of lesbigay subjects in reference works (Santavicca 1977). From private conversations with students, graduates, and teaching faculty, plus open-ended responses to the 1996 survey mentioned above, it is obvious that tenure-track library education faculty feel constrained not to become associated with lesbigay research before receiving tenure, and that library schools are anxious for their graduates to do research in more high-prestige specialties like information science, software applications, or refinements to, and applications of, theory from other fields. Similarly, doctoral students are warned not to become labeled as a lesbigay researcher, as it may impair their chances in the job market. Brenda Marston, for example (see Chapter 11), was told there were no sources for studying lesbigay history, yet after she obtained her history degree, she learned that "it was possible" (p. 133) when she "discovered" lesbigay archives work. Ironically, the appearance of the first biographical dissertation about a lesbigay librarian, Laura Bragg, owes its genesis to the efforts of a heterosexual education major who bene-fitted from the counsel of well-known southern gay historian and education professor, James T. Sears, her dissertation director (Allen 1997). In library education, almost totally devoid of lesbigay role models, it is more likely that the efforts of heterosexual educators will need to be deployed in order encourage reluctant lesbigay doctoral students to plunge into lesbigay research.

LIBRARY HISTORY AND BIOGRAPHY

Perhaps not by accident, librarianship has only occasionally been moved to consider its history, including the field of biography, very seriously. Ironically, ALA's first President, Justin Winsor, was a noted historian of Boston, while one of the twentieth century's most prolific and influential librarians, Louis Round Wilson—also an ALA President—was, among other things, a southern historian. The ALA Centennial of 1976, which resulted in a flurry of historical publishing and conference programs, was presided over by a handful of library historians who had learned to incorporate a warts and all biographical approach to venerable worthies (e.g., Williamson 1963; Holley 1963; Sullivan 1976); who assayed and debated revisionist theories about the motives of the founders of public libraries (Harris 1973; and Dain 1975 are the most celebrated examples of this lengthy debate); and who applied feminist historical analysis of a restrained variety (according to Baum 1992, who distinguishes between "liberal" and "radical" feminism). Apparently few library historians devote their research energies exclusively to library history or biography (Carmichael 1991, 338–39). Even with so much "new" professional history at hand, only one professional biography has raised serious questions about the (hetero)sexual behavior of its subject, Melvil Dewey, since that time (Wiegand, W. 1996), and the field generally lacks three-dimensional biography, which treats the less savory personal and professional aspects of its subjects.

The reasons for librarianship's relatively ahistorical predisposition, and the relatively asexual bent of its focus, have been documented elsewhere, although too few nonhistorians have acknowleged these causes: the tendency of contemporaries to describe the subject only in the most laudatory terms, or to limit their criticisms to the professional sphere; the inhibiting craze of slander or defamation suits; and, most importantly, the self-effacing and self-destructive tendency of librarians collectively, who are expert in preserving the records of civilization, but careless about saving their own (Holley 1967, xvi; Wiegand, S. 1994). A spate of librarian autobiographies leave most questions about personal lives unanswered, and many professional ones unasked (e.g., Powell 1968; Shores 1975; Boaz 1987; McPheeters 1988). Without assuming an unnecessarily Freudian stance, it may be asserted that the lack of meaningful personal context calls into question the lucidity of the professional context, and fails to answer important issues of motive, success, failure, and above all, what it means to be a professional librarian.

In a reactionary social climate and volatile workplace conditions, homosexuality is likely to receive less rather than more scholarly attention than it has in the past unless lesbigay librarians take their concerns into the laboratory (the library), the field (the public, defined variously), and the classroom. Whether change will occur and homosexuality will ever cease being "the last socially acceptable prejudice" (Gaughan 1992) does not depend so much on hostile assault upon immutable workplace structures or administrations; it does, however, require authentic voices to represent the many facets of lesbigay identity, even-handed and ethical challenges to homophobic attitudes and practices—conscious or not—and most of all, the unhesitating commitment of lesbigay librarians to share the wealth of their interpretive tradition among themselves and their colleagues and with the general public. The librarian's relationship to the collection, the patron, and the work environment can never be truly neutral, as some would claim: people bring their own experiences and biases to every situation, professional or not (Scott 1996); judicious but honest discussion of issues about which differences exist may lead to a clearer perspective. Without honesty, however—a clear reflection in the mirror—silence engulfs us, and the dark places of our lives remain unillumined. If the Alcoholics Anonymous adage is true, that we can only be as well as our darkest secret, then what can self-revelation, investigation, and public discussion unveil that is more devastating than the silence and submission of a people afraid to speak their names?

FACELIFTS: ADOPTING NEW RESEARCH ATTITUDES

While library historians have demonstrated an increasingly sophisticated mastery over historical research and narrative techniques in the past several decades, they have not yet fully assimilated an appreciation of various postmodern approaches to narrative discourse and analysis.[5] While in general, library historians are scrupulous in their observation of the formal requirements of oral history, cautious in their avoidance of narrative fallacies, and creative in their use of an increasingly varied arsenal of documentary evidence and aggregate statistical compilation (for example, prosopographical studies such as those of Dain 1991; and Passet 1994), exceptions to the rule of an ontological void in historical and biographical research are rare (for example, all but a few of the biographical sketches in Hildenbrand 1996, refute the traditional sunny, narcoleptic pastiche).

To these relatively minor shortcomings—minor, if one accepts *a priori* the importance of library history as a reflection of the central cultural impulses of society—lesbigay history and research from other fields brings new voices and insights. Black history and women's herstory led the way to deconstruction of western male "history," but gay liberation was "the most thoroughly postmodern" of discourses (Darsey, 1991, 44, quoted in Casey, 1995–96, 227), although like feminist and black identity, "theoretical work in lesbian and gay studies de-essentialized the once apparently stable 'homosexuality' that inquiries had sought to explain, defend, and make visible as a positive life choice" (Patton 1993, 82, quoted in Casey 1995–96, 227). This volatility leaves gay historians to address the traditionally human questions that perceptive biographers have always asked: Whom did they love? What kind of persons were they? How did they resolve their individual identities in society? The postmodern critique subjugates questions of consistency, accuracy, and authority to more basic questions of meaning and import (Reisman 1993; Kleinman and Copp 1993; a good example is Casey 1993). Postmodernists speak of versions of historical accounts, rather than one true story. They speak of history from below. To lesbigays, whose self-documentation efforts have been fragmentary and often totally undone by surviving relatives, these versions may be the only microcosmic view of the gay life from the pre-AIDS era (Berman 1996, 123–94).

Such considerations explain to some extent the somewhat nontraditional variety of approaches employed by the authors in this volume, for all demonstrate aspects of the historical frame: first-person historical narrative, documentary accounts, survey and interview (the survey becomes tomorrow's historical fodder), state-of-the-art descriptions, and personal anecdote and reflections, or a combination of all of these. As editor, I also have reserved the right to respect more than one bibliographic style—endnotes, parenthetical references, and reference lists for essays which cite many secondary sources (Carmichael, Kester), and extensive endnotes for historical accounts relying heavily on primary sources (Robbins). These chapters also represent a variety of subdisciplinary approaches and perspectives, although the intent of the collection is to suggest, rather than to enumerate, the full spectrum of implicated researchers: grass roots gay activists (Gittings, Lahusen, Kepner), seasoned archivist-librarians (Marston, Thistlethwaite), ex-librarians (Cooper, Fishman), new graduates of Masters of Library and Information Studies programs (Forbes, Huffine, and Barnett), plus researchers in American Studies (Gladney), Health and Public Policy (Ryan and Bradford), and Sociology (Williams). The contributors include one Canadian librarian of African extraction (Kester) and two New Zealanders (Parkin and Parkinson). Only one chapter fits the conventional definition of lesbigay library history (Robbins), and its bald but fragmentary facts suggest more concrete reasons why more historical research on lesbigays and libraries has not been forthcoming.

As Louis Menaud notes in a recent collection of essays on academic freedom (1996, 4), postmodernism has transformed the understanding of "disinterestedness," "reason," and "truth," as insupportable abstractions in academic research, and while critics see the demise of Western values in the relativistic historical language of perspective, understanding, and interpretation, the consequences of postmodernism are not necessarily negative if its terminology enables us to appreciate the contributions of minorities, including lesbigays, who are absent from traditional historical accounts. As for traditional research frameworks, the methodological reasons for sensitive research difficulties in the empirical tradition have been discussed elsewhere, although rarely (Lee 1993; Keenaghan 1994).

Caitlin Ryan and Judy Bradford suggest that the difficulties of lesbigay research often are exaggerated within the conventional framework, but by employing a slightly modified version of traditional social science data collection techniques (for example, the "snowballing" sampling technique employed by Woods 1993; or the use of related themes and cohorts, as in Christine L. Williams' study of a subsample of librarians drawn in her larger work on the "feminized" professions) researchers gain a much-needed latitude not permitted by the requirements of representativeness in standard research protocols. By such simple measures as asking subjects to identify their sexual orientation, lesbigay researchers routinely further an historical agenda. In querying both lesbigay and straight respondents, as Williams did, researchers also gain insight into the whole perplex of professional and gender constructs by which professions and individuals are stereotyped. Most importantly, lesbigay researchers must possess sophistication in research methodology, such as that effectively demonstrated in recent lesbigay history outside the library field (e.g., Bérubé 1990; Marcus 1992; Duberman 1993; Chauncey 1995; and especially Sears 1997).

As other writers have remarked, interdisciplinary networking among lesbigay scholars has been boosted by the Internet. Listservs such as Louie Crew's Gay Scholars Listserv, which now counts over 700 subscribers, indicate a use for the Internet beyond providing a sense of solidarity and safety. Norman Kester successfully employed Gary Klein's lesbigay librarians' listserve, GAY-LIBN, to enlist authors in compiling a collection of lesbigay stories and essays. In other cases, such as Louise Robbins' study of the McCarthyism in libraries (Robbins 1996), coincidental evidence of the effects of persecution of gay library employees may surface in the course of another investigation entirely, and merely require that the researcher have an unbiased mind and clear eyes to view documents, and the willingness to publish his or her findings.

Personal dimensions always enter into research, including lesbigay research, but to what extent does self-disclosure—anathema to the psychiatrist, for example—represent a threat or a hindrance to lesbigay research? In the case of Rose Gladney, the needed information about Lillian Smith could not be obtained without full disclosure to Smith's surviving significant other, Paula Snelling, and it is hardly accidental that Gladney's own coming-out process coincided with Snelling's participation in a conversation that women of her generation never had (see p. 51–52).

The publication of Kester's collection of personal stories by lesbigay librarians and their advocates effectively ended the twilight shadow-boxing in which U.S. lesbigay librarians had been engaged since they formed the world's first professional gay organization. Not that they had much help in the past from the historical establishment: a history of social activism in librarianship (Bundy & Stielow 1987, 46, 50, 105, 177) made only passing mention of Task Force activities. While the writers in *Liberating Minds* were by no means representative of all lesbigay researchers and librarians or their advocates, the publication marked an important milestone in making available to other lesbigay librarians personal stories, studies, and reflections on lesbigay materials in libraries. Above all, they set a new standard in the dignity of self-disclosure all but absent from the literature since the formation of the Social Responsibilities Round Table (there are exceptions: examples of these early voices are Guttag 1972; Wolf 1972; see also Broderick 1974 and 1974a, the only library educator to come out in print in the early years).

Gratifying though it may be to have Kester's collection now available to cultural historians, sociologists, and librarians, purely personal stories often avoid the questions important to the future of lesbigays in the profession: Why did gay library pioneers, people who certainly never thought of themselves as any such exalted thing, finally step forward? What are the specific barriers to lesbigay library history? How can lesbigay library historians avoid the pitfalls of reading the present into the past, or of distinguishing between lesbigay ancestors and those whose sexual behavior was either nonexistent or ambiguous? How, indeed, shall researchers define a lesbigay person, when the terrain of that identity has not been fully charted? How can the profession help lesbigay patrons, professionals, and students who, for whatever reason, are having difficulties in their coming-out process, when library administators are not supportive? Most importantly, how are lesbigays to forge an individual identity apart from the stereotypes of mainstream media, lesbigay sub-cultures, or academic hegemonies? How, indeed, are they to conduct their lives without further strengthening the gridlock of public and professional debate between both ends of political and religious extremes?

FACE VALUES: THE GAY TASK FORCE PIONEERS

The ALA GLBTF was headed for sixteen years (1971 to 1986) by Barbara Gittings, who presided at early functions dressed in the same flowered jumper, year after year, which she jokingly claimed was the only dress she owned.[6] Her casual lesbigay ideology suggests a friendlier and less demanding era than that of only several years later, when many lesbians left the group to join ALA's Feminist Task Force.

Gittings was like a great gay scout leader, expert in survival techniques, and politically astute to recognize that humor and friendly confrontation were not inimical within a bureaucracy as large as that of the ALA. The titles of the early programs she planned drew healthy crowds in spite of the controversial subject matter, and her "gay" gay approach to her audience won loyal supporters of the Task Force from across ALA membership rolls. She wasn't even a librarian, just a lesbian library enthusiast who believed in the power of libraries to transform lives. Incidentally, although she founded the first east coast chapter of The Daughters of Bilitis, and edited that organization's journal, *The Ladder*, for several years, the word "lesbian" was never so significant to her as the word "gay," because the former emphasized a person's sex, the latter, a person's sexual orientation.[7] She had even picketed the White House in 1965 for homosexual rights, and with her lover, Kay Tobin Lahusen, was an early household name among the lesbigay community by the time of the Stonewall Riots (Marcus 1992, 104–7; 111–26, 213–22; Thistlethwaite 1994, 225; Streitmayer 1995, 54–57, 77–78). A flurry of controversy had accompanied Michael McConnell's unsuccessful 1970 attempt to enlist the help of ALA in reinstating him as a librarian at the University of Minnesota after he was dismissed for filing for a marriage licence with his lover, Jack Baker—the first time gay issues were brought before ALA's governing council, which still had not resolved the issue five years later when McConnell dropped his petition. Meanwhile, after Israel Fishman turned over leadership of the GLBTF to Gittings in 1971, she unwittingly one-upped the stodgy waffling of the ALA Council by staging a hilarious gay demonstration in Dallas in 1971 that attracted national media attention. The subsequent activities of the GLBTF, which Gittings helped to define, changed the way that many libraries of every description acquired, cataloged, and disseminated gay literature. But more importantly, the Gay Book Award, which Task Force members financed out of their own pockets for fifteen years, helped to foster its growth, and the Gay Bibliography, which was for a time the only such bibliography available to the general public at no charge, contributed to the spread of "lesbigay ideas."

From Gittings' experience, it is perhaps tempting to conclude that first generation lesbigays experienced no ideological schisms, but such was certainly not the case: the first long-lived gay periodical, *ONE* (1947–) , assumed a confrontational, personal, and activist stance, although readers would be hard-pressed to perceive that tone by present-day standards. The rival *The Mattachine Review* sought to assuage the fears of straight America by adopting an accomodationist tone; *The Ladder*, on the other hand, encouraged political solutions at the polls (Streitmayer 1995, 31–48). At its core, then, the modern lesbigay movement before Stonewall tested the limits of individualism and nonconformity during a period of national paranoia, subversion, and repression. The GLBTF came along after most of these early conflicts had already been defined, and by 1970, homosexual rights were only one of many "isms" then being addressed by the Social Responsibilities Round Table. Not every member of the Task Force could cast such a positive light on their experience as Gittings did, since one of the costs of being out could result in dismissal from their jobs.

Israel Fishman founded the Task Force before Gittings arrived on the scene, and his personal experiences reflect the timbre of those of many gay men whose stories remain untold. The cultural baggage of orthodox Judaism weighed more heavily on him than did his professional fears, and his experiences bear many points of similarity with gay people and others of the pre-Stonewall generation. While today some librarians tout a professional stance of neutrality vis-à-vis social issues, Fishman's remembrances make clear how professional standards have sometimes been used to stifle creativity, change, and diversity.

Fishman was not alone among the early leaders in leaving librarianship for good. Janet Cooper, an early Task Force member, has been a cab driver in Boston for many years. Whereas Fishman's defection came by choice, Cooper's change of occupation was the result of harassment, persecution, and discrimination. While her reflection on the meaning of the ALA's Intellectual Freedom Statement purposefully avoids the particular recriminations of a victim—a role she staunchly refuses to fill—her critique of cowardice and lack of character bear important implications for library professionals as well as American citizens generally.

Cal Gough and Ellen Greenblatt's ground-breaking collection of essays on lesbigay library service, now under revision for a second edition, has been almost the only substantial source of information on lesbigay librarianship available to students until Kester's volume appeared. Gough and Greenblatt were the true pioneers of historical research on lesbigay issues in librarianship, although this was not necessarily their intent. Gough's chronology of Task Force history, which closes Part II, is reprinted from the Twenty-Fifth Anniversary Program of the Gay, Lesbian, and Bisexual Task Force (1995) with the permission of The American Library Association and GLBTF.

SAVING FACE: THE ARCHIVAL RECORD

While it has become fashionable in the past fifty years to bemoan the exponential growth and cost of scholarly literature, history can only with difficulty survive without artifacts, documents, and secondary sources. That any account of lesbigay experience from the earlier part of the century survives at all is miraculous, considering the pressures that have been exerted to destroy the papers of self-documenting lesbigays. Hitler's cultural enforcer, Heinrich Himmler, for example, made the burning of the archives of Magnus Hirschfeld's Institute of Sexual Science his first official act (Plant 1986), but as Gittings notes, much of what was on the shelves of American libraries during the same period was prejudicial, misinformed, and pejorative, and the public apparently did not enjoy the same open access to these volumes as it did to others, if the library acquired them at all. Had it not been for the self-conscious attempt to document lesbigay experience and collect gay literature at the grass-roots level, examples of much early gay and lesbian literature would probably not have survived. The late Jim Kepner, who began the first documented gay collection in America, was all the more remarkable for insisting from the first that his personal collection of fiction, memorabilia, and ephemera—now the International Gay Archives of The University of Southern California—should be accessible without restriction. Arthur Schomberg made similar stipulations about his collection of African American history, which eventually became the core of the Schomberg Center for African American Literature of The New York Public Library, but he kept closer control over the collection than Kepner (Johnson-Cooper 1996, 34–38). There are probably few comparable instances in American library history in which a private collection has been made so completely accessible, and Kepner never ceased to write, speak, and agitate generally about the importance of the availability of lesbigay information at the grass-roots level.

Institutional affiliation of lesbigay archives represents a mixed blessing to some researchers. Brenda Marston of the Archives of Human Sexuality at Cornell University presents a review of the common pitfalls of inaccurate subject-headings, hidden content, and artificial subject descriptions that characterize institutionalization of lesbigay archives (see Thistlethwaite 1995, for a complete litany of these errors) and how these have been avoided at Cornell. While the Mariposa Foundation and the university provide the necessary housing and financial support for the collection, the documentary contributions of the lesbigay community continue to supply its fodder. Marston points to the importance of the HIV/AIDS crisis in heightening awareness among the gay community and their family members of the importance of personal papers, letters, and diaries, for it is from these that future generations will assess the impact of government policy and the media on the gay community's recent history.

Separatism has been associated with many religious communities and political movements, with the back-to-Africa movement of Marcus Garvey, for example, as well as modern afrocentricism, the feminist movement, plus a variety of spiritual cults, and a portion of the lesbigay community. It is unfortunate, perhaps, that the reasons behind separatism are not more widely understood. Separatism preserves integrity, ensures safety, and exercises the collective will. Polly Thistlethwaite, associated for more than a decade with the Lesbian Herstory Archives, explains the rationale behind the creation and maintenance of a separatist lesbian/feminist collection, whose policies arose in response to needs. Both Thistlethwaite and Kepner point to the importance of serving a primary constituency first, whatever pressures are brought to bear by the larger historical community. Until antigay discrimination is ended by federal mandate in the United States, the need for such private collections will no doubt remain high, even given the current academic vogue of queer theory and lesbigay studies.

Fortunately, at least one national lesbigay collection already exists in New Zealand, yet it owes its current status as much to repeated persecution as it does to a progay amendment to the Constitution.   Chris Parkin[8] and Phil Parkinson chronicle the beginnings, growth, near-destruction, and present-day governance of the collection in light of emerging national political developments. The authors emphasize the importance of a separate legal identity within the greater institution. Under the U.S. system of elections and legislation, which lacks the flexibility of New Zealand's bicameral parliamentary system, an equal rights amendment for women or lesbigays will not be so easily achieved, and private philanthropy, volunteerism, and grass-roots sponsorship no doubt will be needed more than ever. The New Zealand experience does suggest, however, that a combination of careful planning and serendipity may overturn even the most dour of expectations.

AND THEN, FACE TO FACE

While the benefits of self-disclosure and openness may not be immediately apparent to all segments of the lesbigay community—that is, to persons who have admitted to themselves their same-sex inclinations, whatever their legal or public status—no professional should ever be made to feel that work necessarily equates with pain, boredom, ennui, or the necessity of a hidden dual identity. While the experience of the writer may be more sanguine than that of the reader, I have never regretted the life-saving decision I made nearly twenty years ago to work as I live, and to be as honest as I can be with students, colleagues, and friends about my feelings, my sexuality, and my opinions. My decision to enter librarianship after six disasterous years in banking made such changes possible. While some may view self-disclosure as exhibitionistic, inappropriate, or professionally risky, the alternative of self-denial is ultimately more destructive. The support of lesbigay professors was not personally available to me as a student, but I have been singularly fortunate in my own library education career in maintaining unqualified support from mentors, colleagues, administrators, and students, and I have tried to maintain that same sense of interest and enthusiasm toward all students—whatever their label—whom I am employed to counsel, guide, and teach.

The three chapters with which this volume concludes were all written by recent gay graduates at the University of North Carolina at Greensboro. Like Kester, I had difficulty in obtaining a suitable submission from a lesbian, and I regret that omission, because one of our lesbian graduates had served as a bridesmaid at my straight wedding in 1969. Unfortunately, the requirements of a new job prevented her participation. Nevertheless, these essays represent a variety of generational perspectives (Donald Forbes, like myself, is fifty-one at this writing; John Barnett is thirty-six, and Richard Huffine is twenty-nine). I requested that each of these writers reflect on what librarianship means to them as a gay professional. While these essays seem to bear the general tone of autobiographical reflections, they arose from essentially different circumstances than did those in *Liberating Minds*, because Kester solicited contributors from a variety of sources including e-mail, and I assigned the task to this semi-captive cadre of new professionals. Huffine's chapter was reworked from a paper delivered at the request of Wayne A. Wiegand at the Association of Library and Information Science Education in Philadelphia in

1995 during a program entitled "The Last Socially Acceptable Prejudice," the first discussion of lesbigay issues that that organization had sponsored. Barnett, who was the recipient of a United States Department of Education Diversity Grant (still unfilled after three months because of lack of racial minority applications when Barnett's application appeared, indicating strong interest in lesbigay issues and Hispanic literature), served as my assistant for a year, and worked closely with me on my first two gay studies. Donald Forbes and his partner Lewis Amendola were my close friends long before Forbes entered the library education program at Greensboro. I am deeply grateful to all three of these men for letting me impose upon their sense of duty after their graduate studies were completed.

I will hope that this collection needs frequent future revision; that there always will be unabashed lesbigay librarians to undertake that needed task; and that in the future, lesbigay librarians will never need to study a crime report, read an obituary column, or find familiar names on a quilt to realize that they have a rich professional heritage.

NOTES

1. Rescinded by U.S. District Judge Eugene Nickerson as unconstitutionally imposing special rules on gay groups July 2, 1997, for the second time, in *Able vs. USA*. The regulation, instituted in February 1994, first came under Nickerson's review in March 1995.

2. In the original version of Cronin's paper, which was sent to respondents for a February 1995 program of The Association for Library and Information Science Education in Philadelphia, Cronin indicated that the fact that representatives of the perspectives of multiculturalism (Michael E. Harris), women's issues (Jane Anne Hannigan), gay issues (James V. Carmichael, Jr.), and class issues (Christine Pawley) had been asked to respond to his criticism of library education demonstrated how far library education curricula had drifted away from "The Right Stuff."

3. Caitlin Ryan and Donna Futterman's *Lesbian and gay youth: Care and counseling* (New York: Columbia University Press, 1998), first published by American Pediatrics Association as a journal issue, represented such a crucial area of investigation that the Health, Resources, and Services Administration in the Department of Health and Human Services ordered 4,000 copies in 1997.

4. The P.E.R.S.O.N. Project, largely developed by Jessea Greenman and maintained by Jean Richter, is an online activist network dedicated to lesbigay equity in K–12 education. The mailing list (richter@berkeley.edu) is confidential.   Web address:http://www. youth.org/loco/PERSONProject/.

5. There are exceptions, of course; see Radford and Radford, 1997, for a Foucauldian approach to the librarian stereotype. Such examples are rare.

6. Marie Kuda, "A Pictorial History of the Task Force," Joint Meeting of the ALA Gay, Lesbian, and Bisexual Task Force (GLBTF) and the Library History Round Table (LHRT), Chicago, IL, June 15, 1995.

7. Barbara Gittings, Telephone interview with the author, October 15, 1994.

8. In the course of writing his essay, Phil Parkinson suffered a stroke. I am grateful to Chris Parkin for finishing the essay from Parkinson's notes, and to Parkinson for continuing to contribute to the effort even in rehabilitation.

REFERENCES

Allen, Louise A. (1997). "Laura Bragg: a new woman practicing progressive social reform as a museum administrator and educator." Ph.D. dissertation, University of South Carolina.

Baum, Christina D. 1992. *Feminist thought in American librarianship.* Jefferson, NC: McFarland.

Berman, Paul. 1996. *A tale of two utopias: The political journey of the generation of 1968.* New York: Norton.

Berman, Sanford. 1981. *The joy of cataloging: Essays, letters and other explosions.* Phoenix, AR: Oryx.

Bérubé, Allan. 1990. *Coming out under fire: The history of gay men and women in World War II.* New York: Free Press.

Boaz, Martha. 1987. *Librarian/library educator.* Metuchen, NJ: Scarecrow Press.

Blythe, John; Boswell, John; Bostien, Leon; Kerrigan, William; and Hitt, Jack. "New rules about sex on campus." (Forum discussion). *Harper's Magazine* 287 (September): 33–43.

Broderick, Dorothy. 1993. "Moral conflict about the survival of the public library." *American Libraries* 24 (May):447–48.

Broderick, Dorothy. 1974. "Defending gay librarians." *Wilson Library Bulletin* 49 (September): 31–32.

Broderick, Dorothy. 1974a. "Free U." *Booklegger Magazine* 1 (May/June): 37–39.

Broderick, Dorothy. 1997. "Turning library into a dirty word: A rant." *Library Journal* 122 (July): 42–43.

Bryan, Alice I. 1952. *The public librarian.* New York: Columbia University Press.

Bryant, Eric. 1995. "Pride & prejudice." *Library Journal* 120 (June 15): 37–39.

Bukoff, Ronald N. 1992. "Censorship and the American college library." *College and Research Libraries* 56 (September): 395–408.

Bundy, Mary L. and Stielow, Frederick J. 1987. *Activism in American librarianship, 1962–73.* Westport, CT: Greenwood Press.

Carmichael, James V., Jr. 1997. "A gauntlet for all reasons: The importance of lesbigay library history." In *Liberating minds: The stories and professional lives of gay, lesbian, and bisexual librarians and their advocates,* ed. Norman Kester, 9–24. Jefferson, NC: McFarland.

Carmichael, James V., Jr. 1995. "The gay librarian: A comparative analysis of attitudes towards professional gender issues." *Journal of Homosexuality* 30, no. 2: 11–57.

Carmichael, James V., Jr. 1995a. "Sex in public libraries: An historical primer of what every librarian should know." *North Carolina Libraries* 53 (Summer): 59–64.

Carmichael, James V., Jr. 1992. "The male librarian and the feminine image: A survey of stereotype, status, and gender perceptions." *Library and Information Science Research* 14 (October/December): 411–46.

Carmichael, James V. , Jr. 1991. "Ahistoricity in librarianship: Perceptions of practitioners of biographical research." *Journal of Education for Library and Information Science* 31 (Summer): 329–56.

Carmichael, James V., Jr. and Shontz, Marilyn L. 1996. "'The last socially acceptable prejudice': Gay and lesbian issues, social responsibilities, and coverage of these topics in MLIS/LIS programs." *The Library Quarterly* 66 (January): 21–58.

Casey, Kathleen. 1996. "The arrogance of professional expertise and the virtues of dispossession." Paper, American Educational Research Association, Chicago, IL, October 15.

Casey, Kathleen. 1995–96. "The new narrative research in education." *Review of Research in Education* 21: 211–53.

Casey, Kathleen. 1993 *'I answer with my life': Life histories of teachers working for social change.* New York: Routledge.

Chauncey, George. 1995. *Gay New York, 1890–1940.* New York: Columbia University Press.

Cornog, Martha and Pepper, Timothy. 1996. *For sex education,* see *librarian: A guide to issues and resources.* Westport, CT: Greenwood.

Cronin, Blaise. 1995. "Shibboleth and substance in North American library and information science education." *Libri* 45 (March): 45–63.

Dain, Phyllis. 1975. "Ambivalence and paradox: The social bonds of the public library." *Library Journal* 100 (February 1): 261–66.

Dain, Phyllis. 1991. "Public library governance and a changing New York City." *Libraries & Culture* 26 (Spring): 219–50.

Darsey, James. 1991. "From 'gay is good' to the scourge of AIDS: The evolution of gay liberation rhetoric, 1977–1990." *Communication Studies* 42 (Spring): 43–66.

D'Emilio, John and Freedman, Estelle B. 1988. *Intimate matters: A history of sexuality in America.* Chicago: University of Chicago Press.

Desroches, Frederick J. 1990. "*Tearoom Trade*: A research update." *Qualitative Sociology* 13 (Spring): 39–61.

Dubbert, Joe L. 1979. *A man's place: Masculinity in transition.* Englewood Cliffs, NJ: Prentice Hall.

Duberman, Martin B. 1993. *Stonewall.* New York: Norton.

Fry, Stephen. 1997. "Playing Oscar." *The New Yorker* 73 (June 16): 82–88.

Gaughan, Thomas M. 1992. "The Last Socially Accptable Prejudice" (editorial). *American Libraries* 23 (September): 612.

The gay almanac. 1996. New York: Berkley Books.

"Gay publications under fire In p[ublic] l[ibrarie]s; Sex manuals, juvenile titles and newspapers face ostracism." 1994. *Library Journal* 119 (February 1): 17–18

Geller, Evelyn. 1984. *Forbidden books in American public libraries, 1876–1939: A study in cultural change.* Westport, CT: Greenwood Press.

Gittings, Barbara. 1978. "Combatting the lies in libraries." In *The gay academic*, ed. Louie Crew, 108–117. Palm Springs, FL: ETC Publications.

Gough, Cal R. and Greenblatt, Ellen, eds. 1990. *Gay and lesbian library service.* New York: McFarland.

Guttag, Bianca. [Janet Cooper]. 1972. "Homophobia in library school." In *Revolting Librarians*, ed. Celeste West, Elizabeth Katz, and others, 37–38. San Francisco: Booklegger Press.

Harbeck, Karen M. 1992. *Coming out of the classroom closet: Gay and lesbian students, teachers, and curricula.* New York: Harrington Park Press.

Harris, Michael. 1973. "The purpose of the American public library: A revisionist approach." *Library Journal* 98 (September 15): 2509–14.

Harris, Roma M. 1992. *Librarianship: The erosion of a woman's profession.* Norwood, NJ: Ablex.

Hemmings, Susan.1992. "Separatism: A look back at anger." In *Coming out: An anthology of international gay and lesbian writings*, ed. Susan Likosky, 330–45. New York: Pantheon Books.

Herdt, Gilbert H. 1993. *Children of horizons: How gay and lesbian teens are leading a new way out of the closet.* Boston: Beacon Press.

Hildenbrand, Suzanne, ed. 1996. *Reclaiming the American library past: Writing the women in.* Norwood, NJ: Ablex.

Hofstadter, Richard. 1963. *Anti-intellectualism in America.* New York: Knopf.

Holley, Edward G. 1963. *Charles Evans: American bibliographer.* Urbana: University of Illinois Press.

Holley, Edward G. 1967. *Raking the historical coals: The ALA scrapbook of 1876.* New York: Beta Phi Mu.

Humphreys, Laud. 1970. *Tearoom trade: Impersonal sex in public places.* Chicago: Aldine Publishing Company.

Johnson, Karl E. 1992. *An annotated bibliography of faculty status in library and information science.* Champaign, IL: University of Illinois, Graduate School of Library and Information Science.

Johnson-Cooper, Glendora. 1996. "African-American historical continuity: Jean Blackwell Hutson and The Schomberg Center for Research of Black Culture." In *Reclaiming the library past: Writing the women in,* ed. Suzanne Hildenbrand, 27–51. Norwood, NJ: Ablex.

Joyce, Stephen and Alvin M. Schrader. 1997. "Hidden perceptions: Edmonton gay males and the Edmonton Public Library." *Canadian Journal of Information and Library Science* 22 (April): 19–37.

Keenaghan, Lynn. 1994. "Lost in a 'straight' reality: Lesbians and gay men in social research." In *Re-thinking social research: Anti-discriminatory approaches to research methodology,* ed. Beth Humphreys and Carole Truman. Aldershot, UK: Avebury.

Kinsman, Gary. 1996. *The regulation of desire: Homo and hetero sexualities.* 2nd. ed. Montréal: Black Rose Books.

Kleinman, Sherryl and Copp, Martha A. 1993. *Emotions and fieldwork.* Qualitative Research Methods, no. 28. Newbury Park, CA: Sage Publications.

Lather, Patti and Smithies, Chris. 1995. *Troubling angels: Women living with HIV/AIDS.* Columbus, OH: Athena's Pen DTP, Greyden Press.

Lee, Raymond M. 1993. *Doing research on sensitive topics.* New York: Sage.

Lord, Julia W. 1968. *The cosmic world of childhood: The ideology of children's librarians, 1900–1965.* Ph.D. diss., Emory University.

Marcus, Eric. 1992. *Making history: The struggle for gay and lesbian equal rights, 1945–1990: An oral history.* New York: HarperCollins.

McPheeters, Annie L. 1988. *Library service in black and white: Some personal recollections, 1926–1980.* Metuchen, NJ: Scarecrow Press.

McReynolds, Rosalee. 1997. "Trouble in Big Sky's ivory tower: The Montana tenure dispute of 1937–39." *Libraries & Culture* 32 (Spring): 163–90.

Megill, Allan. 1994. "Four senses of objectivity." In *Rethinking objectivity,* ed. Allan Megill, 1–20. Durham, NC: Duke University Press.

Menaud, Louis. 1996. "The limits of academic freedom." In *The future of academic freedom,* ed. Louis Menaud, 3–20. Chicago: University of Chicago Press.

Miller, Marilyn L. and Shontz, Marilyn L. 1995. "The race for the school library dollar." *School Library Journal* 41 (October 1995): 22–33.

Murden, Steve. 1993. "Gay and lesbian materials: Are Virginia's libraries meeting the challenge?" *Virginia Librarian* 39 (October/November/December): 5–8.

Nardi, Peter M. 1995. " 'The breastplate of righteousness': Twenty-five years after Laud Humphrey's *Tearoom Trade: Impersonal Sex in Public Places.*" *The Journal of Homosexuality* 30, no. 2: 1–10.

Newmyer, Jody. 1976. "The image problem of the librarian: Femininity and social control." *The Journal of Library History* 11, no. 1: 44–67.

Noddings, Nel. 1990. "Feminist critiques of the professions." *Review of Research in Education* 16: 393–424.

"OIF says gay titles top 'most challenged' list." 1994. *American Libraries* 25 (April): 372.

Paris, Marion. 1988. *Library school closings: Four case studies*. Metuchen, NJ: Scarecrow Press.

Passet, Joanne E. 1994. *Cultural crusaders: Women librarians in the American west, 1900–1917*. Albuquerque: University of New Mexico Press.

Patton, Cindy. 1993. "Embodying subaltern memory: Kinesthesia and the problematics of gender and race." In *The Madonna connection: Representing politics, subcultural identities, and cultural theory*, ed. Cathy Schwichtenberg, 81–105. Boulder, CO: Westview Press.

Pharr, Suzanne. 1988. *Homophobia: A weapon of sexism*. Little Rock, AK: Chardon.

Plant, Richard. 1986. *The Nazi war against homosexuals*. New York: Henry Holt.

Powell, Lawrence C. 1968. *Fortune and friendship: An autobiography*. New York: R. R. Bowker.

Preston, John and Lowenthal, Michael, eds. 1995. *Friends and lovers: Gay men write about the families they create*. New York: Plume.

Radford, Marie L. and Radford, Gary P. 1997. "Power, knowledge, and fear: Feminism, Foucault, and the stereotype of the female librarian." *The Library Quarterly* 67 (July): 250–66.

Reissman, Catherine K. 1993. *Narrative analysis*. Qualitative Research Methods, no. 30. Newbury Park, CA: Sage Publications.

Ridinger, Robert B. M. 1997. "Playing in the attic: Indexing and preserving the gay press." In *Liberating minds: The stories and professional lives of gay, lesbian , and bisexual librarians and their advocates*, ed. Norman G. Kester, 92–97. Jefferson, NC: McFarland.

Robbins, Louise S. 1996. *Censorship and the American library: The American Library Association's response to threats to intellectual freedom, 1939–1969*. Westport, CT: Greenwood Press.

Santavicca, Edward F. 1977. *The treatment of homosexuality in current encyclopedias*. Ph.D. diss., University of Michigan, Ann Arbor.

Schiller, Anita R. 1974. "Women in librarianship." In *Advances in librarianship*, ed. M. J. Voight and Michael H. Harris, 103–47. Phoenix, AZ: Oryx.

Schrader, Alvin M. , Herring, Margaret, and De Scossa, Catriona. 1989. "The censorship phenomenon in college and research libraries: An investigation of the Canadian prairie provinces, 1980–1985." *College and Research Libraries* 50 (July): 420–32.

Scott, Joan W. 1996. "Academic freedom as an ethical practice." In *The future of academic freedom*, ed. Louis Menaud, 163–86. Chicago: University of Chicago Press.

Sears, James T. 1997. *Lonely hunters: An oral history of lesbian and gay southern life, 1948–1968*. Boulder, CO: Westview Press.

Shores, Louis. 1975. *Quiet world: A librarian's crusade for destiny: The professional autobiography of Louis Shores*. Hamden, CT: Linnett Books.

Simpson, Richard L and Simpson, Ida M. 1969. "Women and bureaucracy in the semi-professions." In *The semi-professions and their organization*, 196–265. New York: Free Press.

Special Libraries Association. 1990. *SLA Inter-Association Task Force report on image*. Washington, DC: Special Libraries Association (ERIC Microfiche No. ED 329 267).

Steuart, Robert D. 1976. "Writing the journal article." *College and Research Libraries* 37 (March): 153–57.

Stevens, Norman. 1988. "Our image in the 80s." *Library Trends* 36, no. 4: 825–51.

Stewart, Thomas A. 1991. "Gay in corporate America." *Fortune* 124 (February 16): 43–56.

Streitmayer, Rodger. 1995. *Unspeakable: The rise of the gay and lesbian press in America*.

Boston: Faber and Faber.

Sullivan, Peggy. 1976. *Carl H. Milam and the American Library Association.* New York: H.W. Wilson.

Taylor, Marvin J. 1993. "Queer things from old closets: Libraries—gay and lesbian studies—queer theory." *Rare Book and Manuscripts Librarianship* 8, no. 1: 19–34.

Thistlethwaite, Polly J. 1995. "The lesbian and gay past: An interpretive background." *Gay Community News* (Boston) 2 (Winter): 10–11, 24.

Thistlethwaite, Polly J. 1994. "Gays and lesbians in library history." In *The encyclopedia of library history*, ed. Wayne A. Wiegand and Donald G. Davis, 223–27. New York: Garland.

Treiman, Donald J. 1977. *Occupational prestige in comparative perspective.* New York: Academic Press.

West, Celeste; Katz, Elizabeth; and others. 1972. *Revolting librarians.* San Francisco: Booklegger Press.

Whitt, Alis J. 1993. "The information needs of lesbians and bisexual women." *Library and Information Science Research* 15 (Summer): 275–88.

Wiegand, Shirley A. 1994. *Library records: A retention and confidentiality guide.* Westport, CT: Greenwood Press.

Wiegand, Wayne A. 1996. *Irrepressible reformer: Melvil Dewey.* Chicago: American Library Association.

Williams, Christine L. 1989. *Gender differences at work: Women and men in nontraditional occupations.* Berkeley: University of California Press.

Williams, Christine L. 1995. *Still a man's place: Men who do women's work.* Berkeley and Los Angeles: University of California Press.

Williamson, William L. 1963. *William Frederick Poole and the modern library movement.* New York: Columbia University.

Wilson, Pauline. 1982. *Stereotype and status: Librarians in the United States.* Westport, CT: Greenwood Press.

Wolf, Steve. 1972. "Sex and the single cataloger." In *Revolting librarians*, ed. Celeste West, Elizabeth Katz, and others, 39–44. San Francisco: Booklegger Press.

Woods, James. 1993. *The corporate closet: The professional lives of gay men in America.* New York: Free Press.

Part One

Finding Our Names: Theory, Problems, and Context

1

Methodological Issues in Research with Lesbians, Gay Men, and Bisexuals

Caitlin Ryan and Judy Bradford

Many of the methodological challenges in studying lesbians, gay men, and bisexuals are not unique to this population. Researchers face similar challenges and have developed innovative strategies for studying other hidden and hard-to-reach populations, including homeless persons, substance abusers, and out-of-school youth. Research on socially devalued, stigmatized, or illegal behaviors (for example, homosexuality and substance abuse) has required a broader conceptual framework and often a multi-disciplinary approach to effectively sample these populations. These models can and have been successfully applied to studying other hidden populations including lesbians, gay men, and bisexuals.

To say that we lack methodology for studying lesbians, gay men, and bisexuals—as many advocates do—is inaccurate. To conclude that the historic lack of research on lesbians, gay men and bisexuals is attributed to homophobia is simplistic and confounds the multiple causes and contributing factors that have resulted in a lack of visibility and basic information about our lives. Without a conscious effort, however, to share this information across disciplines, to inform and train researchers and information specialists, and to educate political activists and advocates, misinformation about research problems, methods, and effective strategies for studying lesbians, gay men and bisexuals will be perpetuated in our rhetoric, in our research, and in our self-perceptions, which profoundly impact our lives.

HISTORICAL BARRIERS TO RESEARCH ON LESBIANS AND GAY MEN

Research on lesbians, gay men, and bisexuals has been affected by historical, political, and cultural factors that have limited and shaped the information we have about sexual orientation, homosexuality, and earlier expressions of lesbigay identity and culture. These barriers that are overlapping and interrelated include the following:

Evolution of Lesbian, Gay, Bisexual Identity

Lesbian and gay identity as we know it is a twentieth-century invention, evolving in tandem with the development of an organized lesbigay community during the past twenty-five years (Herdt 1992) (see Table 1). The concept of homosexuality only emerged in the nineteenth century out of the medicalization of same-sex behavior, perceived as gender deviant and "inverted." Before that time, gay people had no perceived social identity, and were considered "sodomites" (having a sinful nature, and guilty of capital crime) (Weeks 1979).

These evolving identities, which primarily characterized male homosexuality, have complicated historical research in a variety of ways, including obscuring the expression of same-sex identities and behaviors in lesbians and people of color (Cook 1979; Terry 1991). For social science researchers seeking to study the prevalence of homosexuality and same-sex behaviors, the diversity of sexual behavior (and identity) is further compounded by its expression in people of different racial and ethnic groups, as well as gender, geography, culture, and age.

Table 1
Evolution of Lesbian/Gay Identity

Time Frame	Cohort	Community	Identity	Life Style
1910	Came of age after WWI	no	no	hiding/lived as heterosexual
1940	Came of age during/after WWI	secret	homosexual	secrecy/bars
1969	Came of age after Stone-wall/gay Activism	yes	lesbian/gay	passing/ coming out
1983	Came of Age in the era of AIDS	yes	queer	living "out"

Source: Herdt, 1992.

Lack of Access—Hidden Population

Apart from considerations of identity and behavior, the social and legal sanctions against lesbians and gay men further complicate research with this population, because until more recently, most have been hidden. Early research on gay people was conducted on institutionalized populations (people in prison or psychiatric patients), which significantly skewed results and perpetuated negative stereotypes. Because finding a diverse sample was extremely difficult, initially few researchers tried, and much of the early research on lesbians and gay men was generated from "convenience samples," based on personal networks, clinical populations, and members of social organizations. Respondents were almost entirely white and predominantly male.

Lack of Comparable Definitions and Measures

Early research on gay people generally failed to define how sexual orientation would be measured, or lacked systematic definition so it is often unclear who was actually being studied. For example, a review of 228 studies published on sexual orientation, homosexuality, and bisexuality after 1969 found that 81.6 percent failed to assess respondents' sexual orientation for inclusion in the study, relying instead on reports of others that a participant was appropriate, or assuming that persons who participated in homosexual or heterosexual organizations were themselves homosexual or heterosexual (Shively, Jones, and DeCecco 1983–84). Nearly one out of four studies had no definition for sexual orientation; in all studies, a wide range of methods were used to define and assess sexual orientation, ranging from behavior to attraction to erotic preference to relationships, but no single measure was predominant.

A comparable study to determine how representative samples of lesbians, gay men, and bisexuals had been in health research conducted between 1990 and 1992 found that none of the studies defined the terms "lesbian" or "gay," and only 2.6 percent conceptually defined the population they were studying (for example, behavior, fantasy, or same-sex attraction) (Sell and Petrulio 1996). Moreover, only 2 percent of the studies used probability sampling (a method of randomly selecting part of a group or population so that each person has a known chance or probability of being selected). As a result, few samples were representative even of the groups from which they were drawn (for example, lesbian/gay organizations or clinics).

Similar problems occur in research on substance abuse with lesbians, gay men, and bisexuals. Lack of comparable definitions for chemical dependency (for example, frequency and amount of alcohol consumption) make it impossible to compare or assess rates of addiction in different studies. Coupled with a lack of standardized definitions of sexual behavior and identity, findings cannot effectively be used to plan services, shape policy, or reliably determine needs. However, because information on lesbians, gay men, and bisexuals is so limited, findings are often generalized and used to represent larger populations, even when researchers clearly state the limitations of their study and when the sample includes only openly identified persons in lesbian/gay settings (Sell and Petrulio 1996).

Lack of Interest in the Population—Disreputable Area of Investigation

Until the early 1970s, research on homosexuality was limited and marginalized; most researchers considered homosexuality to be abnormal or pathological, and the topic generally was considered too risky or dubious for scientific study (Hartmann 1996). In fact, researchers who studied homosexuality were under pervasive pressure to condemn homosexuals and were potentially suspect themselves of having a "bad social, moral or scientific character" (xxvi).

Other than Kinsey's landmark study, which established the diversity of human sexuality in 1948 and Evelyn Hooker's research on the psychological adjustment of male homosexuals, which challenged presumed pathology in 1957, little research was conducted on lesbians and gay men until after Stonewall, when increasingly, such research was conducted by lesbian and gay researchers. And with a couple of limited exceptions, no major population studies of sexuality were carried out until nearly forty years after the Kinsey Report was published (Laumann, Gagnon, Michael, and Michaels 1994). This reflects both a lack of interest among researchers as well as ambivalence about sexuality in society, in general. It took the AIDS epidemic to generate interest in conducting a major national survey of sexual practices in 1988. However, the study was derailed by a Congressional amendment forbidding federally funded national surveys of sexual behavior and causing the cancellation of two approved, peer-reviewed grants by the National Institute of Health. The study was attacked by Senator Jesse Helms and Rep. William Dannemeyer on the grounds that "it was a plot by homosexuals to legitimate . . . lesbian and gay lifestyles, was an unwarranted intrusion by the government in private matters, was not needed, [and] should not be supported by taxpayers' money" (Laumann, Michael, and Gagnon 1994, 36). Although this action was condemned by major professional and scientific associations, federal funds have not been used subsequently to support such studies and even more stringent measures have been adopted to prevent research on adolescent sexuality.

Negative Career Ramifications for Researchers

Like gay men and lesbians who have experienced discrimination in other work settings, researchers who are lesbian, gay, and bisexual report negative consequences as a result of being open about their identity /or conducting research on lesbians, gay men, and bisexuals (see Table 2). In a survey of lesbian researchers, representing a variety of disciplines and work settings in twelve countries, approximately one out of four had difficulty either finding or keeping a job, getting a promotion, or obtaining tenure because they were lesbians; nearly one out of five had difficulty teaching at the graduate level because they were lesbians. (Bradford and Ryan 1996). Similar proportions reported negative experiences in finding a mentor, advisor, or consultant, obtaining grant funding, or finding a job because they had conducted research on lesbians.

Table 2
Discrimination and Professional Bias
Reported by Lesbian, Gay, and Bisexual Researchers

Historians	43%
Political Scientists	32%
Sociologists	43%

Lesbian, gay, and bisexual researchers report negative career consequences whether or not they are pro-active on lesbigay issues. In surveys of lesbian, gay, and bisexual members of the Sociologists' Lesbian and Gay Caucus (American Sociological Association) conducted in 1981 and 1992, more researchers were open about their sexual orientation in 1992 (32 percent vs. 54 percent), but greater visibility increased experiences of professional bias (27 percent vs. 43 percent) (Taylor and Raeburn 1995). Among faculty, nonacademic researchers, and graduate students, 67 percent of women and 71 percent of men who were active in their work settings and profession on lesbigay issues reported career-related discrimination, compared with 40 percent of nonactivist women and 30 percent of nonactivist men. Bias experiences included discrimination in hiring, tenure, and promotion, scholarly devaluation, exclusion from social and professional networks, as well as harassment and intimidation.

Among political scientists, 40 percent of lesbian and gay participants in a membership survey of the American Political Science Association said they were "out" in the workplace; of these nearly three-fifths (58 percent) had colleagues who were discriminated against because of their sexual orientation. One out of five said they had been discouraged from conducting research on lesbian, gay, and bisexual topics, while an additional 39 percent reported avoiding such topics because they were not considered to be "serious political science." In a corresponding survey of political science departmental chairs, only 31 percent considered it "acceptable" for faculty or students to self-identify as lesbian, gay, or bisexual in the classroom (Committee on the Status 1995).

Although psychology as a discipline is more supportive of research on lesbian, gay, and bisexual issues, a survey of graduate student members of the American Psychological Association's Division 44 (Society for the Psychological Study of Lesbian and Gay Issues) found that more than half reported negative experiences including exposure to anti-gay or biased textbooks or written course material, offensive and biased comments from instructors, and a range of negative and discriminatory experiences with faculty, administrative staff, and internships (Pilkington and Cantor, in press). Nearly one-third were discouraged from conducting research on lesbian, gay, or bisexual topics, while others experienced discrimination in internships, harassment, and finding supervisors.

Isolation of Lesbian, Gay, and Bisexual Researchers

Lack of access to colleagues, mentors, and other researchers is a major barrier to personal and professional development for lesbians, gay men, and bisexuals and others interested in research on these issues. Nine out of ten respondents to a survey assessing lesbian researchers' experiences and needs in developing an international Lesbian Research Network ranked access to other lesbian researchers as their top priority, while almost as many sought access to information and resources, and three-quarters cited mentoring as their primary need. (Bradford and Ryan 1996). Although many professional associations have established lesbian, gay, and bisexual caucuses or committees which provide opportunities for networking, collaboration, and information sharing within disciplines, a substantial proportion of members are not "out" to professional peers and do not participate in these activities. Inter-disciplinary networking and collaboration is minimal beyond specific research teams or within institutions where multi-disciplinary work may be encouraged. As a result, many lesbian, gay, and bisexual researchers and students feel isolated and lack adequate support for personal development and for pursuing research interests related to sexual orientation.

Because issues related to sexual orientation are significantly affected by history, culture, race, ethnicity, geography, and psychological factors, cross-disciplinary approaches enhance and strengthen research efforts, while expanding our understand-ing of the multi-dimensional impact of identity and sexuality.

Lack of Funding

Lack of funding remains a major barrier to conducting research on sexuality and sexual orientation. Until gay men were included in the hepatitis B trials in the late 1970s and the AIDS epidemic drove new research agendas in the 1980s, large scale studies did not collect information on the behaviors, health needs, and experiences of gay and bisexual men. Women and lesbians had longer to wait, because large scale biomedical research on women was not undertaken until 1990 with the establishment of the Office of Women's Health Research at NIH. It took another five years of advocacy, however, until questions related to the needs and experiences of lesbians and bisexual women began to be included in national women's health studies, and that struggle continues.

Funding also is needed for smaller scale studies, longitudinal research, and research on specific populations such as persons of color who are lesbian, gay, or bisexual. Mainstream foundations are still slow to fund lesbian, gay, and bisexual research outside of AIDS, and competition is high among more limited lesbian and gay funding sources. Nearly three-fifths of lesbian researchers participating in the Lesbian Research Network survey requested help with research funding. When asked to indicate their expertise in this area, however, only one-quarter were able to provide assistance to others in obtaining funding or identifying potential funding sources (Bradford and Ryan 1996).

IMPACT OF SOCIAL CHANGE ON LESBIAN, GAY, AND BISEXUAL RESEARCH

The emergence of an organized lesbian and gay community during the past twenty-five years has had a major impact on the lives of lesbian, gay, and bisexual people, stimulating the development of an identifiable culture and providing social, professional, and political support that has made it possible for that culture to be expressed, recorded, and shared with the broader society. The availability of an organized community also fosters lesbian, gay, and bisexual identity development, including earlier self-identification and coming out at younger ages, which further informs and invigorates the development of lesbigay culture.

Access to support and an increasingly visible community has helped buffer the threat of negative career ramifications as a result of coming out and professional involvement with lesbian, gay, and bisexual issues. Increasingly, students and younger researchers are open about their lives. The introduction of lesbian, gay, and bisexual studies courses and related courses on human development and clinical issues, provide a vehicle to expand research on this population and to consolidate the transmission of lesbigay culture.

IMPACT OF GENDER AND RACE ON LESBIAN/ GAY/ BISEXUAL RESEARCH

Although lesbian, gay, and bisexual culture and its expression in our lives is remarkably diverse, documentation of the experiences of lesbians, bisexuals (particularly women), and people of color is remarkably limited. Among psychologists, who publish most frequently on lesbian and gay issues, a review of *Psychological Abstracts* shows that less than fifty articles per year have been published on lesbian issues since 1987 (Rothblum 1994). Moreover, a survey of graduate faculty members by the American Psychological Association found that eight out of ten who were involved with lesbian and gay research, coursework, or student supervision with lesbian and gay clients were men; of the few women included, most were studying either gay men or HIV/AIDS (American Psychological Association 1993).

A review of research on sexual orientation published in 1984 found that less than one in seven specifically targeted lesbians (Shively, Jones, and DeCecco 1983–84). In a similar review conducted on health-related research published between 1990 and 1992, the majority of studies focused on gay men, while approximately 13 percent targeted bisexual men, and only 3 percent concerned bisexual women (Sell and Petrulio 1996). The disparity is even greater when considering the dearth of information on lesbians, gay men, and bisexuals of color where the complex interaction of sexual orientation and ethnic identity shapes the development and expression of sexual and social identities. Outreach and sampling strategies that actively recruit openly identified white lesbians and gay men will not effectively target ethnic and racial minorities who are lesbian, gay, and bisexual, or others who are not affiliated with the identified lesbian and gay community or open about their sexual orientation. While several researchers have focused on developing appropriate research methods to study these groups, much work is needed to assess and express the true diversity of nonheterosexual communities.

Although the AIDS epidemic has added to an already larger body of research focusing on gay men, it also has increased the proportion of lesbian and gay researchers studying HIV, and resulted in more intense focus on issues related to sexual orientation, behavior, networking, identity development, and life stages. In addition, mainstream researchers have increasingly become involved with studying HIV and issues related to sexual orientation. The growing interest in research with this population is underscored by the proliferation of journals on lesbian, gay, and bisexual issues, which have emerged during the past few years.

NEED FOR TRAINING AND SUPPORT

Building the research capacity of lesbian, gay, and bisexual researchers and enhancing the quality of research on lesbian, gay, and bisexual issues requires the planning and development of research networks, the development of formal mentoring systems, and the establishment of standard definitions and measures for key concepts and terms. One such project—an international Lesbian Research Network (LRN)—currently is under development to provide access to information, resources, mentoring, and technical assistance for lesbians who do research on lesbian-related and other topics in a broad range of settings and disciplines. The LRN has conducted an international survey of lesbian researchers to identify needs and experiences and prioritize planning and programs; a Directory of Lesbian Researchers, indexed by location, topic, and discipline is planned.

IMPLICATIONS FOR THE FUTURE

The opportunities for expanding and enhancing the quality of research on lesbian, gay, and bisexual issues have never been more promising. Electronic networking and journals can connect researchers throughout the world and rapidly transmit information, exponentially increasing access and placing lesbian, gay, and bisexual issues on a par with other mainstream areas of investigation. Increased access will stimulate research in neglected areas of investigation: people of color who are lesbian, gay, and bisexual; lesbians; and bisexual women. However, caution is warranted: the proliferation of journals on lesbian, gay, and bisexual issues and increased interest in these populations among students and other researchers does not mean that underlying methodological problems will be addressed or that the quality of their work will warrant publication and dissemination. A lack of understanding of these issues by peer reviewers and editors, inappropriate use of findings by the media, and our failure to develop research literacy among lesbian, gay, and bisexual advocates who routinely interpret research in community settings, serve to perpetuate the myths and misinformation engendered by inaccurate research.

Librarians and information specialists play a unique role in helping collect, document, and preserve information about lesbigay culture and making that information available to the world. For all the rapid expansion of research; lesbian, gay, and bisexual programs; and community projects, the body of knowledge about this population still is evolving. There is much to be done in refining our research capacity and much to be discovered and shared when we apply those skills in more effective and creative ways.

REFERENCES

American Psychological Association. 1993. *Graduate faculty in psychology interested in lesbian and gay issues*. Washington, DC: American Psychological Association.
Bradford, Judy and Ryan, Caitlin. Survey of lesbian researchers—preliminary analysis. Presented at "Teaching to Promote Women's Health," Toronto, Ontario, June 15, 1996.

Committee on the Status of Lesbians and Gays in the Profession, American Political Science Association. 1995. Report on the status of lesbians and gays in the political science profession. *PS: Political Science & Politics* 28 (September): 561–74.

Committee on Women Historians' Report on the Lesbian and Gay Historians Survey. 1993. *Perspectives* (April): 13–15.

Cook, Blanche W. 1979. "The historical denial of lesbianism." *Radical History Review* 20 (Spring/Summer): 60–65.

Hartmann, Lawrence. 1996. Foreword. *Textbook of homosexuality and mental health*, eds. Robert P. Cabaj and Terry S. Stein, xxv–xxxi. Washington, DC: American Psychiatric Press.

Herdt, Gilbert. 1992. "'Coming out' as a rite of passage: A Chicago study." In *Gay culture in America*, ed. Gil Herdt, 29–67. Boston: Beacon Press.

Laumann, Edward O.; Michael, Robert T.; and Gagnon, John H. 1994. A political history of the national sex survey of adults. *Family Planning Perspectives* 26, no. 1: 34–38.

Laumann, Edward O.; Gagnon, John H.; Michael, Robert T.; and Michaels, Stuart. 1994. *The social organization of sexuality: Sexual practices in the United States*. Chicago: University of Chicago Press.

Pilkington, Neil W. and Cantor, James M. In press. "Perceptions of heterosexual bias in professional psychology programs: A survey of graduate students." *Professional Psychology: Research and Practice*.

Rothblum, Esther. 1994. Personal communication with the author. April.

Sell, Randall L. and Petrulio, Christian. 1996. "Sampling homosexuals, bisexuals, gays and lesbians for public health research: A review of the literature from 1990 to 1992." *Journal of Homosexuality* 30, no. 4: 31–47.

Shively Michael G.; Jones, Christopher; and DeCecco, John P. 1983–84. "Research on sexual orientation: Definitions and methods." *Journal of Homosexuality* 9 (Winter/Spring): 127–33.

Taylor, Verta, and Raeburn, Nicole C. 1995. "Identity politics as high risk activism: Career consequences for lesbian, gay and bisexual sociologists." *Social Problems* 42 (May): 252–73.

Terry, Jennifer. 1991. "Theorizing deviant historiography." *Differences: A Journal of Feminist Cultural Studies* 3 (Summer): 55–73.

Weeks, Jeffrey. 1979. "Movements of affirmation: Sexual meanings and homosexual identities." *Radical History Review* 20 (Spring/Summer): 164–79.

2

A Lesbigay Gender Perplex: Sexual Stereotyping and Professional Ambiguity in Librarianship

Christine L. Williams

Many librarians lament that people outside of their profession have distorted stereotypes of librarians. One author refers to the popular image as "the old-maid-Marian-Librarian, or if the case may be, the fairy-Harry-Librarian image" (Glab 1972, 20). Contained within these stereotypes are beliefs about the librarian's sexuality: if female, the assumption is that she is a sexually repressed spinster; if male, the assumption is that he is gay.

Scholarship has contributed to the popular notion that male librarians are feminine. In the 1960s, psychologists built the stereotypes into survey instruments intended to measure personality attributes. The popular California Personality Inventory, for example, considers an expressed interest in librarianship an indication of femininity (Turner 1980, 236). Several researchers have used such scales to ascertain the gender identity of men in librarianship and other predominantly female professions (e.g., Morrisey and Case 1988; Turner 1980; Wilson 1982, 119–20). Most of these studies have found little difference between men librarians and "normal men"; indeed, it is astonishing that the consistent finding of "no difference" continues to make the scholarly headlines. However, this repeated scrutiny of men in nontraditional occupations serves as a constant reminder that their masculinity—and hence, their sexuality—is in question.

Even some who are sympathetic to the plight of gay men in the workforce occasionally draw upon these stereotypes in their research. Martin Levine, who was one of the first sociologists to study discrimination against gay men, argued that widespread homophobia in society "drives many gay men away from men's work and into sissy jobs, which functions to reinforce prevailing images of gay men as effeminate" (Levine 1989, 273). Among the "sissy jobs" he lists are dancer, florist, secretary—and librarian.

But if the "outside world" believes that librarianship is a haven for gay men, they are deeply mistaken. Lesbian and gay librarians have documented an extensive history of discrimination against them by their profession (Carmichael and Shontz

1996; Gittings 1990; Gough and Greenblatt 1990; Thistlethwaite 1994). The recent controversy over a photo of the ALA Gay and Lesbian Task Force marching in the 1992 San Francisco Freedom Day Parade published on the cover of *American Libraries* illustrates the scope of this hostility. The magazine printed several letters to the editor condemning the publication of the photograph. One writer tied his outrage to the image problem:

The library profession is too often identified in academe as a place where the odd, the different, and the unwanted in other departments can be easily cached. Consequently, many, if not most, males in librarianship are thought of as being gay. Whether it is true or not does not matter. The perception inhibits many from entering the profession as freely as one enters computer science, statistics, or chemistry. Your cover helps with the impression that the profession is open to all types of peoples, all types of ideas, and of course, all types of information; but it doesn't further our profession as part of mainstream America. ("More on gay cover-age" 1992, 738)

Others were less reflective about their negative reaction to the cover photo. One wrote in that he "wanted to puke" when he saw it ("Editorial discretion advised" 1992, 625). Another was "disgusted, appalled, and nauseated to see my professional association supporting a sexually perverse movement" ("AL's gay pride cover" 1992, 844). Although, to their credit, *American Libraries* printed several supportive letters and editorials condemning this hostility, the point is clear: librarianship is not an especially welcoming place to gays and lesbians.

Why does the popular stereotype that librarianship is a haven for "the odd, the different, and the unwanted" bear such little resemblance to the actual experiences of gay and lesbian librarians? This chapter explores this paradox, focussing on gay men. This chapter is based on research I conducted on men in four predominately female occupations: nursing, librarianship, elementary school teaching, and social work (Williams 1995). The first part discusses some of the historical reasons for the popular stereotypes. The second part explores the interpersonal and organizational dynamics within libraries that perpetuate discrimination against gay librarians.[1]

THE GENDERING OF LIBRARIANSHIP

To understand the origin of the sexual stereotypes about librarians, it is important to review the history of the feminization of the profession. Although librarians have been around for centuries, the occupation as practiced today began in the late nineteenth century, with the enormous expansion of publicly-supported libraries. As historians have amply documented, the proportional representation of women in library jobs grew as the number of jobs did. In 1870, only 20 percent of the 213 librarians in the United States were women; by 1930, women comprised over 90 percent of the more than 30,000 U.S. librarians (Schiller 1979; U.S. Census 1943). The rapid feminization of librarianship was promoted by library leaders who argued that women were, by nature, best suited to its occupational demands. Women were preferred because of their housekeeping abilities, which emphasized tidiness, order, peace, and decorum. In 1889, the following advice was offered to library planners: "Something may be said of the desirableness of making the library wear a pleasant and inviting look. The reading-room offers perhaps the best opportunity for this. A reading-room lately seen has a bright carpet on the floor, low tables, and a few rocking-chairs scattered about; a cheerful, open fire on dull days, attractive pictures on the walls, and one can imagine a lady librarian filling the windows with plants. Such a room is a welcome in itself, and bids one come again" (quoted in Garrison 1972–73, 136). Furthermore, women's putative patience for accurate, tedious work made them ideal candidates for cataloging, and their maternal inclinations suited them for work in the children's collections, a library specialty that has been almost exclusively female since its inception in 1900 (Weibel and Heim 1979; Garrison 1979).

This definition of librarianship as suitably feminine and domestic was developed to justify the employment of educated single white women into what in the early nineteenth century was considered an occupation of dubious social status. Middle class parents had to be convinced that sending their unmarried daughters to work in libraries would not impugn the dignity of their families or interfere with their future marriage plans. The ideology of femininity, which linked librarianship to domesticity, paved the way for the employment of young single women in libraries.

The library leaders' determination to hire these women for the new positions was ultimately motivated by economic concerns. Because libraries were funded by private donations and public money, labor costs had to be kept down as much as possible, and well-educated women would work for a fraction of the salaries commanded by "comparable" men. Women worked for less pay than men because their employment options were gravely restricted at the time, but employers justified the lower pay on the grounds that women did not use their incomes to support a family, as men presumably did. Women's meager pay was based on a social consensus regarding the bare minimum amount of money believed necessary for individual subsistence—not the social value or importance of the job (Kessler-Harris 1990).

In contrast, the men who remained in librarianship during the period of feminization were consistently paid higher salaries than the highest paid women; in fact, men typically earned double the salaries of their female counterparts (Garrison 1979). This higher wage was justified in part by appeals to men's breadwinning responsibilities. But equally important, male librarians were financially rewarded for their newly acquired administrative and supervisory roles. As the number of library jobs grew, the profession became hierarchically organized and managed, with the top administrative positions reserved for men only.

Stereotypes of masculinity were used to defend the hiring of men for the top library positions. Trustees, philanthropists, and politicians were believed to prefer business dealings with male administrators. Men were lauded for their abilities to sustain criticism, use resources efficiently, and even to be rough and aggressive. Speaking at the 1892 meeting of the American Library Association (ALA), a library trustee explained:

My reason for preferring a man for the head of a library in a large city . . . is connected with the business side of the library profession. Unfortunately women are hedged about with rules of decorum and courtesy which somewhat interfere with their usefulness in many

relations in a municipal or a business community; with the trustees, for instance, who may
. . . comprise men of rough or at least of downright and positive character. A man's relations
with such a board are freer and more likely to be influential than a woman's, because he can
talk right *at* them and *with* them, without offense on either side. He is usually accustomed
to hasty and unfair criticism and knows how to meet it effectively. With the city
government—especially the council who make appropriation—a man can work far more
efficiently than a woman can . . . . With the rougher class of the community, with laborers
and artisans, a man, for obvious reasons, can do more effective work. (Quoted in Weibel and
Heim 1979)

Gender stereotypes were thus built into the library profession. Women were to
be the rank-and-file library workers, as their supposed feminine attributes made them
amply suited to maintaining a pleasant, orderly reading room atmosphere, performing
tedious cataloging work, and controlling children. Men were to be the directors and
administrators because their forceful natures and no-nonsense reasoning abilities.
The pay structure further reinforced this gender segregation. Paying women very
little money fostered their continued dependence on the family for support, whereas
rewarding men for their accomplishments with high salaries encouraged them to be
ambitious and career-minded.

The contemporary stereotypes of librarians as spinster women and gay men are
more understandable in light of this history. Gender roles patterned on the
heterosexual nuclear family are embedded in the occupational roles and the pay
structure of library jobs. The jobs were designed for unmarried women preparing for
their future domestic role. Consequently, for a man to work in a rank-and-file
position, the popular view is that (a) he doesn't have a wife and children to support,
and (b) to be successful in his job he must possess feminine attributes such as a
penchant for tidiness and knowledge of the rules of decorum. For most Americans,
these assumptions confirm their image of gay men. These stereotypes are the legacy
of employers' efforts to extract cheap labor from educated women; they bear no
necessary resemblance to the work of librarianship, any more than they resemble
work in traditionally male jobs such as accounting and pharmacy. Nevertheless, like
all stereotypes, they have influenced how librarianship is perceived by outsiders, and
they have had important consequences for the gender dynamics within the
profession.

MASCULINITY IN LIBRARIANSHIP

The ideology of femininity has been contested within librarianship throughout
the twentieth century, particularly as some library leaders sought to enhance their
professional status. In response to a growing dissatisfaction over the low status and
pay of library work, leading librarians and researchers began blaming women for the
problems of their occupation. The failure to obtain true professional status was
attributed to women's feminine orientation, especially to their low aspirations and
erratic commitment to the labor force. Men, in contrast, were seen as possessing just
that combination of qualities needed to enhance librarianship's status. This curious
analysis sparked recruiting drives to encourage more men to enter librarianship. In
the 1960s, for example, the ALA consciously targeted men by issuing recruitment

brochures with the titles, "The Librarian—Merchant of Ideas," and "The Librarian—Idea Consultant." College scholarships were set aside for men, and special libraries hired men with promises to place them "in the areas of administration, science and technology, and computer information systems" (O'Brien 1983, 63). In the 1970s, *American Libraries* published a photo essay entitled "Who We Are," commemorating the 100th anniversary of the ALA, which contained the following image of the male librarian, here described by Pauline Wilson:

The male librarian featured most prominently is a burly individual with heavy, craggy features and big hands. He is shown in rubber boots and a knitted skull cap working the rigging of his fishing boat. In another shot he sits in a deck chair in his rough, outdoorsy clothes, cigarette dangling from his mouth Humphrey Bogart style, a pair of big binoculars grasped in his hands while he gazes out to sea. The accompanying text relates that he is an athlete as well as a fisherman who sells his catch commercially. The reader is told that he was a boxing champion and that he plays handball and likes to challenge his staff to a game of racquetball from time to time. (Wilson 1982, 35)

Clearly, the library profession preferred a specific expression of masculinity from the men in its ranks—the ambitious, technical, outdoorsy type. The concern was frequently expressed that recruiting mediocre men would do nothing to enhance the overall status of the profession.[2] Often implicit in these concerns was the suspicion that the men currently employed in librarianship were inadequately masculine. One writer, lamenting the "predominant public image of the male librarian [as] a kindly and sometimes effeminate misfit," argued that with better publicity "a new and more vigorous type of male librarian will become more prevalent" (Angoff 1959, 555–56).

This preference for only certain types of men in librarianship reinforces what sociologists call "hegemonic masculinity." This term, coined by Robert Connell, suggests that different styles of masculinity compete for preeminence in society. The hegemonic, or socially privileged form today is represented by men possessing entrepreneurial spirit, athleticism, rationality, and, importantly, heterosexuality. This particular configuration of masculinity has not always held its privileged position in our society, and it is constantly contested by other forms, including various gay masculinities. But the preference for hegemonic masculinity is built into many occupations and organizations, thus reproducing heterosexism, and contributing to the homophobic environment experienced by many gays and lesbians in the work place (Connell 1987, 1992; Segal 1990; Williams 1995).

According to my in-depth interviews with librarians throughout the United States, men in general continue to receive preferential treatment in graduate school admissions, hiring, and promotion to the top positions. This observation is born out by the statistics: although the majority of professional librarians are women, men continue to be overrepresented in the top positions of academic and public libraries, and on average, they earn more money than their female colleagues (Dowell 1988; U.S. Labor Department 1991, 223). However, it is still the case that only those who demonstrate appropriately masculine qualities benefit from this preference. In the remainder of this chapter, I will draw upon my in-depth interviews to illustrate the informal ways that hegemonic masculinity is reproduced and rewarded in the profession.

I interviewed twenty-nine librarians (twenty-two men and seven women) in four U.S. metropolitan areas (Austin, Boston, Phoenix, and San Francisco) as part of my study of men in predominately female professions.[3] Nearly all had encountered the stereotype that male librarians are gay and effeminate. Very few believed that the stereotype was accurate, but some felt uncomfortable because of it. According to one California librarian: "The perception is that an incredibly large percentage of men who are librarians are gay . . . I had one friend in library school . . . he was six-foot-something and very good looking, had been in a rock band, dressed all in black all the time, and it really bothered him—the stereotype of librarians. He had a hard time saying to people, 'I am a librarian.' He was straight, but he wore an earring, so he was afraid everybody would think he was gay."

His fear may have been founded on his own homophobia. But it also is likely that he believed that appearing gay would result in discriminatory treatment against him. Employers may avoid hiring gay men and promoting them to leadership positions. Although none of my respondents had any direct experience of such job actions, several felt that anti-gay sentiment was prevalent within libraries. One Massachusetts librarian recalled a job interview where his sexuality was indirectly questioned: "I went to an interview for a librarian position not long ago and it was in a school where it was total female faculty, the principal, everything. The only male there was the janitor. And that was one of the questions asked me: 'Do you think you would be comfortable in a faculty with all women?' There were two principals in the room, and before I could answer the question, the other principal said, 'Well, that'd be heaven, wouldn't it?' And so I laughed right along with it."

As a school librarian, this man probably was subject to unusually intense scrutiny about his sexuality. Several respondents claimed that there is both a greater suspicion and greater intolerance for gay men working in schools and in the children's collections at public libraries. One man described an interview at a school where the principal insisted on physically looking him over before he was offered the job. He successfully obtained that position, but when he later applied for a job at a public library, he was asked if the reason he was leaving was because he had "trouble with boys"—implying that men in school librarianship are sexually interested in the male pupils.

The stereotype that gay men have a prurient interest in boys can result in men being transferred to positions considered more appropriate for men. In one case, a children's librarian was promoted to assuage the fears of parents in the community:

R: Some people had said that they didn't want a man doing that job (storytelling). I thought that I did a good job. And I had been told by my supervisors—they came out and did an evaluation, just before all of this happened—and I was told that I was doing a good job.

CW: Have you ever considered filing some sort of lawsuit to get that other job back?

R: Well, actually, the job I've gotten now . . . it's a reference librarian; it's what I wanted in the first place. I've got a whole lot more authority here. I'm also in charge of the circulation desk. And I've recently been promoted because of my new stature. So, no, I'm not considering trying to get that other job back.

Hegemonic masculinity is reasserted through such discriminatory job actions.

To assuage the homophobia of the community, this man was transferred out of a job closely associated with the feminine role of child care, to a job emphasizing intellectual and managerial authority. Employers often assume that men are better suited than women for leadership positions. As this example indicates, heterosexual men, and gay men who remain closeted, actually can benefit financially from this discrimination (Connell 1992).

Blatant bias against gays thus bolsters hegemonic masculinity. However, because hiring and promotions decisions usually happen behind closed doors, it is impossible to comprehend the full scope of anti-gay discrimination in any profession. In their study of gay professionals, Woods and Lucas contend that the exclusion of gays and lesbians is typically accomplished in more subtle and informal ways:

The traditional white-collar workplace is "heterosexist" in the sense that it structurally and ideologically promotes a particular model of heterosexuality while penalizing, hiding, or otherwise "symbolically annihilating" its alternatives. Like racism, sexism, and other isms, heterosexism encompasses not only blatant, isolated displays of prejudice (a bigoted remark, a hate crime), but also the more subtle, unseen ways which lesbians and gay men are stigmatized, excluded, and denied the support given their heterosexual peers. (Woods and Lucas 1993, 9–10)

Woods and Lucas identify the forced invisibility of gay employees, the public celebration of heterosexual mating rituals, and the masculine values embedded in bureaucracies as contributing to the anti-gay culture of most work organizations.

Respondents provided many examples of these subtle yet institutionalized forms of bias in libraries. For instance, in many libraries, employees regularly celebrate heterosexual engagements, weddings, and baby showers. It is not uncommon for heterosexual professionals to wear wedding bands, decorate their offices with photos of their family members, or invite their spouses to office social functions. Gays and lesbians forced to remain closeted at work can feel excluded and isolated because of these practices.

Co-workers and clients make assumptions about male librarians that further reinforce hegemonic masculinity and contribute to the marginalization of alternative gay masculinities. For example, several men told me that they are often called upon to perform special tasks, such as lifting heavy boxes of books, or even acting as security guards. This was the case in a large metropolitan public library system, where most of the men worked in the central library instead of the neighborhood branches. One of these men explained the reason for this segregation: "We didn't have security guards [in the central library building]. Since the administrator worked in this building, and she could move people from the branches, she decided she wanted to have men in the main library to sort of double as security guards." In this example, all men are presumed to be capable of defending the library against rowdy and potentially violent patrons. Those men who have this ability are clearly privileged by this administrator; alternative expressions of masculinity are ignored, trivialized, or devalued in comparison.

Several of those interviewed believed that men bring additional special qualities and abilities to the practice of librarianship. This opinion became especially apparent when I asked respondents if they thought more men should be recruited into the profession. Many responded affirmatively because they believed that men would enhance the technical practice of librarianship. When asked what the profession should do to attract more men, one Texas librarian answered: "Since automation has become part of the profession, more and more men are coming. I think that men are looking more for prestigious careers, and automation has given that to the profession. Not just organizing books, but applying technology to the process."

In addition, some claimed that libraries need the special expertise in sports and auto repair that men could bring to the profession. One woman maintained that more men were needed in collection development for this reason: "I'm unusual in my library because I know sports. One woman had a question about Wayne Gretsky; she didn't know who he was. She came to me and asked, 'Who's Wayne Gretsky?' I said, 'Well, ma'am, he's the most famous hockey player in the world.' She said, 'Oh, that helps.' And I remember being astonished that nobody in the library had any sports knowledge; they had like zero. And yet that's a whole section in the library that's fairly popular. And unfortunately, as it stands, it tends to be something that men are more interested in, although not necessarily."

Although she recognizes that not all men know a lot about sports (and some women, like herself, know a great deal), she nevertheless believes that more men should be hired for the special expertise they could contribute in this area. This illustrates the intractable nature of gender stereotypes: they often persist despite countervailing experience and evidence. All men potentially benefit from this belief, and those who can demonstrate proficiency in masculine topics may be privileged in seeking jobs.

Finally, several mentioned that more men are needed in the profession to act as role models for children, especially in school libraries: "In schools, in general, where there's so few male teachers compared to female teachers, I think that they're eager to have them as role models. A lot of these kids come from single-parent families where they're living just with their mother. I think they really like the idea of having men in the schools."

Of course, not all men are welcome: as we have seen, there is a great deal of prejudice against gay men working with children. Only heterosexual men displaying the right paternal qualities are preferred as role models for children.

Thus, it is not uncommon for those who work in libraries to assume that men possess special qualities and abilities that are needed in the profession. These include leadership skills, strength, computer expertise, sports and automotive knowledge, and fatherly qualities. It certainly is not the case that gay men lack abilities in these areas; I am not arguing that heterosexual men have a monopoly on these abilities. However, the privileging of these hegemonic masculine qualities does tend to undermine and diminish alternative expressions of masculinity. Those men who do not conform to the social expectations contained within hegemonic masculinity—either willfully or not—do not receive the benefits accruing to men throughout the profession. Consequently, many gay men feel marginalized and excluded in librarianship, and like gays in so many other professions, they feel pressure to remain closeted.

CONCLUSION

The paradox of heterosexism in a "gay" occupation reflects the dynamic ways that gender and sexuality are negotiated in organizations. Because librarianship was designed as a career for well-educated single white women in the nineteenth century, it retains its association with femininity and domesticity in the popular imagination today. But it is precisely this association that marks the occupation as low-status, low-paying work. Efforts to attract and retain more men in the profession is a response to society's sexist devaluation of women and the work they do. The fact that masculine men have been viewed as a panacea to the problems of the profession stigmatizes and excludes those men who fail or refuse to conform—including those expressing alternative gay masculinities.

Librarianship ought to redesign its occupational structure to recognize and celebrate the diversity of talents and abilities among librarians. It is just as wrong to privilege displays of hegemonic masculinity today as it was to privilege domestic femininity at the end of the nineteenth century. Uncoupling gender stereotypes from occupational roles is a crucial step toward ridding the workplace of heterosexism and achieving equality of opportunity for all workers.

NOTES

This paper was prepared while the author was a Fellow at the Center for Advanced Study in the Behavioral Sciences, Stanford, California. I am grateful for financial support provided by the National Science Foundation (#SES–9022192) and the University Research Institute of the University of Texas, Austin.

1. This paper does not address lesbian experience in the profession because my data are limited to men. I believe that a separate analysis is needed to understand the specific forms of discrimination and special treatment accorded to lesbians in librarianship.

2. For examples, see the editorial forum, "The Weaker Sex?", *Library Journal* 63 (March 15, 1933): 232, and responding letters to the editor (294–96, 342–43, 438); Ralph Munn, "It is a mistake to recruit men," *Library Journal* 74 (November 1, 1949): 1639–40, and responses, *Library Journal* 75: 66, 98, 422, 478, 518, 520; Charles Joyce, "The Suppliant Maidens", *Library Journal* 86 (December 15, 1961): 4247–49, and responses, *Library Journal* 87: 356, 358.

3. The complete study was based on 99 interviews with men and women in four professions. Of the 76 men interviewed, five told me they were gay. See Williams 1995.

REFERENCES

"AL's gay pride cover: Pro and con." *American Libraries* 23 (November 1992): 840–44.

Angoff, Allan. 1959. "The male librarian—an anomaly?" *Library Journal* (February 15): 553–56.

Carmichael, James V., and Shontz, Marilyn L. 1996. "'The last socially acceptable prejudice': Gay and lesbian issues, social responsibilities and coverage of these topics in MLIS/MLS programs." *The Library Quarterly* 66 (January): 21–39.

Connell, Robert W. 1987. *Gender and power.* Stanford: Stanford University Press.

Connell, Robert W. 1992. "A very straight gay: Masculinity, homosexual experience, and gender." *American Sociological Review* 57: 735–51.

Dowell, David R. 1988. "Sex and salary in a female dominated profession." *Journal of Academic Librarianship* 14: 92–98.

"Editorial discretion advised,"*American Libraries* 23 (September 1992): 625.

Garrison, Dee. 1979. *Apostles of culture: The public librarian and American society, 1876–1920.* New York: The Free Press.

Garrison, Dee. 1972–73. "The tender technicians: The feminization of public librarianship, 1876–1905." *Journal of Social History* 6: 133–59.

Gittings, Barbara. 1990. *Gays in libraryland: The Gay and Lesbian Task Force of the American Library Association: The first sixteen years.* Philadelphia: By the author.

Glab, Kathleen. 1972. "The sensuous librarian." In *Revolting librarians,* ed. Celeste West and Elizabeth Katz, 19–21. San Francisco: Bootlegger Press.

Gough, Cal, and Ellen Greenblatt, eds. 1990. *Gay and lesbian library service.* Jefferson, NC: McFarland & Company.

Kessler-Harris, Alice. 1990. *A woman's wage: Historical meanings and social consequences.* Lexington: University of Kentucky Press.

Levine, Martin. 1989. "The status of gay men in the workplace." In *Men's Lives,* ed. Michael Kimmel and Michael Messner, 261–76. New York: Macmillan.

"More on gay cover-age." *American Libraries* 23 (October 1992): 738.

Morrisey, Locke J., and Case, Donald O. 1988. "There goes my image: The perception of male librarians by colleague, student, and self." *College and Research Libraries* 49 (September): 453–64.

O'Brien, Nancy Patricia. 1983. "The recruitment of men into librarianship following World War II." In *The Status of Women in Librarianship,* ed. Kathleen Heim, 51–66. New York: Neal-Schuman Publishers.

Schiller, Anita R. 1979. "Women in librarianship." In *The role of women in librarianship,* ed. Kathleen Weibel and Kathleen M. Heim, 222–256. Phoenix, AZ: Oryx Press.

Segal, Lynne. 1990. *Slow motion: Changing masculinities, changing men.* New Brunswick, N.J.: Rutgers University Press.

Thistlethwaite, Polly J. 1994. "Gays and lesbians in library history." In *The encyclopedia of library history,* ed. Wayne A. Wiegand and Donald G. Davis, 223–27. New York: Garland.

Turner, Robert L. 1980. "Femininity and the librarian—another test." *College and Research Libraries* 41 (May): 235–41.

U.S. Census. 1943. *Comparative occupation statistics for the United States, 1870–1940.* Washington, DC: Government Printing Office.

U.S. Labor Department. Bureau of Labor Statistics. 1991. *Employment and Earnings* 38: 223.

Weibel, Kathleen, and Heim, Kathleen M., eds. 1979. *The role of women in librarianship.* Phoenix, AZ: Oryx Press.

Williams, Christine L. 1995. *Still a man's world: Men who do "women's work."* Berkeley: University of California Press.

Wilson, Pauline. 1982. *Stereotype and status: Librarians in the United States.* Westport, CT: Greenwood Press.

Woods, James, and Lucas, Jay. 1993. *The corporate closet: The professional lives of gay men in America.* New York: The Free Press.

3

Biographical Research on Lesbigay Subjects: Editing the Letters of Lillian Smith

Margaret Rose Gladney

The publication of *How Am I to Be Heard? Letters of Lillian Smith* in the fall of 1993 marked the culmination of fifteen years of research and writing about a woman whose life and work had influenced mine for over twenty years. When Jim Carmichael asked me to participate in the twenty-fifth anniversary celebration of the American Library Association's (ALA) Gay, Lesbian, and Bisexual Task Force (GLBTF), although I welcomed the opportunity to reflect on my research in a somewhat different light, I also wondered, at first, how my study of Lillian Smith might relate to the subject of gay and lesbian library history. As I learned more about the founding of the first professional GLBTF, however, I began to see clearly that the research, writing, and publishing of *How Am I to Be Heard?* was very much a product of the history I had been invited to celebrate.

Significantly, I discovered, the GLBTF from its beginning had included and recognized the work of activists within and outside scholarly and established professional organizations. A collaborative effort, like my work on Lillian Smith, its work embodied and reflected the efforts of many people who are part of a much larger and longer process: the movements for social change that have defined and made real our highest ideals of social justice and human liberation in a democratic society, especially the African American liberation and civil rights movements, which inspired both the women's liberation and lesbian, gay, bisexual, and transgendered liberation movements. Because of the work of those movements I, a southern white woman, could earn a Ph.D., be employed in a Deep South state university, find redress in the courts when I initially was denied tenure at that university, subsequently secure institutional support from that university to write a book about Lillian Smith, a woman whose life and work challenged her culture's fundamental ideas about race and sex, and have that book published by a southern university press, with a feminist editor, and in a series devoted to works on gender and culture.

Reflecting on that history, I remembered the collective and interconnecting work of many who have gone before, and many who continue to challenge the prescribed limits of social and political categories. Such is the work of the ALA's Social Responsibility and Library History Round Tables (SRRT and LHRT). Remembering that history, I considered how Lillian Smith's letter to the Student Nonviolent Coordinating Committee (SNCC) in the early 1960s might be helpful in addressing the sometimes bitter debate on the place of lesbigay issues in the ongoing dialogue about librarians' social responsibilities.[1]

Organized in April of 1960 to coordinate the activities of the student-initiated sit-ins protesting segregated public facilities throughout the South, SNCC quickly became the most radical arm of the civil rights movement. From the first sit-in in Greensboro, North Carolina, Lillian Smith supported them and encouraged her friends in older civil rights organizations to support the bold activism of those black and white students. She was invited to speak at their first conference in Atlanta, and a number of the SNCC leaders visited Smith in her mountain home near Clayton, Georgia. By December 1962 or January 1963, when she wrote the letter excerpted here, violent resistance to the sit-ins, marches, and demonstrations was increasing throughout the South and the young activists were, understandably, discouraged.

Dear All of You at SNCC:
I read your Newsletter with a sinking heart. It sounds so terribly bad. But things are breaking and thawing: we must hold on to that. A frozen river is a quiet thing; in thaw it is a roaring monster. We are in thaw in the South: there is bound to be much noise, much individual cruelty, much collective madness. But underneath, change is taking place—not only in streets and places but in human hearts. And this we must every one remember. I remember when I first began writing my magazine *South Today* things were so frozen that people actually thought I was mad. (And not only the Ralph McGills—but truly wise and good people thought so). I remember the stunned faces in Raleigh N.C. at a meeting of the Southern Churchmen (their faces were all right-the audience's collective face is what I remember) when I quietly said segregation is morally wrong, psychologically wrong, culturally wrong: all of us, white and Negro are harmed by it. The whites' souls are harmed, the Negroes' bodies and minds. That gasp from the audience. This was in 1943. I kept on writing, speaking out, and more important, thinking, thinking, letting this dilemma, this sickness relate, as it must, to all the other sicknesses of our soul and confusions of our mind. And people thought I was half out of my mind! Of course. That was the frozen period. If you think this thaw is bad, I wish you could have experienced the hard frozen sterile quality of those times. I say this not to minimize the horror of today but to give perspective, to help us see that sometimes noise and blood and screams and blows are not a sign of things worsening but of things getting better.[2]

Two of Smith's observations seem particularly appropriate in light of the increasingly heightened resistance to any effort to act openly or inclusively in support of lesbian, gay, bisexual, and transgendered peoples. First, it is important to remember that we, too, are in "a time of thaw"—Smith's perspective that evidence of increased resistance to civil rights activism was itself a sign of what happens, naturally, inevitably in the course of working for social change. Second, it is significant how she addressed the most pressing social dilemma of her time, her society's response to racial differences: by "letting this dilemma, this sickness relate, as it must, to all the sicknesses of our soul and confusions of our mind." Lillian

Smith is remembered today not only because she spoke against racial segregation in a time when few other whites of her class and region were doing so; her work remains significant because she insisted that issues of race cannot be understood in isolation, apart from every other aspect of human mind and heart, or to phrase it in contemporary language, from any of our other social constructions of class, gender, or sexuality.

I did not begin to write about Lillian Smith with the idea of writing lesbian history or biography. When I began my research in the summer of 1978, I did so as a southern, white feminist, especially interested in the way Smith had stretched and challenged the limits imposed by the traditional construction of southern white ladyhood.

Long before the publication of her magazine *South Today* and her best-selling novel *Strange Fruit* established Lillian Smith as the South's most liberal white writer, she was known to hundreds of young white women and their families throughout the South as "Miss Lil," director of Laurel Falls Camp, a highly popular, educationally innovative summer camp for girls in the mountains of northern Georgia. It was through her work with the camp that Smith first began systematically to examine and then confront her society's concepts of race and gender. Thus I began my study of Smith as an oral history project in which I interviewed over fifty women who had been Laurel Falls campers or counselors, including Paula Snelling, whom I knew first as Smith's "life-long friend and companion," assistant camp director, and co-editor of the magazine.

Invariably, when I presented my first papers about Smith and Laurel Falls Camp at regional and national women's studies meetings, the question came from the audience: What was the nature of the relationship between Lillian Smith and Paula Snelling? Always my answer was: How can we know? Smith didn't identify herself as lesbian. Of course the obvious way to "settle the question" was to ask Paula Snelling. She was still alive, though by then in a nursing home, paralyzed on her left side from a stroke. I had interviewed her on several occasions about Laurel Falls Camp, but had never asked her about the "nature" of her relationship with Lillian Smith.

What did I think she would say? Why hadn't I asked her? Here was the tricky part, and a prime example of why questions of sexual identity or sexual expression cannot be fully examined in isolation. Ironically, the very characteristics that had initially led me to identify so closely with Smith and her worldview—our both being born female into small-town, upperclass, white southern families—now served to inhibit and blind my research. How could I ask Paula Snelling about her sexual relationship with Lillian Smith? That was her private business, wasn't it? What difference did it make? That was the question I asked myself. That was the question my closeted lesbian friends and lovers asked me. And I could not give an answer. I was blinded by my own class and gender socialization and by my closeted lesbian sexuality. So long as we hold the illusion of sexuality and sexual expression as purely private matters, it is too easy to dismiss the questions about same-sex relationships in historical research as mere speculation or gossip, or the insidious desire of those queer others to project their own queerness onto historically recognized figures. I knew I wanted to believe that Lillian Smith and Paula Snelling were lovers, but I feared that was only because I so admired Smith and her stand as a southern white woman for racial justice that I wanted her to affirm the lesbian love I was afraid to acknowledge. Still blind to the power of compulsory heterosexality to distort and inhibit personal as well as cultural and systemic analyses, I stood firm publicly on scholarly objectivity and said, of Smith's sexual identity, "we simply cannot know." At the 1981 Berkshire Conference on Women's History, when a representative from the Lesbian History Archives left her card on the podium requesting a copy of my paper on Smith and Laurel Falls Camp for the Archives, I never responded. Trying so hard to be professional (i.e., safe) especially when dealing with socially taboo areas of sexual expression, I allowed my own unexamined fears to become my most effective censors.

A year later, in the summer of 1982, I spent two weeks in Lillian Smith's home near Clayton, Georgia, at the request of Lillian's sister and brother, Esther and Frank Smith, sorting and collecting the papers that had not previously been donated to the major Smith collections at the University of Georgia and University of Florida. Larry Gulley, archivist for the University of Georgia special collections, drove up from Athens to help me. We examined thoroughly every file drawer, closet, cabinet, and chest in the remodeled camp cabins occupied by Lillian Smith, before she died in 1966, and Paula Snelling, until her stroke in 1978. We even recorded the titles of several hundred books in the camp library. After four days of sorting and packing, Larry left with his pickup truck filled with archival boxes and I went back to what had been Paula Snelling's house to lock the door before returning to Alabama. As I made one last safety check to be sure nothing was left open, I found a small leather case, stuck back in a cabinet. How had we missed it before? It is one of the intriguing mysteries of which many biographers and historians tell. It was not locked. I opened it. There, among old photographs, picture postcards from Snelling to her brother and parents when she was at Columbia University, and a brown paper bag containing Paula Snelling's parents' courtship letters, lay a small packet of letters marked "private." In it were a handful of letters, dated in the 1940s and 1950s, from Lillian Smith to Paula Snelling, and a few from Snelling to Smith.

There I read what I had found nowhere else in Smith's correspondence: unmistakably clear expressions of their physical as well as intellectual intimacy. Writing to Paula from Brooklyn, N.Y., where she lived while working on the Broadway production of *Strange Fruit*, in February 1946, Smith closed with these words: "I'd love to feel your lips on mine . . . and I can imagine other feelings too. Better guard these letters."[3] The letter that stood out for me, however, was one in which Smith confessed ambivalence about her sexuality. In June 1952, again from her apartment in Brooklyn, Smith wrote Snelling:

Paula—
     What a nice letter you write me! It did you good to go through the old letters, didn't it. The picture of you swung me back through the years. You were so darned cute and attractive. You are "sweeter," "finer" now but you had something then that was so young and—nice, that bi-sexual charm which no one dares admit is seductive—except in real life.
     I am sorry my letters are burned, that is my ambivalence. My shame about

something different and completely good. It has been that shame that has destroyed the keen edge of a pattern of love that was creative and good. Blurring it, dulling it.[4]

The letters had been guarded and I continued to guard them. I knew I had to show them to Paula Snelling, but it took me several months to arrange the time and work up my courage to see her. Happily surprised to see the contents of the case, she told me she thought all her personal papers had been destroyed. "I don't know why I saved these," she said, "except perhaps to read in my very old age!" Snelling asked that her parents' letters be deposited at Emory University with the Snelling family papers because, she said, the subjects—her parents—were long-since dead, and besides, she added, "their relationship was normal." When I told her I thought her relationship with Lillian Smith was also normal, she smiled and said, "I know you do, but . . . "

When I asked Paula specifically about the nature of her relationship with Lillian Smith, she replied: "We shared everything; we loved each other very much, and sometimes we expressed that love physically."

But she did not agree with those who said Lillian Smith was a lesbian. No, she insisted, Paula was the lesbian in the relationship, because she never desired a relationship with a man. Lil, on the other hand, could have been happily married, had the right man come along.

That evening I left the letters with Paula Snelling. When I returned the next morning, Paula asked me to do something I had never expected. She asked me to read some of the letters aloud to her. It was a rare moment of intimacy I shall never forget.

What emerged as the most important lesson from that experience was not that I had by some fluke found the evidence to confirm the sexual nature of a relationship between two women. Rather, it seems now far more significant that the presence of those letters opened an opportunity, created a new space, for communication based on trust between Paula Snelling and me. After I read those letters to her, Paula said to me: "I have talked more intimately with you than I have with anyone except Lil." As I read and asked questions, Paula added comments, clarifying some part of a letter from her perspective, and at times saying, "Lil was just wrong about that." She talked openly about her own life, as well as about Lillian Smith's, in ways she had not done before, telling about her childhood and her relationship with her family as compared to Lillian Smith's family life.

I did not uncover a consciousness on Snelling's part of having lived what we would call today a lesbian lifestyle. In *Odd Girls and Twilight Lovers,* Lillian Faderman described middle class, especially professional, lesbians in the 1930s and 1940s as being totally closeted, even to other lesbian friends.[5] When I asked her specifically if she and Smith had ever discussed their relationship with other women friends, even those I thought seemed to have lived as lesbian couples themselves, Snelling said no, their friendships with the other women were based on other shared interests and activities. Most importantly, in the course of that conversation I gained a much fuller sense of Paula's personality and attitudes, and indirectly of Lillian Smith's as well, thereby confirming for me one of the reasons it is so important to acknowledge sexual expression in historical research. Something very liberating can happen when part of a person that has been previously hidden, denied, or demeaned is finally affirmed.

Snelling clearly accepted her lesbian sexuality, defining it as an abnormality of her genes, but not a sin, and nothing to feel ashamed about. She said she felt Smith hid their relationship, not to deny it but to protect it. Sadly, though not surprisingly, her lifetime sense of the necessity of protecting and guarding was not easily changed. Paula told me more than once how much she appreciated my bringing those letters to her, but in the end, she also said I must destroy them. "You want me to destroy these?" I asked incredulously. Then came my reprieve, my escape valve: "When you are finished with them," she replied. That last clause was all I needed; after consulting with Larry Gulley, I deposited the letters at the University of Georgia with the rest of Smith's papers.

Even though the letters were saved, the question remained: How could I use them in writing about Lillian Smith? Could they even be included in a volume of her collected letters? They were, after all, still guarded, still restricted material. Historian Blanche Weisen Cook observed in the introduction to her biography of Eleanor Roosevelt that the restrictions on Eleanor Roosevelt's papers reflect the restrictions on women's lives and, therefore, our knowledge of women's history. She further noted that Eleanor Roosevelt herself and her friends exercised control over those letters and over the construction of their public lives, and that it was very important to them to maintain that control.[6]

Like Eleanor Roosevelt, Lillian Smith was quite conscious of herself as a historically significant figure. She wanted her life to be remembered. With the exception of the correspondence between her and Snelling, which I discovered in the hidden leather case and which Snelling herself had intended destroyed, it is no accident that Smith's letters were available for publication. At least for the last decade of her life, she kept carbons of her correspondence and arranged for her papers to be preserved. Yet, the voice preserved in Smith's letters often is a public voice, for most of her personal papers were destroyed. A fire in 1955 destroyed Smith's home and with it many of her unpublished manuscripts, as well as her personal correspondence with her family. Even before 1955, however, it seems evident that Smith and Snelling intentionally destroyed most of their correspondence with each other, at least in part because they feared the disclosure of the intimate sexual nature of their relationship. Like Eleanor Roosevelt, and most people I know, Lillian Smith and Paula Snelling had sought to exercise and maintain control over the construction of their public and private lives.

The problem, or question for me as biographer was must I honor their desire to remain closeted? Was it possible, in effect, to write with integrity while trying to perpetuate the illusion that the supposedly offending expressions of sexuality could be effectively separated from all other aspects of their lives? Or, would it be more helpful to address the question of why it was so important to Smith and Snelling to keep the full nature of their relationship hidden? What was the source of Smith's ambivalence and shame about her sexual attraction and love for Snelling? Was she ambivalent because she was attracted to men as well as to women? Or, as Smith so effectively demonstrated through her novels, *Strange Fruit* and *One Hour*, perhaps her ambivalence stemmed from her acute perception of the inadequacy of language, the inevitable failure of all labels to convey the depth and complexity of human relationships. As Paula Snelling once remarked to me, "There's no word for what we do with words! As soon as we open our mouths to speak, we limit communication."

Yet, having finally acknowledged and begun to accept my own lesbian sexuality, I knew I could ignore neither the nature of Smith's relationship with Snelling nor the fact that her struggle with the ambivalence in her own heart greatly influenced not only her choices of self-definition, but also the structure and content of her work. After months of indecision and avoidance, I began to see how the power behind the heterosexual/homosexual dichotomy that kept Smith closeted was likewise inhibiting my ability to write about her. Determined to confront my own demons, I began writing an essay on Smith's treatment of homosexuality. In the process, I realized that even while acknowledging the arbitrary and limiting nature of categories or labels, it was critical to redefine and push the limits of those categories, thereby claiming the power to create a new and more inclusive view of Smith, her life, and her work.

Then, just as I decided I must return to Paula Snelling and ask her permission to use the letters she had told me to destroy, she died, in February 1985. In March I presented the paper, but before I could determine how to gain permission from the Smiths to publish the quoted passages from some of the private letters, I received a letter from Frank Smith, Lillian's brother, saying an unnamed source had told him about my recent paper, which he called "a little coup." He threatened to sue me if I published anything referring to Lillian Smith as a lesbian. Shocked, I called to discuss the letter with Frank and reminded him that Paula had discussed their relationship with me. His response was that Paula was sick and had no right to say what she did. I called another member of the Smith family, a niece, whom I felt might reason with Frank. She asked to see a copy of the paper, which I sent. I then received a letter from Esther saying, "You have killed my sister." I realized that my naming Lil as a closeted lesbian had in fact killed Esther Smith's image of her sister. The first time I met Esther, she had greeted me with these words: "I adored my sister." Clearly, she could not—at least at that moment—adore a sister who was lesbian.

It was a scholar's nightmare. Without the Smiths' permission, I could not submit that essay for publication. For the next four years I felt effectively silenced, blocked in my writing, and I often wondered if Lillian Smith would ever be heard in her own full voice. Still, I continued to search for and collect Smith's letters, and tried to keep open the door of communication with the Smith family, but our formerly warm and supportive relationship was deeply strained. I felt Esther and Frank Smith felt I had betrayed their trust. I was plagued, at times, not only by a strong sense of rejection but also by grave doubts about my own perceptions, my own reading of Smith's life and work.

Finally, however, I realized I would complete the project of editing Smith's letters only if, once again, I faced my own fears, listened to my own voice, and wrote about her life as I saw it. As feminists and African American historians had done before with issues of gender and race, I moved the question of Smith's sexuality from the margin to the center, honoring her closeted relationship with Snelling as a source of power and inspiration, as well as ambivalence and shame in Smith's life. Then, and only then, did the pieces of her life—her work as camp director, journalist, novelist, social activist, her personal and public friendships—begin to fall into place and to assume the clarity I had not seen before.

I am not saying writing the book was then easy. I labored for three more years to complete the manuscript, never knowing whether at the end the Smith family would grant permission to publish the letters. As it turned out, my editor at the University of North Carolina Press was correct in believing that the value and power of the whole portrait would persuade the family not to censor what taken in isolation they had so vehemently condemned and denied. Furthermore, after reading the manuscript in its entirety, Esther Smith gave not only her permission to publish, but also her praise.

Our expressions of sexuality, like our expressions of gender, race, and class, do not exist in isolation, but emerge in relationship with each other. All are necessary in any effort to create a full portrait, whether of an individual or of a people, in any time or place. Lillian Smith was fond of saying that racial segregation was both symptom and symbol of the fragmented age in which she lived. Something similar may be said of the dichotomized structuring of sexual expression, which leads us to honor only what we call heterosexual, or any one definition of lesbian or gay. While we cannot address sexuality in isolation, neither can we create the new, more nearly complete portrait of a subject until we can move what has been marginalized to a place of honor and respect. We have to step through the internalized as well as externally imposed boundaries of heterosexism. We have to step out of that seemingly safe spot called normality to make a new space from which to view the multi-faceted subjects of our research, the complexity of ourselves and of our world.

NOTES

This chapter is a revised version of a talk given as part of "The Importance of Gay and Lesbian Library History" session sponsored by the American Library Association's Library History Round Table and Social Responsibilities Round Table in honor of the twenty-fifth anniversary of the Gay, Lesbian, and Bisexual Task Force, June 24, 1995.

1. See especially *American Libraries*, "Reader Forum," July/August, September, October, November1992; July/August, September 1993; January 1994.

2. Margaret Rose Gladney, ed., *How am I to be heard? Letters of Lillian Smith* (Chapel Hill: University of North Carolina Press, 1993), 301.

3. Lillian Smith Collection #2337, Hargrett Rare Books and Manuscript Library, University of Georgia Libraries, Athens.

4. Gladney, 136.

5. See Lillian Faderman, "Wastelands and oases: The 1930s," *Odd girls and twilight lovers* (New York: Columbia University Press, 1991).

6. Blanche Weisen Cook, *Eleanor Roosevelt* (New York: Viking, 1992).

4

A Closet Curtained by Circumspection: Doing Research on the McCarthy Era Purge of Gays from the Library of Congress

Louise S. Robbins

To paraphrase Winston Churchill's famous description of the Soviet Union— "a riddle wrapped in a mystery inside an enigma"[1]—trying to uncover the story of the purge of gays and lesbians from the Library of Congress (LC) during the McCarthy era is like trying to peer behind a curtain inside a closet inside a tightly-guarded chamber. The problems are manifold. The nature of the federal Cold War era loyalty programs (within which context the purges took place) and the studied circumspection of LC administrators are compounded by the taboos regarding homosexuality and the difficulty of interpreting the record.[2] The direct documentary evidence from which information about the purge of homosexuals can be drawn is scant indeed: three highly repetitive Senate documents, one letter, and a few entries in the diaries and reports of the chief assistant librarian, Verner Clapp, and the director of the administrative department, John C. L. Andreassen, from May through July 1950, and a few ambiguous entries through mid-1951.

The loyalty and loyalty-security programs that surrounded the homosexual purges began under President Harry S. Truman in 1947 and became more harsh under President Dwight D. Eisenhower in 1953. Truman's Executive Order 9835, signed March 22, 1947, set up a procedure to check all current executive branch employees and job applicants. The Civil Service checked names against FBI, military intelligence, House of Un-American Activities Committee, and other pertinent files. If it found any "derogatory" information, a full FBI field investigation was mandated. Each agency established loyalty boards to review dossiers, conduct hearings, and make recommendations concerning the disposition of cases. Dismissals could be appealed to the administration's specially-appointed Loyalty Review Board, which also coordinated agency programs. Employees should be dismissed if "reasonable grounds" of disloyalty were found to exist. Evidence to be used in determining disloyalty ranged from sabotage and espionage through the advocacy of the use of violence to overthrow the government to "affiliation with or sympathetic association with" any organization designated by the Attorney General "as totalitarian, fascist, communist, or subversive" or seeking to overthrow the government.[3]

Because the LC is a legislative branch agency, it was not covered by the executive order. Librarian of Congress Luther H. Evans, however, voluntarily brought the library under the loyalty program in hopes of garnering confidence—and larger appropriations—from a Republican-dominated Congress that viewed his earlier connections with the New Deal's Works Progress Administration and the Democratic administration with suspicion.[4] Considering the mood of Congress and the temper of the times, as well as the fact that the library had voluntarily brought itself under other Civil Service regulations in earlier years, it is difficult to imagine Evans taking any other course. Although it took two years for LC to secure access to investigative machinery and to the appeals machinery of the Loyalty Review Board, investigations of LC employees began in spring 1948.[5] Within months the Civil Service had cleared more than half of LC's 1,632 incumbent and 97 new employees.[6] Verner Clapp, chief assistant librarian, was in charge of LC's loyalty program and chaired its loyalty panel. Although he confessed "loss of sleep over this business," in August he promptly suspended several employees against whom the FBI's "evidence of disloyalty" was strongest.[7]

During the loyalty program's first three years, 2,524 LC employees were checked; 70 full field investigations were completed or in process. The LC loyalty board, however, had made unfavorable determinations in only two cases out of the fifty-one it had adjudicated. Four additional employees had resigned. Clapp's instructions that LC's loyalty panel write their reports so carefully that they could not be overturned apparently were successful; only seven out of forty-seven cases were re-opened following a Loyalty Review Board audit.[8] Although apparently only two LC employees were discharged following a loyalty investigation during Clapp's 1947–1956 tenure as head of the program, it is clear that a much higher number of employees weathered suspicions, suspensions, investigations, and hearings before the storm cleared.

Additional trouble was brewing, however, for some LC employees. They were among many victims of a broad purge launched on February 28, 1950, just a few weeks after Sen. Joseph McCarthy's Wheeling, WV, speech, which catapulted him to center stage with attacks on Communists in the State Department. John Peurifoy, a State Department official testifying in Congress, made a chance remark that ninety-one employees dismissed for "moral turpitude" were homosexuals, not Communists. With the Republicans looking for ways to discredit the Truman administration, testimony at a subsequent Senate hearing by the Washington, D.C., Police Department vice-squad chief that thousands of "sexual deviates" worked for the government set in motion an "unprecedented" government-wide investigation.[9] A committee chaired by Senator Clyde Hoey conducted hearings into "the medical, psychiatric, sociological and legal phases of the problem" as well as the "security risk" involved in hiring homosexuals. These investigations were carried out in executive session, in sharp contrast to McCarthy's highly publicized inquiries into alleged subversive activity.[10] Partly for that reason, these investigations and their effects have drawn little notice and little research.[11] Interestingly enough, it appears that until the investigation began, few agencies actively sought to ferret out their gay and lesbian employees.[12] Once the investigation began, however, action to purge "perverts" or "deviates" was swift. While only four resignations and two firings can definitely be linked to nine years of the loyalty program, between ten and fifteen LC employees lost jobs as a result of the 1950 purge of "homosexuals and other sex perverts" from the federal government, according to the Senate report that documented the investigation and resulting dismissals.[13]

The investigation and the move to rid the government of homosexuals technically was not related to the loyalty program: those accused did not go through the review process that those charged with disloyalty did. Nevertheless, the arguments made for removing gay men and lesbians from government service tarred them with the brush of subversion. As Sen. Kenneth Wherry reported, a score of government officials agreed that "moral perverts are bad national security risks; that they are dangerous persons to entrust with knowledge of security secrets or access to documents containing security secrets because of their susceptibility to blackmail on threat of exposure of their moral weakness."[14]

The Hoey report not only echoed Wherry but cited prevailing Freudian thinking, calling gays and lesbians "immature" and suffering from arrested or "inverted" sexual development. Although homosexuals who had a "genuine desire" to be cured could be helped, many did not want to change their "way of life." "Perverts" were likely to "lack the emotional stability of normal persons," the report stated, and to have weakened their "moral fiber" to the extent that they were unsuited for responsible positions. These characteristics also made them "susceptible to the blandishments of the foreign espionage agent." Burdened by the stigma of their "sex perversion," they were perceived as prime targets for blackmail attempts which would compromise confidential government secrets—another trait that made them a greater security risk than heterosexuals. In addition, the report charged, by "enticing" normal people to engage in "perverted practices," homosexuals were a "corrosive influence" on their colleagues. "One homosexual," the report said, "can pollute a Government office."[15]

Whether or not the LC was concerned about "pollution," it is quite likely that Librarian Evans had strong anti-gay as well as anti-communist feelings. Poetry consultant Karl Shapiro reported that Evans told him plainly that "we don't want any communists or cocksuckers in this library."[16] On the other hand, the report's figures reveal that LC had made no move against homosexuals before the 1950 Senate investigation made it imperative. According to Dan Lacy, who spent several years at LC (mostly as an assistant to Evans), the investigation was "something of a problem" for LC because "while there were not any subversives, there were lots and lots of homosexuals" at LC, which had been happy—especially during the War years—to hire "young men with an education" who could not get into the military.[17] Nevertheless, according to the daily diaries kept by Verner Clapp, his reports to Evans, and the daily reports by administrative chief John C. L. Andreassen, the LC responded to the Senate investigation, as did other agencies, by trying to identify homosexuals and terminate their employment.

By early May, 1950, the LC sought information from the FBI on which to base its charges and dismissals. The FBI, however, referred the library to the District of Columbia Police Department, which apparently gave LC the "run-around." Clapp instructed personnel director Jacob Mason to put his request to them in writing. A few days later, Mason reported that he was "getting somewhere" with the Civil Service Commission in his inquiries regarding "perverts."[18] By May 22, 1950, the day after he reported a "long talk with Clapp on perversion problems,"[19] Andreassen and Mason were beginning to formulate guidelines and take action. The rule of thumb was to "get rid of probationary and indefinite cases; invite medical counsel for all the others," Clapp reported to Evans.[20]

Two temporary employees were to get "medical assistance," Clapp noted on May 22.[21] Others were not so fortunate. Clapp's diaries contain a cryptic note for May 23, 1950: "Perversion. 2 resignations (1 prob, 1 indef) rec'd."[22] No other comment or explanation follows. Clapp generally did not identify by name people who were currently under investigation, whether for subversion or perversion.

One exception to that general rule appears in the diary and report entries for May 25, 1950. The case is revealing of the problems of doing research on the largely invisible history of gay men and lesbians: what kinds of conclusions is it safe, or ethical, to draw from a document—or harder yet, from hints in a document? When the term "perversion" refers not only to homosexual behavior, but also to a whole range of other behaviors outside the prevailing norm, what do we know about an individual charged with "perversion"?[23] What can be concluded from proximity in space and time of bits of evidence? What can be read into silences? The case is—or may be—also revealing because of the different way in which this case of "perversion"—if it was one—was handled.

Because such explicit information apparently is rare, it is worth sharing the text of two entries from Clapp's May 25, 1950, report to Evans (which expands on his diary for the same day): "3. Mason [the personnel director] informs me PV [Paul Vanderbilt, according to the diary] is arranging through Personnel for psychiatric attention . . . 11. Mason reports that Mortell, chief psychiatrist, P[ublic] H[ealth] S[ervice], advises getting rid of perverts as political liability, and offers no medical aid or advice."[24] Can one draw a connection between Vanderbilt's seeking psychiatric help and the apparent belief within the LC administration that homosexuality was susceptible to psychiatric treatment and thus conclude that Vanderbilt was gay?[25] Did he seek treatment for some other difficulty, sexual or not? Was Vanderbilt being given special treatment by being encouraged to seek help rather than being forced to resign? Vanderbilt was the head of the Prints and Photographs Division, not a rank and file employee. (The division was controversial in its own right because it held such collections as the Farm Services Administration photos of Dorothea Lange and Walker Evans that reflected badly on "the American way of life" by exposing the abject poverty of the Depression era agricultural worker). A letter from Luther Evans—in Italy on UNESCO business—to Verner Clapp, dated May 21, 1950, (earlier than the report entry) but received May 26 (later than the report entry) adds mystery to the enigma. In a paragraph that is filled with unrelated tidbits of unfinished business, but no illumination of the topic at hand, Evans writes, "I fear that Paul Vanderbilt will have to go."[26] And by the end of 1950, Vanderbilt was gone.[27] He went to Wisconsin, where he founded the Visual Archive of the State Historical Society. His successor in the job, Jack Holtzheuter, an "out" gay man, met with Vanderbilt daily for many years and says he was *not* gay. What then is known about Paul Vanderbilt's case? Only that he left the LC under some kind of duress and landed on his feet.

The circumspection with which Clapp usually handled names also is carried forward to the June entries. He instructed Mason to "go ahead with all" those charged with perversion "except K."[28] He noted in his diary that "one of the p[erverts] (G.) is married. Lay off. One other ( ) [sic] has resigned."[29] Andreassen was not so careful, listing three days later the names of three people who had resigned.[30] Were they, too, victims of the purge of gays? One of the men had been mentioned earlier in the diaries as the subject of a loyalty probe, but the timing of their resignations makes their dismissal as gays probable, as does the fact that they were reported at all. The routine departure of employees in a bureaucracy of some 2,000 normally is not mentioned by top administrators.

One June series of entries in Clapp's diaries and Andreassen's reports indicates that the LC administration followed a practice that earned criticism in the Senate report. The report chastised government agencies for a "head-in-the-sand attitude toward the problem of sex perversion." If the agencies made a real effort to investigate allegations of homosexuality they "eased out these perverts . . . in as quiet a manner as possible."[31] On June 5, Clapp apparently charged an employee with being homosexual and met with a denial. Said Clapp, "I told him if he admitted the charge I would have recommended resignation." Two days later, both Andreassen and Clapp recorded his resignation.[32] A month later, when asked about a reference for him, Clapp instructed Andreassen to report on his "work record only, making this clear."[33] Although Clapp allowed him to resign quietly, his "outing"—if that's what it was—still had a cost.

Attention to "perverts" or "deviates," as homosexuals were variously labeled in the diaries and reports, lasted into July 1950, with three cases mentioned in mid-month, and "perversion," along with loyalty, discussed by Mason with Clapp toward month's end.[34] While the diaries reveal enormous amounts of time and energy expended during the remainder of Clapp's tenure on loyalty and loyalty-security cases, by the end of July the library seems to have left the cases of "perversion" and shifted its gaze to other problems, especially to the protection of the library's most precious holdings from the possibility of destruction as a result of the Korean War, which clearly was feared as the first potential confrontation between nuclear super powers. One January, 1951, resignation may have been related to the search for homosexuals in government, but the evidence is very murky.[35]

So what do we really know about the purge of gays at the LC? We know that the library apparently knowingly hired gays during World War II and did not seek their ouster until the 1950 investigation began. We know that the purge lasted intensely only from April through July of 1950.[36] We know that the library sought the help of the District of Columbia Police, the Civil Service Commission, and the FBI to identify homosexuals, and that the library encouraged at least some of those suspected of homosexuality to seek medical help. We know that most of those charged were allowed to resign. Finally, we know that between ten and fifteen LC employees were among the approximately four hundred federal employees across the country who lost jobs during the 1950 purge of homosexual employees.[37] Ascertaining anything else, however, is difficult.

The difficulty stems in part from secrecy. The purge of gays from government service—like the loyalty program—was shrouded in secrecy. Thus the very nature of the purge makes its toll impossible to calculate. In fact, as Max Lerner observed in his *New York Post* column, "[O]nly the accusers and the hunters—Senate probers, security officers, police officials—get their names in the papers. The hunted remain anonymous—unspecified, uncounted, nameless men."[38] People accused of disloyalty frequently resigned before receiving interrogatories or without demanding a hearing in hopes of being able to escape the taint of the charge. The same was true of those charged with perversion. In fact, President Dwight D. Eisenhower's 1953 loyalty-security program simply included "sexual perversion" as one of the grounds for which an agency chief had absolute discretion to fire an employee; any significant distinction between subversion and homosexuality was removed.[39]

Not only does the very nature of the 1950s purges and the difficulty of measuring their tolls complicate matters (how does one calculate sleepless nights, concern for one's livelihood, harassment through late-night telephone calls?) but so does the circumspection, indirection, and guardedness of the library's administrators. It is not surprising that Verner Clapp instructed those examining the loyalty cases not to mention the names of individuals in their daily diaries, and that great care was taken with the files. Clapp was concerned with both security and reputation. But the silence regarding the purge of gays at the library was more intense. While several discussions about the loyalty program—and its evils—took place among top administrators at the weekly Librarian's Conference, there is no indication that the purge of gays was ever discussed. In addition, government employees in those days—and perhaps today as well—simply tried to avoid speaking much about sensitive political issues and kept their opinions to themselves. Outspokenness was not a virtue.[40]

One type of silence becomes nearly deafening as one pieces together whatever can be known about this disturbing era of library life: where are the women, the lesbians? Surely, the question of whether there were lesbians on the staff must have been raised, given a substantial number of women employees at the library. Yet never is a feminine pronoun used, or a woman's name mentioned. Certainly, middle-class lesbians generally were more closeted in the 1950s than were working-class lesbians or gay men, and female friendships generally have been less suspect than male friendships. In addition, gay men were much more likely to frequent Lafayette Park or other public places where the District of Columbia or Park Police might pick them up.[41] Thus police blotters, used by the Civil Service to identify homosexuals, would not have been as revealing a source of information about lesbians. This silence, this absence, draws a curtain around one aspect of this closeted tale.

Without additional sources of information one can know very little for certain about the 1950 purge of gays and lesbians in the LC.[42] Until we uncover those other sources, the full story will remain veiled by a curtain within a closet within a chamber of circumspection.

NOTES

1. Broadcast, October 1, 1939.

2. One of the main problems of historical research is the tendency to read the present into the past; this is especially true in the case of lesbigay history, since language pertaining to sexual matters is so coded, and mores and self-understandings have changed so radically within the last fifty years.

3. See Eleanor Bontecou, *The Federal Loyalty-Security Program* (Ithaca, NY: Cornell University Press, 1953) for an examination of Truman's loyalty program and subsequent executive orders and legislation. Ralph S. Brown's *Loyalty and security: Employment tests in the United States* (New Haven, CT: Yale University Press, 1958) looks at not only the federal program, but programs applied to state and private sector employees as well. The full text of Executive Order 9835 can be found in Bontecou, Appendix I.

4. Librarian's Conference Minutes, April 7, May 5 and 14, 1947, Box 517, ADM 23-1, Library of Congress Central File (MacLeish-Evans), Manuscripts Reading Room, Library of Congress, Washington, D.C. (hereafter cited as LC); George A. Pughe interview with author, July 14, 1992, Washington, D.C.; Charles A. Goodrum and Helen W. Dalrymple's *The Library of Congress* (Boulder, CO: Westview Press, 1982), 47–50.

5. "Chronology of Congressional Authorizations of LC's Loyalty-Security Programs," June 17, 1954, Subject File: Loyalty Program, Record Group 32, Verner W. Clapp Papers, Manuscript Reading Room, Library of Congress (hereafter cited as Clapp Papers).

6. *Annual Report of the Librarian of Congress for the Fiscal Year Ending June 30, 1948* (Washington: The Library, 1949); Verner W. Clapp to John Taber, [August 26, 1948], Security 2-2, Box 1069, LC.

7. General Order 1319, ORG 1-1, Box 907, LC; [Burnis] Walker's Notes, August 25, 1948, Administrative Department Daily Reports, Vol. 8, Record Group 553, LC. For an examination of LC's participation in loyalty programs during Clapp's tenure as chief assistant librarian see Louise S. Robbins, "The Library of Congress and Federal Loyalty Programs, 1947–1956: No 'Communists or Cocksuckers'," *Library Quarterly* 64 (October 1994): 365–85.

8. *Annual Report of the Librarian of Congress for the Fiscal Year Ending June 30, 1950* (Washington, D.C.: Library of Congress, 1951), p. 159–60; Frederick Wagman, who served on the panel with Clapp, remembered that the panel saw itself as "saving people, saving reputations," according to a telephone interview with the author, January 26, 1993.

9. For the context of the investigation and purge, see John D'Emilio, *Sexual politics, sexual communities: The making of a homosexual minority in the United States, 1940–1970* (Chicago: University of Chicago Press, 1983), p. 41; see also D'Emilio's "The homosexual menace: The politics of sexuality in cold war America," in *Passion and power: Sexuality in history*, edited by Kathy Peiss and Christine Simmons (Philadelphia: Temple University Press, 1989), p. 227.

10. "Employment of Homosexuals and Other Sex Perverts in Government," Senate Document 241, 81st Congress, 2nd Session; Serial Set Vol. 11401; Dan M. Lacy, an administrator at LC during part of this time, in an interview with the author (February 19, 1993, Irvington-on-Hudson, NY), commented on the lack of publicity compared to the

McCarthy hearings; Martin Duberman, in his introduction to excerpts from the Senate report in *It's about time: Exploring the gay past*, rev. and expanded ed. (New York: Penguin Books, 1991), p. 178, calls the Senate report "the key document . . . which fully enunciates official sentiments and 'solutions'" regarding homosexuals in the 1950s. Two other documents, "Report Made by the Senior Senator from the State of Alabama, Mr. Hill, with Reference to Testimony on Subversive Activity and Homosexuals in the Government Service," Unpublished Committee Print, CIS Number S4178, 81st Congress, 2nd Session, [May] 1950; and "Report of the Investigations of the Junior Senator of Nebraska on the Infiltration of Subversives and Moral Perverts into the Executive Branch of the U. S. Government," Unpublished Committee Print, CIS Number S4179, 81st Congress, 2nd Session, [May] 1950, provide the background and impetus for Hoey's investigation.

11. Another reason for the lack of research may be that no gay men or lesbians challenged the purges. See David K. Johnson, "Homosexual citizens: Washington's gay community confronts the Civil Service," *Washington History* (Fall/Winter 1994–95): 54–55.

12. Before the loyalty program, homosexuals would not have been immune from attack. Senator Wherry of Nebraska apparently began his campaign to rid the government of "alien-minded radicals with low standards of morality" in 1943, according to "Report of the Investigations . . . ,"p. 1. Johnson, however, in "Homosexual Citizens," dates the intensification of enforcement against homosexuals in the District of Columbia, and an interest in their place of employment, to October 1947, after the loyalty program began operating (p. 52).

13. The figures are reported in "Employment of Homosexuals and Other Sex Perverts. . . ," Appendix III.

14. "Report of the Investigation of the Junior Senator of Nebraska . . .," p. 2.

15. "Employment of Homosexuals and Other Sex Perverts. . . ."

16. According to Karl Shapiro, Poetry Consultant for 1946–47, the first thing that Luther Evans ever said to him was, "Shapiro, we don't want any communists or cocksuckers in this library." Shapiro is quoted in Natalie Robins's *Alien ink* (New York: Morrow, 1992), p. 291. I confirmed the statement in a telephone interview with Shapiro on March 31, 1994.

17. Dan M. Lacy, interview with author, February 19, 1993, Irvington-on-Hudson, N.Y.

18. Entries for May 8, May 9, May 10, and May 15, 1950; Diaries, Box 1, Clapp Papers.

19. Entry for May 21, 1950, Daily Reports, Director, Administrative Department, Vol. 13, Record Group 558, LC.

20. Entry for May 22, 1950, Daily Reports, Chief Assistant Librarian, Vol. 3, Record Group 538, LC.

21. Entry for May 22, 1950, Diaries, Box 1, Clapp Papers.

22. Entry for May 23, 1950, Diaries Box 1, Clapp Papers.

23. Dan Lacy, in an addendum to his interview with the author, recounted an event that illustrates the range of behaviors included under the "perversion" rubric: "We had one tragedy—an otherwise fine man who was a pedophile and an occasional alcoholic, who sometimes lost control when drinking. He was also deeply religious. His past was known to the Library, who nevertheless continued his employment under his promise of sobriety. He, however, fell one more time and committed suicide." Names of suspected "perverts" were taken from police records and may have included many behaviors other than engaging in homosexual sex. According to "Employment of Homosexuals in Government . . .," p.

20, most homosexuals were charged with disorderly conduct. Generally they chose to forfeit $25.00 bond, according to "Report Made by the Senior Senator from the State of Alabama . . . ," p.3.

24. Entry for May 25, 1950, Daily Reports, Chief Assistant Librarian, Vol. 3, Record Group 538, LC. Vanderbilt's name is spelled out in the Clapp diary entry of the same date.

25. Psychiatrists were at this time moving more and more into sex therapy and marriage counseling, with a number claiming some expertise in the treatment of the "sexual immaturity" or "inversion" as homosexuality was labeled. The Public Health Service's (PHS) reluctance to involve itself in the "treatment" of homosexuality probably indicates that the PHS was quite clear about the political lay of the land.

26. Luther H. Evans to Verner W. Clapp, May 21, 1950, General Correspondence, Box 6, Clapp Papers.

27. *Annual Report of the Librarian of Congress for the Fiscal Year Ending June 30, 1951* (Washington, D.C.: The Library, 1952), p. 6.

28. Entry for June 8, 1950, Diaries Box 1, Clapp Papers.

29. Entry for June 9, 1950, Diaries Box 1, Clapp Papers.

30. Entry for June 12, 1950, Daily Reports, Director Administrative Department, Vol. 13, Record group 558, LC. I have declined to use the names of individuals mentioned in the diaries and reports unless I know they are deceased.

31. "Employment of Homosexuals and Other Sex Perverts. . . ," p. 10.

32. Entry for June 5, 1950, and June 7, 1950, Diaries Box 1, Clapp Papers. Entry for June 7, 1950, Daily Report, Director Administrative Department, Vol. 13, Record Group 558, LC.

33. Entry for July 3, 1950, Diaries Box 1, Clapp Papers.

34. Entry for July 13, 1950, Daily Reports Director Administrative Department, Vol. 14, Record Group 558, LC; Entry for July 29, 1950, Diaries Box 1, Clapp Papers.

35. See entries for January 16 and 17, February 6, 13, and 28, and March 5, 1951, Daily Reports, Director Administrative Department, Vol. 15, Record group 560, LC. Only initials common to earlier inquiries regarding "deviates" link some of these entries with the purge.

36. This research covers only the period from 1947 through 1956, during which time there is no indication of another campaign to rid the library of homosexual employees. It is safe to assume, however, that the library avoided hiring people it suspected of being homosexual.

37. The figure of 400, derived from the Hoey report, is taken from Johnson, "Homosexual Citizens," p. 47.

38. Max Lerner, "The Washington sex story," *New York Post*, July 10, 1950, cited in Johnson, "Homosexual Citizens," p. 54.

39. Executive Order 10450, *Federal Register* 18 (April 29, 1953) found in ADM 15-15, Record Group 931, LC.

40. I thank Professor Don Krummel at the University of Illinois Graduate School of Library and Information Studies, a former Library of Congress employee, for reminding me of this factor.

41. Johnson, "Homosexual Citizens," p. 52.

42. According to a telephone conversation with Professor Athan Theoharis, Marquette University, who has extensively used the Freedom of Information Act to gain access to FBI files, the policy file on the homosexual purges still exists, but the personnel files of those investigated as a result of the policy were destroyed some years ago by the FBI with the permission of the National Archives and Records Administration. The best hope for

recovery of this piece of the past lies in those who were immediately affected coming forth and telling their stories.

5

Queer Histories/Queer Librarians: The Historical Development of a Gay Monograph

Norman G. Kester

A monograph detailing the coming out stories and professional work of queer librarians could not have come about without the existence of a professional organization of lesbigay librarians, namely the American Library Association's (ALA) Gay, Lesbian and Bisexual Task Force (GLBTF), nor without previous research in the field of gay studies, which have affected our work. The nature of these stories and the development of my collection, *Liberating Minds: The Stories and Professional Lives of Gay, Lesbian and Bisexual Librarians*, has something to say about the evolution of the varied professional identities of lesbigay librarians over time. Moreover, as recent general lesbigay literature attests, the telling and retelling of our stories can be the catalyst for creating more diverse library/information environments in the future (e.g., Diamant 1993; Woods 1993; Friskopp and Silverstien 1995; Winfield and Spielman 1995; Powers and Ellis 1995; and Rasi and Rodriguez-Nourges 1995).

As editor, I posed several questions when I was planning this pioneering collection. Would queer librarians finally be willing to write about their professional experiences? Would they have anything positive to say about working in libraries that were part of a larger heterosexual (that is, homophobic and discriminatory) world? Gay-bashing among librarians is not unknown, however civil or reasonable its tone (see Berger 1995, for example, who outlined *Library Journal*'s "disturbing, continuing fascination . . . with the gay and lesbian scene . . . [in] promoting and glamorizing of immoral homosexual behavior"; and a fitting refutation by Carmichael October 15, 1995; see also Williams 1995, 92–93, who supplies copious examples of discriminatory attitudes in social work). Would there be a diversity of contributors, including queer librarians of color and lesbians, who wanted to write about their coming out and other experiences? What would compiling such a collection mean for the future of our professional work and activism as lesbigay librarians and library educators? And finally, would a publisher be willing to accept such a work?

These concerns, in a country that still largely confuses homosexual acts with lesbigay identity, have been somewhat assuaged by the development of queer theory and the burgeoning gay press. At the same time, professional prejudice and misunderstandings are still common enough to warrant exploration, although dispassionate discussion of such issues in librarianship is rare, and sophisticated research has been almost totally lacking. Getting an edited work into print is not easy in the best of circumstances, and for editors of lesbigay writing, may be complicated by other issues. This account identifies and explains these problems as they arose for me in the course of compiling *Liberating Minds*, in the hope that it may serve as a primer for those unfamiliar with the obstacles of translating lesbigay ideas into mainstream print.

TWENTY-FIFTH ANNIVERSARY OF THE GLBTF

Reaching Inside Out, the preconference in Chicago (June 1995) coordinated by the ALA's GLBTF to celebrate that organization's twenty-fifth anniversary, served as the perfect opportunity to meet with American lesbigay librarians and others who had experience and contacts in the publishing world. Some of these conferees became contributors, including Cal Gough, James E. Van Buskirk, Martha Cornog, Jerry Perry, Sanford Berman, and James V. (Jim) Carmichael, Jr.

Many lesbigay librarians had already expressed interest in my work, although some initially were skeptical about the importance of documenting their activisim and work in libraries. As word of my call for submissions was heard through various listservs on the Internet and in library journals, however, more librarians became convinced of what I saw as the urgent value of recording for posterity our minority professional experience. I later wrote three articles to document what had transpired at the conference (Kester July 21, 1995; September 1995; "Cherishing the Past"). These further alerted prospective queer contributors that I was seeking submissions for my edited collection. Another important aim of my attendance at the GLBTF celebration was to encourage lesbian librarians and librarians of color to submit writings for the collection. (It is worth noting in passing that until a gay listserv was created, queer librarians had no means of identifying each other other than by attending GLBTF functions.)

THE PROBLEM OF ASSESSING CONTRIBUTORS

My first, and perhaps most pressing problem was devising a method for reaching possible contributors. I began by sending out a call to lesbigay bookstores, archives, and libraries. I also contacted individual librarians who had previously contributed to Cal Gough and Ellen Greenblatt's (1990) groundbreaking work. There was a minimal response by librarians to my first notice, but fortunately, both Sanford Berman and Martha Cornog, two progressive librarians, were among those who responded positively. They provided names of many other potential contributors, and suggested networks of referral. The first lesson, then, was learning the value of seasoned professionals to a project like mine.

Another problem I encountered was my own uncertainty caused by a lack of any proven record that would indicate whether queer librarians were able to write of experiences such as coming out, censorship of gay and lesbian materials in libraries, homophobia, sexism and racism, and developing lesbigay library collections. Certainly, Gough and Greenblatt's collection of essays had discussed some of these issues, but the focus of the collection was not personal. I feared that lesbigay librarians might lack the requisite force of expression and coherence to frame their experiences, especially if they had not fully integrated their sexual and professional identities. Furthermore, even among gay activists, internalized homophobia and self-censorship may lead to the "toning down" of written forms of expression. Most obvious of all was lack of a clear precedent for such stories in librarianship: the dilemma of not knowing how and what to write about one's work as it relates to activism as queer professionals, or full integration of one's personal and professional identities. I reasoned, however, that those who would submit contributions would be motivated by a deep longing to relate their stories as a way of further "coming out" truthfully to themselves and to the library profession.

An informal survey of the tentative contributors indicated to me that at least among this small group of lesbigay librarians, such a project was long overdue. Most of my contributors were out in the workplace and very comfortable being labelled as gay, lesbian, or bisexual librarians. Hence, it would be (emotionally) easy for most of them to write about their coming out and other experiences as queer librarians. By writing about their experiences, these writers hoped to provide comfort, confirmation, and encouragement for other queer librarians. Some saw it as a coming-out call for other queer librarians, a risk-taking venture whose price was unequivocal openness and honesty among peers, the aim of which was self-acceptance on a holistic plane. These initial contributors, at least, were ready to speak their minds openly on a range of issues in a full volume of coming-out stories, something that until now they had not had the opportunity to do.

Cal Gough had suggested that I might broaden the scope of my book to include queer booksellers, library users, journalists, publishers, and volunteers of community archives. He may have feared, as I did, that there might not be enough librarian-contributors for such a work, but at any rate, such inclusions were entirely appropriate considering the cross-over between publishing, the book trade, and librarianship. Moreover, because the user is central to the librarian's professional credo, some input from activist library volunteers seemed appropriate. For example, I received one contribution from a library user who had struggled unsuccessfully to develop a gay and lesbian collection in Sedalia, Missouri (Evans 1997). As for the book trade, I heard from the manager of a lesbian and gay bookstore—Glad Day—in Toronto (Mistysyn 1997). Only in the case of lesbigay publishers did my contacts—Sasha Alyson (formerly of Alyson Publications), Barbara Grier (Naiad Press), and Makeda Silvera (Sister Vision Press, Toronto)—fail to yield results.

One quick and efficient method to identify potential contributors emerged from the signed book reviews of gay and lesbian titles in *Library Journal*. This source yielded at least one contributor, and James E. Van Buskirk of the San Francisco Public Library agreed to write for the collection (Van Buskirk 1997). Sharon Malinowski's essential lesbigay literary companion and bibliography provided other contacts (Malinowski 1994; 1995). Postings in library journals also were helpful in reaching those librarians who might not be connected to the Internet.[1]   Various issues of the *GLBTF Newsletter* and *Lambda Book Report* were consulted for other contributors. It is worth noting in this regard how essential the output of lesbigay presses and publications is in identifying gay writers, because such people may, but usually do not, publish with the same avidity in the mainstream ("straight") press. More significantly, many mainstream journals still do not review queer titles, although this situation has radically improved in recent years.

I also made it known that anonymous submissions would be accepted, because I reasoned that assurances of anonymity might increase the number of submissions to the collection. Most contributors were willing to have their own names included in the collection. Interestingly, more women then men wanted to write using a pseudonym, apparently to safeguard their privacy at their libraries. Such a result is to be expected because lesbians may be discounted even more than gay men in the work place, and gender bias is by no means confined to the straight community (Carmichael 1995, 40–47).

The most productive method of accessing possible contributors was through posting notices on the gay librarian listserv (GAY-LBN) the listserv for African American scholars (AFSL), and in the *GLBTF Newsletter*.[2] Because I was not personally connected to the Internet at my home library, I contacted a librarian at the University of Toronto who graciously made her resources available to me. Finally, attending the GLBTF preconference also helped to generate interest in the book and convinced more queer librarians that their participation in the project was vital.

Some librarians and library educators write personal coming-out stories, pass them among queer friends for their edification, without serious thought of publication. Jim Carmichael was good enough to send me one of these from a New Zealand–born library consultant who was interested in re-editing his work for my collection. The consultant came from an older generation of gay librarians who married early in their careers, and who realized only many years later that they could be free of the ambiguity and duplicity they felt in their heterosexual unions. However, the fact that he feared that his coming out in print might hurt his ex-wife may have prevented him from finishing his work.

LIBRARY EDUCATORS

Although I received support from library associations in both Canada and the United States when I advertised my call for submissions, support from library educators was slow in coming. Initially, I didn't know if library educators, with the publish or perish pressures that prompt many of their efforts, would consider a project like mine worthy of consideration.

I was thrilled to learn, therefore, that both Jim Carmichael (University of North Carolina, Greensboro) and Alvin M. Schrader (University of Alberta) were eager to send me submissions for the collection (Carmichael 1997a, 1997b; Schrader 1997). Carmichael had written to inform me of his support: "I think you are brave and brilliant and prescient to have initiated this project, which to my knowledge is the first of its kind in the profession, and long overdue. It will no doubt be cited for many years to come, especially as there is so little literature available in the field" (Carmichael 1995c). I was moved by this letter because it said to me that my struggle to find contributors—and the nature of my research—had not gone unnoticed.

Meanwhile, Schrader had hit upon an idea: "Although I had thought about doing something when Jim [Carmichael] sent me your call for submissions, it wasn't until I was reading over the proofs for my new book *Fear of Words: Censorship and the Public Libraries of Canada*, being published by the Canadian Library Association next month, that I suddenly realized a possible contribution was looking me right in the face—an indepth analysis of antigay challenges that were reported in my 1988 survey of Canadian public libraries" (Schrader 1995b). Roma Harris from the University of Western Ontario's Graduate School of Library and Information Science also responded: "I'm amazed at your energy and applaud your efforts to bring to light gay and lesbian issues in librarianship. I'm sure [your book] will be a huge success" (Harris 1995).

Both Harris and, more recently, Carmichael had conducted research in queer issues in the library profession (Harris and Creelman 1990; Carmichael 1995a; Carmichael and Shontz 1996). So, they may have been aware of what I was up against in terms of professional disdain and lack of support from some quarters. One must also acknowledge the seminal work of Cal Gough and Ellen Greenblatt, two practicing librarians, in creating the circumstances that made documentation of lesbigay librarian lives and research in lesbigay library issues inevitable (Gough and Greenblatt 1990; 1992; Greenblatt and Gough 1995). Their collection of essays, concerned primarily with lesbigay collections and clientele, led the way for other librarians and scholars to conduct research in the field of queer issues in libraries (see for example, Lukenbill 1995; Sweetland and Christensen 1995).

The fact that librarians rather than library educators initially provided the impetus to explore queer themes might seem to indicate a resistance of library educators to conduct research in this area. The findings of Carmichael and Shontz (1996) would certainly seem to support this conclusion, and it is confirmed in other fields. One particular study has charted the negative feedback received by gay and lesbian sociologists who conducted research on queer issues in terms of promotion and tenure decisions. Taylor and Raeburn (1995, 266–68) note that "many also emphasized that their research on gay or lesbian topics is not only marginalized but often characterized as mere *activism* [my emphasis] rather than serious scholarship." The study further indicated that coming out to colleagues, conducting research, and teaching in queer studies "can have significant professional and personal costs." Queer library educators probably have feared—and do fear—the same. Scholarly gay studies such as those recently undertaken by Gladney in American studies (Gladney 1993) and Carmichael and Shontz (1996) in librarianship, both at southern universities, may help academics in these environments appreciate the value of gay studies. The latter work will lend credibility to lesbigay issues as a subject with significant implications for the profession, particularly in light of fundamental professional documents, emerging legal precedents, and the social responsibilities mandate.

WHERE ARE THE LESBIANS?

Barbara Gittings's classic piece, "Gays in Library Land" (see Chapter 6), provided me with personal inspiration to start *Liberating Minds*. Barbara is an unusually affable person who provided an example of courage and derring-do to gays *and* lesbians during the sixteen years she headed the GLBTF. People like Barbara are rare, however, and even more so in the ALA and in libraries, which are essentially bureaucratic institutions with conservative to moderate leanings. Ironically, the tendency not to rock the boat is endemic among those who supposedly uphold ALA's Intellectual Freedom Statement. My initial dilemma was whether lesbian librarians would feel comfortable in submitting their writing to such an *out* work, and one edited by a man, at that. Already midway during my call for submissions, a retired lesbian feminist librarian, who had anonymously contributed a piece to the collection, decided that because of the "stress" of coming out, she could not have her essay included. This woman, who had been active very early on in the women's movement (she had written and contributed to the professional literature anonymously over many years), was still, for all her activism, basically overwhelmed by her very real fear of owning her lesbian identity. It seemed as if other (older) lesbian librarians also might remain silent for a variety of personal and professional reasons that I had no difficulty in imagining. Moreover, the initial call for submissions had not yielded many pieces from lesbian librarians, so I felt an urgent need to access other potential women contributors, for if the monograph was to be creditable, it would have to include a balanced gender ratio among writers.

When, in the late summer of 1995, Sanford Berman passed along an article that was sent to him from Heike Seidel in Munster, Germany, I was elated. She had written Berman to ask his opinion of an article she had submitted to a German library journal on lesbian users in libraries (Seidel 1995). I jumped at the opportunity to ask her whether or not she would like to submit something for my book. Very quickly she responded with an essay which I received in November (Seidel 1997). I was doubly pleased that her contribution would further broaden the book's international scope. My efforts finally resulted in more contributions from women. Through postings on the Internet, Deborah Turner from the University of California, Santa Cruz and Holly Edwards from New Zealand learned of my project and submitted their coming out stories. By early December I also had received two other submissions from a lesbian library student in Toronto, and an older lesbian librarian from Albany, New York.

Morgan and Brown have explained why lesbians are not out at work: fear of job discrimination, lesbophobia, and sexual harassment are only some of the constraints placed upon lesbians, a situation that is compounded by masculinist bias. Workplace assault rates for lesbians can be high—up to 20 percent (Morgan and Brown 1993, 267). In fact, coupled lesbians may face further discrimination in the workplace as same-sex relationships are not recognized and "women who come out at a later age may be faced either with changing careers, or with leaving to integrate their lesbianism with the career they have chosen, a process which itself may have the effect of slowing the coming-out process" (274, 278). My female contributors, some of whom are just coming out now, also have alluded to how their coming out experiences, in their work and personal lives, as compared to gay men, have taken a much lengthier period of time (see, for example, Klein 1997; Stone 1997; and Gomez 1997). Younger generations of lesbian librarians have experienced less difficulty in coming out at work: such contributors as Bonita C. Corliss (despite coming out in a most difficult setting—a prison library) and Jill Holman ably testify to at least two more encouraging life histories (Corliss 1997; Holman 1997).

While it took lesbians longer to respond to my call, more submissions from women came my way, many more than I expected, especially toward the end of my call for submissions during November and December. Although I couldn't use every submission, I was very happy that a wide sample of lesbians representing different ages, ethnic identities, countries of origin, and social classes wanted to include their voices in this collection.

BISEXUALITY: PROBLEM OR NOT?

The name change of ALA's Gay and Lesbian Task Force to The Gay, Lesbian and Bisexual Task Force in 1995 was not achieved without considerable controversy among GLBTF members. Memory of the discussions surrounding this issue led me to believe that it was important to also include the experiences of bisexual librarians, whose organizing efforts in librarianship has been a fairly recent phenomenon. Only midway during my various calls for sumissions did I make this decision, partly because of my own lack of knowledge about bisexual issues and challenges. Cal Gough referred me in March of 1995 to Michael S. Montgomery who had been instrumental in petitioning the Task Force to include the term "bisexual" in its title. I informed Montgomery that as of yet I had received only one submission from a bisexual librarian, and that other such submissions would be welcome, since they would only "help to broaden the scope of the work, and make it much more inclusive" (Kester, 1995a). Montgomery complied with alacrity (Montgomery 1997).

For bisexual librarians, even self-identifying as bisexual may be very difficult. In fact, "biphobia" among gay men and lesbians is not uncommon, since some gay and lesbian librarians may feel that their bisexual counterparts are catering to heterosexual privilege (Stayton 1994). Moreover, "as long as a person is labelled bisexual, he or she faces problems in obtaining consistent support from homosexuals" and the necessity for secrecy is an even more apparent reality among bisexuals than among their gay and lesbian counterparts (Weinberg, Williams, and Prior 1994, 119, 123).

Compounding the bisexual paradox even further, communities of color may define homosexuality and bisexuality differently than white communities. The distinctions between bisexuals and homosexuals may be less rigid in communities of color, although this theory has yet to be tested. At any rate, such a scenario augments the dysfunctions of coming out for persons of color, and particularly bisexuals. These factors may explain why I received only one story from a black bisexual (Turner 1997).

SILENCING QUEER LIBRARIANS OF COLOR

One of my most important tasks as editor was to encourage queer librarians of color to submit their writings for this collection. This seemed more apparent as time passed, because initially, there were only two submissions, one from myself, and another from a Latina librarian (Gomez 1997). At the GLBTF preconference reception for gay author Quentin Crisp and local queer writers at the Gerber-Hart Library and Archives in Chicago in 1995, I had made an important contact with an African American gay librarian, and was eager to meet others. On the other hand, my efforts at corresponding with other potential contributors of color had so far yielded poor results. I was particularly disheartened when two African American librarians failed to respond to my letters. It was November before I received another submission from a person of color, a multicultural librarian at the University of California, Santa Cruz. An African American children's librarian, who got word of my call for submissions late in the fall, was interested in writing about living with HIV, but he was somewhat hesitant because he didn't know how his wife might respond to him contributing to such a collection. My final deadline of December 15 was fast approaching.

My difficulties were not entirely unanticipated. I well understood the reservations lesbigays of color might experience in adding their names to such a seemingly activist work. Black queer librarians have a lot to fear: homophobia from the black community and racism from the white community. My own piece for the collection indicates how racism and homophobia cloud the coming out process for black gay and lesbian librarians. It is astounding that some come out at all, never mind adding their names to a published lesbigay work (Kester 1997a; see also Kester in press).

Asian Americans also were difficult to reach. In Chicago, I had met up with Asian American librarian Daniel C. Tsang at the GLBTF preconference activities, and implored him to write for my collection. I followed up our meeting with a plea: " I hate to focus on minority lesbigay librarians and our issues, but it's obvious that there are so few of us who are *out* there in library land, and there is so little written about our experiences from our own perspectives, that I think it would be crucial that you consider writing something for the collection" (Kester 1995c). Alas, I did not receive a response.

I also sent personal messages and had these posted on the African American Studies and Librarianship listserv. These messages were more successful in reaching a number of interested librarians in early and late fall of 1995. My message to queer librarians of color who were subscribers to AFAS-L was straightforward: "No doubt, some of you may have wanted to submit something for this collection, yet privately you may have not wanted to 'come out' in print—so soon. I too, as a black gay librarian, have had to ask myself several times, if I wanted to speak so privately about my various identities. [Yet], as Audre Lorde once said, [so truthfully and clearly] 'our silences will not protect us'" (Roddy 1995).

I wanted to impart to queer librarians of color that I not only understood their issues, but that I was among them and that this work would be comprehensive enough to represent their issues, too. That African American lesbigay librarians might feel they were African American first, and gay, lesbian, or bisexual, second, has been documented, and according to Gutiérrez and Dworkin (1992), the "perceived lack of support both from the White gay and lesbian cultures and from the heterosexual African American cultures affects [and delays] gay identity development" (142).

I also contacted Bruce Morrow in New York, editor of a recently published work of short fiction by black gay writers (Morrow and Rowell 1996). I had submitted an article to his work, and through him, I was able to get a listing of black queer groups in the United States. From there, I sent out my call to these groups (hoping that there might be interested librarians among them) without much success. I also made use of *The Gay and Lesbian Address Book* to access other related groups including AIDS Information Resource Centers, hopeful that there might be librarians volunteering there who would want to write of their professional experiences (*Gay and Lesbian*).[3]

That more lesbigay librarians of color did not contribute, and none from the Native American community, despite my efforts, testifies to the difficulty that already marginalized populations experience in claiming a lesbian or gay identity, much less a bisexual identity, and this situation complicates the task of accurately portraying the totality of the lesbigay experience.

FINDING A PUBLISHER

Naturally moving toward the most familiar target, I initially approached the notable gay publisher, Alyson Publications, which had already published a volume about gay teachers (Jennings 1994), about the possibility of publishing my work. My reception was lukewarm and noncommittal. Meanwhile, Sanford Berman suggested that I call McFarland & Company Publishers' President Robert Franklin with whom he had dealt over the years. McFarland had published Gough and Greenblatt's highly successful (1990, now going into a second edition) book of essays on gay and lesbian library service. I contacted Franklin, who encouraged me to send him a proposal, which he received enthusiastically. This news was of great excitement (and relief) for my contributors and myself. Of course, this account minimizes the barriers that would have been faced in publishing houses that shy away from new markets, unproven authors, or texts whose potential cannot be estimated because of the lack of firm statistical data on the lesbigay population. Perhaps some publishers have yet to learn of the boom in lesbigay publishing, now evident in prominently-labeled gay and lesbian sections in major bookstore chains across the country. Some scholarly publishers, such as Sage and Yale University Press, are limited by considerations of scholarship rather than subject matter. It is remarkable that besides Haworth, Greenwood, and McFarland, few library publishers have interested themselves in this very promising field, and it would be difficult to say whether it is the lack of lesbigay library authors, or publishers interested in their domain, or both, that contributes most to the paucity of queer library studies. It is clear from my experience, however, that the burden of proof remains with the production of a proposal and a manuscript worthy of publication. Given a good manuscript, and belief in the project, publishers can now be found.

A WORLDWIDE LESBIGAY LIBRARY CULTURE

Positive contacts with the German lesbian library assistant mentioned earlier and a lesbian librarian in New Zealand encouraged me to broaden the geographical coverage of the monograph. Several librarians and archivists who I had approached earlier were unable to submit contributions, so I decided to interview them and provide the edited text of these interviews in the book. These included interviews with a gay librarian living with AIDS who had worked for the Toronto Public Library (Kester 1997b) as well as with Harold Averill, archivist at the Canadian Lesbian and Gay Archives (Kester 1997c). Because HIV/AIDS has devastated queer communities, I also felt it important to document the existence of those librarians living with HIV/AIDS, and to ask them to submit their thoughts and ideas about how the disease had impacted their personal and professional lives. Moreover, an interview with African Caribbean Canadian women public librarians in 1993 convinced me of the significance of the personal narrative and the taped unstructured interview as a valid means to document the professional experiences of previously ignored minority librarians (Kester, in press; and 1995).

The collection would now not only document the development of queer librarians' work and professional lives in the United States, but also in Canada, Germany, and New Zealand. It would suggest the continuum of queer experience in library work, and testify to the fact that our activism was a worldwide phenomenon. Indeed, there seems to be a worldwide lesbigay culture in which queer librarians have done much to provide access to the lesbigay heritage to countless library users, and while I had encountered many seemingly insurmountable obstacles in identifying the cohort, gathering entries, and obtaining a representative sampling of voices, by late fall, 1995, I realized that I should be gratefully amazed at my success.

In a profession that extols itself on meeting the needs of its users first, *Liberating Minds* is not only about liberating and empowering queer library users who have been influential in initiating the development of queer collections in libraries, but also about liberating librarians. It speaks boldly about our past, our present—and our future. It gives credence to the idea that queer librarians have always been a part of the profession, often playing challenging and pivotol roles in providing equitable library services and collections to lesbigays and other minority communities, as well as the straight community.

Further research needs to address the professional development of queer librarians, as well as to uncover the rich history of our activist past. No doubt, *Liberating Minds* will provide further insight into our divergent histories as lesbigay librarians. My work as editor for *Liberating Minds* has been encouraging yet challenging. In the end, the fact that well over thirty-five submissions were received, a great number—beyond my wildest dreams—proved to me that there were queer librarians in at least four different countries, especially in the United States, who were willing to speak candidly about their professional lives. Among these, U.S. librarians are overrepresented, yet perhaps this is inevitable since public librarianship as we know it originated in the efforts of American founders. Realizing the full potential of the American library founders' promises of a democracy of ideas, however, may indeed call for global participation. This is not to minimize the difficulty of the personal act of courage involved in the writing of each of the essays. There still are valid historical and cultural reasons why some lesbigay librarians, who continue to remain silent about their professional lives at work, are simply unable to contribute. Fear of being found out among the timid, and indifference among the weary are, sad to say, all too prevalent. Still, the willingness of contributors and the publisher should amaze anyone familiar with our relatively recent attempts to document our history. The meaning and significance of the revolution that took place in the ALA in 1970, when a small group of queer librarians decided they had nothing more to gain by their invisibility, has been largely forgotten outside the GLBTF. It is a story that deserves to be better known among library school students and practicing professionals, for in it is contained the philosophical core of librarianship: make accessible, make available, make visible, provide, supply, empower.

My book is just a beginning: much more work needs to be done professionally, not just in the United States, but also in Canada, Germany, and New Zealand where professional associations of lesbigay librarians have been established in the past, and where our professional work will continue to flourish—and create access to our lives, histories, and cultures.

Each generation of queer librarians brings with it different and new expectations of what it is to be gay, lesbian, or bisexual—different senses of how *out* one might be in libraries given the social, political, and legal norms of the times. Bigoted attitudes can only be changed slowly; what ultimately remains within our control are our own attitudes. With the publishing of *Liberating Minds*, it is hoped that future generations of lesbigay librarians will not have to suffer the ignominy and loneliness of professional invisibility, with all the attendant self-hatred, anguish, and fear that queer existence has usually implied in the past. It is hoped that queer librarians will develop more comfortably and successfully as well-integrated, empowered, and self-respecting members of the library profession in the future. If, in the future, these stories generate among queer librarians even a modicum of dignity and pride, and a sense of continuity with those who have preceded them, then the publication will have more than merited these collective efforts.

NOTES

A word of thanks to Douglas Frayne (Professor, Department of Near Eastern Studies, the University of Toronto), and to James B. Drake (Information Broker and Librarian,

Mississauga Library System, Mississauga Central Library, Business Department) for their invaluable advice and editing as I prepared this chapter.

1. Queries for my call for submissions were posted in *Public Libraries, School Library Journal, MSSRT Newsletter, Lambda Book Report, The Lesbian Review of Books, Feminist Bookstore News, PT News, ILGA Bulletin*, the *GLBTF Newsletter*, and, in November 1995, *American Libraries*. In Canada, postings were made in Canada's library journal, *Feliciter, Inside OLA*, and *CENTER/FOLD: The Newsletter of Toronto Center for Lesbian and Gay Studies*. The lesbian and gay press, *Xtra!* (Toronto), *Capital Xtra!* (Ottawa), and *Xtra!-West* (Vancouver) also ran my queries over the course of a year.

2. Available e-mail for GAY-LBN: GAY-LBN@VM.USC.EDU; for AFAS-:LISTSERV @KENTVM.

3. I contacted the AIDS Committee of Toronto's Resource Center, which boasts one of the largest book and video collections in a Canadian community setting relating to HIV/AIDS, but the response for my project was less than enthusiastic.

REFERENCES

NB: Kester, *LM* = Kester, Norman G. 1997. *Liberating minds: The stories and professional lives of gay, lesbian and bisexual librarians*. Jefferson, NC: McFarland.
* * *

Berger, David. 1995. Letter. *Library Journal* 120 (September 1): 100.

Berman, Sanford. 1997. "Agitating/Innovating: A Sandy Berman Grabbag." In Kester, *LM*, 25–45.

Carmichael, James V., Jr. 1995a. "The gay librarian: A comparative analysis of attitudes toward professional gender issues." *Journal of Homosexuality* 30 (2): 11–57.

Carmichael, James V. Jr. 1995b. "Glamorized heterosexuality." *Library Journal* 120 (October 15): 8.

Carmichael, James V., Jr. 1995c. Personal letter to the author, May 31.

Carmichael, James V., Jr. 1997a. "Coming out as a form of individualism: A pre-Stonewall relic." In Kester, *LM*, 46–50.

Carmichael, James V., Jr. 1997b. "A gauntlet for all reasons: The importance of lesbigay library history." In Kester, *LM*, 9–24.

Carmichael, James V., Jr. and Shontz, Marilyn L. 1996. "'The last socially acceptable prejudice': Gay and lesbian issues, social responsibilities, and coverage of these topics in M.L.I.S./M.L.S. programs." *The Library Quarterly* 66 (January): 21–58.

Clifford, Violet [pseud.]. 1997. "A lesbian in hinterland." In Kester, *LM*, 123–25.

Corliss, Bonita C. 1997. "A threat to the security of the institution." In Kester, *LM*, 139–42.

Diamant, Louis, ed. 1993. *Homosexual issues in the workplace*. Washington, DC: Taylor and Francis.

Elrod, J. McRee. 1997. "The 'About your sexuality' kit." In Kester, *LM*, 73–75.

Encyclopedia of social work. 1995. 19th edition. Washington, DC: NASW Press. Q.v. "Bisexuality" by Jean S. Gochros.

Evans, Robert. 1997. Rising tide and ocean of compassion in Midwest. In Kester, *LM*, 135–38.

Friskopp, Annette and Silverstien, Sharon. 1995. *Straight jobs, gay lives: Gay and lesbian professionals, The Harvard Business School, and the American workplace*. New York: Scribner.

The gay and lesbian address book. 1995. New York: Berkley Publishing Group.

Gittings, Barbara S. 1990. *Gays in library land: The Gay and Lesbian Task Force of the*

American Library Association: The first sixteen years. Philadelphia: The author.

Gladney, Margaret R. 1993. *How am I to be heard?: Letters of Lillian Smith.* Chapel Hill: University of North Carolina Press.

Gomez, Barbara. 1997. "Connecticut public and school libraries: a 40 year user's perspective." In Kester, *LM*, 129–34.

Gough, Cal and Greenblatt, Ellen, eds. 1990. *Gay and lesbian library service.* Jefferson, NC:McFarland.

Gough, Cal and Greenblatt, Ellen. 1992. "Services to gay and lesbian patrons: Examining the myths." *Library Journal* 117 (January): 59–63.

Greenblatt, Ellen and Gough, Cal . 1995. "Gay and lesbian library users: Overcoming barriers to service." In *Diversity and multiculturalism in libraries*, ed. Katherine H. Hill, 197–213. Greenwich, CT: JAI Press.

Guitiérrez, Fernando J. and Dworkin, Carl H. 1992. "Gay, lesbian, and African American: Managing the integration of identities." In *Counseling gay men and lesbians: Journey to the end of the rainbow.* Alexandria, VA: American Association for Counseling and Development.

Harris, Roma H. 1995. Personal letter to the author, July 26.

Harris, Roma H. and Creelman, Janet A. E. 1990. "Coming out: The information needs of lesbians." *Collection Building* 10 (Summer/Fall) : 37–41.

Holman, Jill. 1997. "Loving women, loving learning—linking the lesbian and the librarian." In Kester, *LM*, 198–204.

Jennings, Kevin, ed. 1994. *One teacher in ten: Gay and lesbian educators tell their stories.* Boston: Alyson.

Kester, Norman G. 1995. "Bringing the word and the book to the people—Rita Cox retires from Toronto Public Library." *Feliciter* 41 (February): 26–29.

Kester, Norman G. 1995a. Letter to Michael S. Montgomery, March 12.

Kester, Norman G. 1995b. "The likes of Quentin Crisp: Librarians need to look at what they're not collecting." *Xtra!*, (21 July): 36.

Kester, Norman G. 1995c. Personal letter to Daniel Tsang, July 4.

Kester, Norman G. 1997a. "Cherishing the past/planning for the future: Queer librarians celebrate 25 years of activism in libraries and society." In Kester, *LM*, 98–101.

Kester, Norman G. 1997b. "Living with AIDS in the library: An interview with Michael Pearl of the Toronto Public Library." In Kester, *LM*, 164–74.

Kester, Norman G. 1997c. "Queering the historical record: An interview with Harold Averill of the Canadian Lesbian and Gay Archives." In Kester, *LM*, 108–20.

Kester, Norman G. 1998. "Empowering and liberating minds: The African Caribbean Canadian public librarian." In *Civil rights, libraries and Black librarianship*, ed. J. Mark Tucker. Champaign, IL: University of Illinois, Graduate School of Library and Information Science.

Kester, Norman G. (In press). *Brother, warrior: The black gay librarian-writer: Some personal reflections.*

Klein, Pauline M. 1997. "Why being OUT is necessary for me." In Kester, *LM*, 190–92.

Lukenbill, W. Bernard. 1995. "Providing HIV-AIDS information for rural communities: A role for the rural public library." *Public Libraries* 34 (September/October): 5.

Malinowski, Sharon, ed. 1994. *Gay and lesbian literature.* Detroit: St. James Press.

Malinowski, Sharon, ed. 1995. *The gay & lesbian literary companion.* Detroit: Visible Ink Press.

Mistysyn, Kimberly-Lei. 1997. "Managing the local gay & lesbian bookshop." In Kester, *LM*, 161– 63.

Montgomery, Michael S. 1997. "Of books and bisexuality." In Kester, *LM*, 55–59.

Morgan, Kris S. and Brown, Laura S. 1993. "Lesbian career development, work behavior and vocational counseling." In *Psychological perspectives on lesbian and gay male experiences*, Linda D. Garnets and Douglas C. Kimmel, eds. New York: Columbia University Press.

Morrow, Bruce and Rowell, Charles H., eds. 1996. *Shade: An anthology of gay fiction by men of African descent*. New York: Avon.

Powers, Bob and Ellis, Alan. 1995. *A manager's guide to sexual orientation in the workplace*. New York: Routledge.

Rasi, Richard A. and Rodrigues-Nourges, Lourdes, eds. 1995. *Out in the workplace: The pleasures and perils of coming out on the job*. Los Angeles: Alyson.

Roddy, Mary. 1995. Letter to African American gay, lesbian, and bisexual librarians, October 24. Original sender Norman Kester (October 28, 1995). Available e-mail: AFAS-L on LISTSERV@KENTVM.

Schrader, Alvin M. 1997. "Community pressures to censor gay and lesbian materials in the public libraries of Canada." In Kester, *LM*, 149–60.

Schrader, Alvin M. 1995. *Fear of words: Censorship and the public libraries of Canada*. Ottawa, Ont.: Canadian Library Association.

Schrader, Alvin M. 1995a. Personal letter to the author, May 13.

Seidel, Heike. 1995. "Sexuelle minderheiten in bibliotheken - zum beispiel: Liesbische frauen." *Buch und Bibliothek* 47 (November/December): 1024-1029.

Seidel, Heike. 1997. "Step by step." In Kester, *LM*, 209–13.

Stayton, Wayne. 1994. "Bisexuality." In *Human sexuality: An encyclopedia*, eds. Vern L. Bullough and Bonnie Bullough, eds., 64–65. New York: Garland.

Stone, Martha E. 1997. "My destiny: librarianship." In Kester, *LM*, 79–83.

Sweetland, James H. and Christensen, Peter G. 1995. "Gay, lesbian and bisexual titles: Their treatment in the review media and their selection by libraries." *Collection Building* 14 (2): 32–41.

Taylor, Verta and Raeburn, Nicole C. 1995. "Identity politics as high-risk activism: Career consequences for lesbian, gay and bisexual sociologists." *Social Problems* 42 (May): 252–73.

Turner, Deborah A. 1997. "Where should the closets be in a library without walls?" In Kester, *LM*, 143–48.

Van Buskirk, James E. 1997. "A queer career." In Kester, *LM*, 214–18.

Weinberg, Martin S., Williams, Colin J. and Prior, Douglas W. 1994. *Dual attractions: Understanding bisexuality*. New York: Oxford University Press.

Williams, Christine L. 1995. *Still a man's world: Men who do "women's" work*. Berkeley: University of California Press.

Winfield, Liz and Spielman, Susan. 1995. *Straight talk about gays in the workplace: Creating an inclusive, productive environment for everyone in your organization*. New York: American Management Association.

Woods, James D. 1993. *The corporate closet: The professional lives of gay men in America*. New York: Maxwell Macmillan International.

Part Two

Telling Our Names: The Pioneers

6

Gays in Library Land:
The Gay and Lesbian Task Force
of the American Library Association:
The First Sixteen Years

Barbara Gittings

> "I don't see why those people are getting all the publicity when we have so many famous authors in town."
> —Librarian at 1971 ALA conference, commenting on TV coverage of the Task Force's kissing booth.

A kissing booth at a librarians' convention? A *gay* kissing booth? What on earth were Those People up to?

Getting ourselves noticed, that's what. Making a gay presence to highlight gay issues in a setting where homosexuality wasn't typically viewed as a concern for the profession.

When the gay group in the American Library Association (ALA) formed in 1970, it was the first of its kind, the first time that gay people in any professional association had openly banded together to advance the gay cause through that profession. Why didn't this happen first among gay professionals in law or religion or the behavioral sciences, the fields that had been treating homosexuality as a special concern?

It was just good luck for ALA to be the pioneer.

A year before, at ALA's annual conference, social activists had launched a new official unit of ALA, the Social Responsibilities Round Table (SRRT), under whose wing self-created task forces began to tackle neglected issues in librarianship.

When Israel Fishman formed the Task Force on Gay Liberation (TFGL), it was promptly endorsed by SRRT and was allocated a share of SRRT's small money pie (derived from dues separate from ALA dues). The TFGL drew a handful of other gay librarians who also were fired up by the Stonewall rebellion in 1969[1] and were eager to change gay literature and gay people's lives. Janet Cooper and Fishman met at SRRT gatherings at ALA's 1970 conference in Detroit. They talked about not running scared any more, and about using their professional standing and skills to openly influence library holdings on homosexuality.

I, too, was keen to push for change. Back in 1949, when I was a freshman in college, the confusion finally cleared and I put the label on and said to myself, "Homosexual—that's what I am, I'm one of those." So what were those? What did it mean to be homosexual? What was in store for me? There wasn't anyone I could ask. So naturally I went to the library for information.

Today, when I speak to gay groups and mention "the lies in the libraries," listeners over thirty-five know instantly what I mean. Most gays have at some point gone to books in an effort to understand about being gay or to get some help in living as gay. In my time, what we found was strange to us (they're writing about me but I'm not like that!) and cruelly clinical (there's nothing about *love*) and always bad (being this way seems grim and hopeless).

I flunked out of college at the end of my freshman year because I had stopped going to classes so I could run around to libraries and spend my time reading— reading about myself in categories such as Sexual Perversions—and wondering and worrying. When I returned home in disgrace, I couldn't explain to my parents what was wrong, and I still knew no one I could approach to talk to—so back to the stacks I went.

This time I was luckier. I found the fiction of homosexuality. In these stories, homosexuality often was an agony and the endings usually were unhappy. Still, the characters weren't case histories but people who had feelings and who loved and who even had times of happiness. From Stephen Gordon, the earnest strong dyke of Radclyffe Hall's *The Well of Loneliness*, to Compton Mackenzie's *Extraordinary Women*, the exotic figures of fun, they all made me feel much better about being a lesbian.

Soon I had my first mutual love affair, and soon after it ended I left home and landed in the nearest big city. After seeing to my most urgent needs—a job, a place to live, and a choral group to sing with—I devoted most of my spare time to my continuing education. I spent hours in the Rare Book Room reading Havelock Ellis and John Addington Symonds, and many more hours browsing in secondhand bookshops hoping to turn up gay novels.

Eventually I read Donald Cory's *The Homosexual in America*[2] and was thrilled to find extensive checklists of literature in the back of his book. I arranged to meet Cory, and through him I found the then-tiny gay movement, which I officially joined in 1958. Now I had less time for reading and collecting. At first, I did social and political organizing. Later, I was picketing and marching for gay rights, battling homophobic bureaucrats, appearing on radio and later on TV, and editing *The Ladder*, the first national lesbian magazine.

But working in the movement kept reminding me that the written word has such a long-range effect, that the literature on homosexuality was so crucial in shaping the images that we and others have of ourselves, and that these distorted images we were forced to live with must not be allowed to continue. I knew that the lies in the libraries had to be changed, but I didn't have a clear sense that we gay people could do it.

Then for a few months in 1970 I was asked to report gay news on New York's WBAI-FM. One day, in the station's mail slot for the gay broadcast, I found a news release from the Task Force on Gay Liberation of the American Library Association. A group of gay librarians had formed and was inviting others to join.

Gay books? Libraries? That rang bells for me!

I went to early meetings of TFGL in New York in the fall of 1970 and was welcomed. The group was ambitiously planning a sizeable annotated bibliography. Meanwhile, a short list of the most positive materials available was wanted for distribution at the midwinter conference of ALA, and I helped put together that first nonfiction bibliography, dated January 1971, with thirty-seven entries—books, pamphlets, and articles. That first list was easy. We were still ten years away from the great explosion of gay materials that would mean Reader's Delight Equals Listmaker's Plight.

Israel Fishman was TFGL's first coordinator, and his talent for making a flamboyant presence helped put the group boldly on the ALA map that first year. For the annual conference in June 1971 in Dallas (I was there, I was now thoroughly hooked!) the group planned solid, professional program events: the first Gay Book Award; talks by Joan Marshall and Steve Wolf under the joint title "Sex and the Single Cataloger: New Thoughts on Some Unthinkable Subjects"[3]; and a talk by Michael McConnell, who had lost a new library job in 1970 after he and his lover Jack Baker applied openly for a marriage license, and who was fighting his job discrimination case in the federal courts.

But solid, professional program events need audiences. We needed publicity. At the biggest meetings during the conference, we aggressively leafletted with 3,000 copies of a revised edition of our list, which now was titled "A Gay Bibliography" and had forty-eight entries including a few periodicals and featured a bold "Gay Is Good" logo at the head. We posted notices of our activities all around the conference premises—and kept replacing them as they disappeared. We ran a hospitality suite in the main convention hotel where we offered free copies of gay periodicals and a place to relax and talk.

We took over the microphones at a huge meeting of the Intellectual Freedom Committee at which fictitious value games were being played, and claimed the audience's attention with a real example of intellectual freedom abuse: the case of Michael McConnell, whose earlier appeal to the IFC had been brushed aside even though IFC's own policies were clearly applicable to his situation. We were afraid to pre-empt a tame meeting and give it some guts.

And we learned, with the help of McConnell's lover Jack Baker, how to do news releases. Late each night we were in ALA's on-location offices using the typewriters and photocopying machines to produce short write-ups of our past or coming activities, always including not only the main facts but a lively quote or two ("Catalog librarians declare that 15 million gay Americans refuse to be called Sexual Aberrations"). Then we went around Dallas hand delivering the releases to newspapers, wire services, and radio and TV broadcast stations.

What a heady time! We were activists. We were innovative, bold, imaginative, full of fun and energy, full of love for promoting our cause.

Predictably, it was our gay kissing booth that really threw us into the limelight. All the SRRT task forces had been invited to use a booth in the conference exhibit hall for a couple of hours each. We could have devoted our turn to a nice display of books and periodicals and our "Gay Bibliography." But Israel Fishman decided to bypass books and show gay love, live.

We called it Hug-a-Homosexual. On the bare grey curtains forming the back wall of the booth, we hung signs reading "Women Only" at one end and "Men Only" at the other, and there we waited, smiling, ready to dispense free (yes, free) same-sex kisses and hugs.

The aisles were jammed. But no one entered the booth. They all wanted to ogle the action, not be part of it. Maybe the *Life* photographer and the glaring lights from two Dallas TV crews made them feel shy.

Hundreds of exhibit visitors crowded around and craned their necks as the eight of us in the booth hugged and kissed each other, called encouragement to the watchers, kissed and hugged each other some more—and between times handed out our bibliography to those in the throng.

Librarians at that 1971 conference learned fast that lesbians and gay men are here and everywhere, that we won't go away, and that we will insist on our rights and recognition. Result: in the last days of the conference, we got both the Council (the elected policy-making body of ALA) and the general membership to pass our pro-gay resolution.[4] Maybe some librarians voted for it because it seemed innocuously vague, and maybe others voted for it in hopes we would embarrass ALA with another Hug-a-Homosexual stunt. Still, the resolution did become official policy of ALA.

Our group's aim to change library holdings on homosexuality coincided with a shift in the book business itself. In 1969, even the best nonfiction writing on gays was mostly by nongay authors, and it hedged about us, sniped at us, clucked over us, or dissected us.

But the Stonewall uprising of 1969 galvanized many gay people to new action. Some produced book manuscripts that caught editors' fancy as the major trade publishers sighted a whole new market. At the time our gay group sprouted in ALA, publishers were processing the first major crop of gay-positive books by gay authors. There were a dozen of them, and they boosted by 50 percent the books section of the June 1972 edition of our "Gay Bibliography." Now the first title on the list was no longer Atkinson's *Sexual Morality* but Abbott and Love's *Sappho Was a Right-On Woman*.

Our first Gay Book Award in 1971 also reflected the publishing transition. Isabel Miller, a published writer under her own name Alma Routsong, could not, in 1968-69, sell her novel about a lesbian couple homesteading in the early 1800s. So she published it herself in 1970. At the time she came to Dallas in 1971 to receive our Gay Book Award for *A Place For Us*, she was negotiating with McGraw-Hill for a hardcover edition of her novel to be retitled *Patience and Sarah*—and McGraw-Hill was one of the publishers who had turned it down before. We had found a way to honor our own gay authors just as the first wave of general recognition was breaking.

I loved working with the TFGL. So when Israel Fishman wanted to step out as coordinator and suggested me for the job, I was delighted to accept. I took out membership in ALA (ALA accepts lay members) to facilitate the necessary working-through channels within the association. Since we now had a formula for success at ALA conferences, we used it in Chicago in 1972. Again, posting notices and handing out the "Gay Bibliography" at large meetings kept people aware of us, and this time our main events also were listed in the official conference program.

Michael McConnell brought an overflow audience up to date on his case: a federal appeals court, reversing a lower court's ruling in his favor, had said that while there was no question he was fully qualified for the library job he was denied, the university was entitled to renege because he demanded "the right to pursue an activist role in *implementing* his unconventional ideas" (court's emphasis).

Joan Marshall spoke again wittily on the queer ways gay books are classified, and she told about one positive change, the Library of Congress's new number, HQ 76.5, for works on "Gay Liberation Movement."

The authors of *Lesbian/Woman*, Del Martin and Phyllis Lyon, and *The Gay Mystique*, Peter Fisher, were on hand to receive jointly the second Gay Book Award. And there were poetry readings from Sappho, Walt Whitman, Constantin Cavafy, and Gertrude Stein, reminding our audience of 250 that these writers whose works they value on library shelves had a homosexual dimension to their lives and their art.

Our hospitality suite that year was large and, thanks to enthusiastic gay friends in Chicago, was kept open twelve hours a day for people to talk, browse in gay books, walk through a display of photos of gay love and gay liberation activities, and examine a set of art works by famous artists (Rodin, Homer, Hockney, and so forth) showing same-sex couples. When the wife of the ALA president came to look us over, we felt we'd really arrived.

But our job was as much to unsettle ALA over gay issues as to settle into the ALA fabric. With good gay reading for adults fairly launched, what about gay reading for kids? In February 1972, *School Library Journal* published an article about our group by Mary McKenney, who noted that school libraries owe, but rarely give, good service to young gay people or to any students who want sensible information about homosexuality.

At the ALA conference in June of that year, we unveiled our first gay primer, *Fun With Our Gay Friends*, in which Dick and Jane and their playmates casually meet same-sex adult couples as a natural part of the world around them. Frances Hanckel, another nonlibrarian in TFGL, insisted the primer deserved more attention than mere display. So, spoofing ALA's Newbery-Caldecott Awards for children's books, we created and bestowed the New Raspberry-Cold Cut Award. Alas, there was no rush of publishers to put this winner into mass circulation. But we knew we'd come back to the theme of gay reading for youngsters.

We skipped the 1973 conference and the Gay Book Award for that year. None of our core members could get to Las Vegas, and there was no outstanding book we wanted to honor. Still, we tried to maintain our presence at ALA by means of a flier, which we asked friends in SRRT to post and hand around at the conference.

We were unmistakably present in New York City in 1974. Our smiling leafletteers, all two of them, blitzed the conference in its first three days with 4,000 copies each of our "Gay Bibliography" and a flier announcing our activities. Almost 300 people turned up to hear "Let's Not Homosexualize the Library Stacks," Michael McConnell's reasoned appeal to move from "Homosexual" to "Gay" in subject headings to spur needed changes in attitude.

Appropriately, our first Gay Book Award author, Isabel Miller, presented the 1974 award to *Sex Variant Women in Literature* by Jeannette Foster, a retired librarian. Dr. Foster too had had publishing trouble. When in the mid-1950s she finished her critical survey of lesbianism and sexual variance in literature from Sappho through twentieth-century writings in English, German, and French, no publisher would touch it, not even a university press. She had to go to a vanity house in 1956 to see it in print, and then wait almost twenty years more to see it properly republished. We were pleased to recognize her pioneer work.

By now we had a reputation for putting on programs that appealed to librarians' professional interests and were also entertaining. Over 400 people attended our 1975 program on negative gay themes in teenage novels, "The Children's Hour: Must Gay Be Grim for Jane and Jim?" It struck sparks. The lively debate it triggered convinced us to do a follow-up panel discussion as part of the next year's program. And the energy momentum drove the program's architects, Frances Hanckel and John Cunningham, to prepare a set of "Guidelines for the Treatment of Gay Themes in Children's and Young Adult Literature" (September 1975), to write an article for the library press called "Can Young Gays Find Happiness in YA Books?"[5] and to collaborate on a trade book titled A *Way of Love, a Way of Life: A Young Person's Introduction to What It Means To Be Gay* (Lothrop, Lee and Shepard, 1979).

Other popular programs included:

- "Serving the Fearful Reader" (1976), a series of skits about what can happen when patrons who are timid or confused about homosexuality approach the reference desk, plus a superbly acted pantomime on the stolen-book problem called "Now You See It, Now You Do"
- "Gay Film Festival" (1978), eighteen nonfiction gay/lesbian films including the just-released blockbuster *Word Is Out*
- "An Evening with Gertrude Stein" (1979), a re-creation by actress Pat Bond that was so moving that one librarian told us afterward, "You know, I've never read Gertrude Stein, but I'm going to read her now"
- "Gay Materials for Use in Schools" (1980)
- "It's Safer To Be Gay on Another Planet" (1981), about gay themes in science fiction/fantasy, with author Robert Silverberg as panel moderator
- "The Celluloid Closet: Lesbians and Gay Men in Hollywood Film" (1982), Vito Russo's now-famous lecture with film clips from 1895 to today, including several startling outtake scenes
- "Why Keep All Those Posters, Buttons, and Papers? The Problems and Rewards of Gay/Lesbian Archives" (1983)
- "Closet Keys: Gay/Lesbian Periodicals for Libraries (1984)
- "You Want to Look Up WHAT?? Indexing the Lesbian and Gay Press"; also, "Blind Lesbians and Gays: The Lavender Pen on Cassette and in Braille" (1985)

Our programs were always open to the gay community in the host city. We publicized our ALA events through local gay groups and publications, and we let people know they didn't need to be registered for the conference, they didn't even need to be librarians. They were welcome to walk in—and they did.

Also, we were shy about asking host-city people for help with everything from bringing refreshments, to donating flowers to dress up the podium, to leafletting with us around the conference. Occasionally, local activists would set up a bonus event for the benefit of TFGL members. Examples: in Los Angeles, the national president of Parents and Friends of Lesbians and Gays, Adele Starr, and her husband Larry Starr came to our business meeting to talk about their work with libraries and to exchange ideas; in New York City, we went to showings of films about May Sarton and Christopher Isherwood, arranged by the Gay Teachers Association.

Our open-door policy was partly due to our having, in the early years, several nonlibrarians besides myself in key roles in the Task Force—most notably Jack Baker; Frances Hanckel, who was active in the group for over seven years; and Kay (Tobin) Lahusen, who for fifteen years contributed vision, practical help, and a photo history of our activities. Publicity and propaganda were as much needed as librarian skills, and there was plenty of work for everyone who wanted to boost gay materials and their handling in libraries.

Participation by nonlibrarians not only brought extra energy and talent to our group, it also was good for ALA's image. Hundreds of gay men and lesbians across the United States who wouldn't dream of being involved in professional meetings of doctors, historians, and the like—except perhaps to demonstrate against them—found themselves happily rubbing elbows with librarians at ALA conferences.

The lay-professional mix in the Gay Task Force (GTF—as it was renamed in 1975 so the word Gay would hit the eye first) was aided by ALA's and SRRT's few rules about structure and membership, and by the very loose organization of GTF itself. For its first sixteen years, including the fifteen years I served as coordinator, GTF had no elected officers, no membership requirements, no dues. As coordinator, I handled most of the ongoing scut work: ALA paperwork and deadlines, SRRT meetings and reports, correspondence, set-up and printing of fliers and the "Gay Bibliography" and other publications, the mailing list, program arrangements, and recruiting. Other jobs were done by those willing to do them, for the fun and satisfaction.

In outreach beyond the library field we scored best with "A Gay Bibliography." We had begun this list as a selective guide to the small crop of gay-supportive books just beginning to appear in 1970-71, plus a few key gay periodicals and pamphlets. Naturally, we wanted the list to reach not only librarians who buy for their libraries, but also gay people who might be searching for the sparse gay material then available in libraries and bookstores.

By dint of our efforts to promote our one-of-a-kind guide, we began getting mentions of our bibliography and our group in books then being published, such as *Sappho Was a Right-On Woman* (1972) and *Lesbian/Woman* (1972). Even in 1990, the GTF hears from people who have just come across these books and who write "I hope there's still somebody at this address after all these years."

For some who write to us, it's their first contact with a gay/lesbian group. The "information" they often need is more than finding gay reading—it means finding other gay people. What a boon it's been to have *Gayellow Pages* to which to steer them!

Our "Gay Bibliography," issued yearly at first, soon got harder to revise so often. The sixth edition, in March 1980, with 563 entries including audio-visuals, took more than a year to put together and cost several thousand dollars to produce. We had to take a breather. Fortunately, we had ordered a big printing run, and over the next few years more than 38,000 copies of that edition were distributed in and out of libraries.

As gay materials grew in quantity and quality, we began getting requests for shorter lists, lists crafted for a particular audience or focussing on one topic. For example, an aide to a midwestern state legislator asked for no more than a dozen basic gay items to start educating lawmakers who knew little about homosexuality. "If you give them a long list, it's too much to grasp and they won't look at anything," she said. We complied.

Other inquiries came from lesbians and gay men who wanted guidance to novels, since our bibliography's book titles were nonfiction and biography. Founders of the early Parents-of-Gays groups sought to pinpoint materials about gay peoples' relationships with their families. And once a librarian at a men's prison wrote that some inmates wanted to be able to use gay materials without advertising the fact; would we make up a list of gay male books without the words "gay" or "homosexual" in the titles or showing on the covers? We did.

There was one challenge we could meet: the occasional request to "Please send all available information on homosexuality. My term paper is due next week."

Out of the requests we got most often came a series of short lists, including "Gay Resources for Religious Study," "Gay Materials for Use in Schools," and "Gay Aids for Counselors," all launched in 1978 and revised several times, and "Gay Teachers Resources" (1979, 1980). "A Short Lesbian Reading List" (also first issued in 1978) prompted more than one reader to ask, "Is it for tall lesbians too?"

One special list we started in 1976, "Gay Books in Format for the Blind and Physically Handicapped," was eventually adopted, with our gratitude, by another organization far better equipped to keep it up to date and circulate it, the Lambda Resource Center for the Blind in Chicago.

We also drew up a short list aimed specifically at librarians. In 1976, John Cunningham pointed out that H. W. Wilson's *Public Library Catalog* recommended only two books on homosexuality: Merle Miller's *On Being Different* and Peter and Barbara Wyden's anti-gay *Growing Up Straight*. Cunningham's efforts to deal directly with the catalog editors got mired in the Wilson company's complicated national-jury system for its selections. So we prepared a "Gay Materials Core Collection List" (1976, updated annually through 1980) as a buying guide for small and medium-sized public libraries. For five years we did our best to counteract the inadequacies of Wilson's recommendations, which continued to lag far behind publishing trends in the choice of gay titles.

As more good gay literature came out, lay people too were itching to get the stuff into libraries. Stuart W. Miller headed our committee of eight who produced a pamphlet of tips for nonlibrarians, "Censored, Ignored, Overlooked, Too Expensive? How to Get Gay Materials into Libraries" (1979). This booklet explained library selection policies in a general way, and told what groups and individuals could do to promote gay books and periodicals in their public and college libraries. It included sections on what to do if your request is turned down, on why gay books are sometimes kept where you have to ask for them, and on donating materials to the library.

Ordinary libraries weren't our only concern. Gay and lesbian libraries and archives had begun forming in the 1960s, to provide concentrated collections and preserve materials that wouldn't be acquired by most mainstream libraries. Each such library/archive had to create its own classifications and subject headings, because existing schemes for organizing information, such as Dewey and Library of Congress, weren't intended for the depth and scope of specialized collections. But why keep inventing the wheel? In 1985, Joseph Gregg and Robert Ridinger began developing a master thesaurus of subject terms that will make it easier for gay libraries to coordinate with each other and for their users to find materials.

Much of GTF's work was guidance and encouragement with respect to gay materials produced by others. The one kind of information on homosexuality we hoped to influence directly was encyclopedia articles. Encyclopedias are a first source of information for many readers, and they carry authority, especially with school students who assume the material in them is the best available. What students read about us in encyclopedias in the 1970s ranged from dismal to depressing. As for accuracy, it had as much relevance to our lives as a skin doctor writing about black people. Our committee on encyclopedia changes reviewed the major encyclopedias[6] and also planned to ask gay psychiatrists and psychologists, whose "expert" credentials might more readily impress encyclopedia editors, to work with us to effect changes.

So many avenues for us to explore! For a few years in the early 1980s we turned our midwinter meetings into mini-programs—mini only in the size of the rooms allotted us, since at the smaller Midwinter conference of ALA each January, ALA units were supposed to have only working sessions for their members, no programs for large audiences. Thirty to forty people would cram GTF's small room to hear our unofficial programs:

- In 1981, two librarians who came to explain the case of a Virginia Beach gay newspaper that was removed from a freebie table in the public library's lobby
- In 1982, "The Family Protection Act vs. First Amendment Rights"
- In 1984, "Gay-Lesbian Publishing and the Library of Congress: Coming Out and Going In"
- In 1985, "Gay Materials in Smalltown, USA?"

At the 1986 midwinter conference we did arrange a full-scale, big-room program on "AIDS Awareness: The Library's Role." Despite co-sponsorship by the Public Library Association, a major division of ALA, there was a very disappointing turnout for this excellent presentation of the AIDS Information Project at the Chicago Public Library in cooperation with the Chicago Department of Health. We were ahead of our time in raising the AIDS issue in ALA in early 1986.

We had other disapppointments too.

For instance, there was our experiment with sign language interpretation. Lyn Paleo, a speaker at our 1981 panel "It's Safer To Be Gay on Another Planet," happened to be a signer, and she offered to interpret the whole program. We announced this in advance. A number of deaf librarians attended the program and told us afterward how pleased they were to have something they could go to at the conference outside of the few signed sessions devoted to deaf concerns.

We thought we'd latched onto a good thing. So the next year we paid for interpreters for our main and secondary programs, both lectures with audio-visuals: "The Celluloid Closet: Lesbians and Gay Men in Hollywood Film" by Vito Russo, and "From 'Boston Marriage' to the Tell-All 1970's: One Hundred Years of the Lesbian in Biography" by Marie Kuda. Again, we advertised the signing. This time, not a single person wanting sign interpretation showed up. It was a worthy but expensive gesture and we didn't repeat it.

Then there was the fizzle of our gay mediagraphy for teenagers. After Frances Hanckel and John Cunningham set ALA buzzing about young-adult gay materials in 1975-76, the Media Selection and Usage Committee (MSUC) of the Young Adult Services Division invited two GTF members as consultants to help MSUC prepare a mediagraphic essay on the gay experience. Here was a great chance for us to influence a recommended basic-collection list to be issued by an influential group in ALA. After a couple of productive meetings to review films and books, the project fell apart, then was put back on track by a new MSUC chair, then collapsed again. Why was never clear.

We also fared badly with a project strictly our own, our discrimination survey in 1978. We wanted to know, beyond our small group, what are the concerns of gay and lesbian library workers about discrimination or censorship on the job? We crafted a questionnaire to find out. To reach as many people as possible, we satu-rated the 1978 conference with the questionnaire: copies in stacks right near conference registration documents that everyone would pick up, copies handed out to everyone at doorways to meetings big and small, even copies laid on audience chairs in advance of some meetings. No one needed to feel singled out in getting a copy.

The result after several thousand questionnaires were distributed? Only 135 were returned. Most of the respondents reported they didn't feel any pressures strong or subtle affecting themselves or gay materials for their libraries. This "No Problem" picture struck us as skewed, but at the time we had no other way to discover different stories.

Certainly there *was* prejudice in library land. We had a prime case to prove it: Michael McConnell. For four years starting in 1971, McConnell and others in GTF protested his job loss at Council and Membership meetings. Each time the case was bumped along for "study" or "investigation"—to the IFC, to the desk of ALA's Executive Director, to the Staff Committee on Mediation, Arbitration and Inquiry.

Each report recommended "No action," citing in part such technicalities as the fact that the university that dumped McConnell in 1970 wasn't violating any ALA policy in force at that time. Since ALA did adopt our 1971 gay support resolution (see note 4) and in 1974 an equal employment policy including the phrase "regardless of . . . individual lifestyle," it's plain that ALA failed the spirit if not the letter of fairness by refusing even in 1975 to go to bat for McConnell.

ALA was a bit less squeamish about gay rights by the time Anita Bryant launched a national crusade against gay rights in 1976. Anita Bryant, until then best known as a Christian singer and a publicist for Florida orange juice, expected her "Save Our Children" campaign to roll back gay civil rights laws and to undo other gains toward equality achieved by our movement.[7] In 1977, GTF got the ALA Council to pass a resolution reaffirming "its support for equal employment opportunity for gay librarians and library workers" and reminding libraries of "their obligation under the Library Bill of Rights to disseminate information representing all points of view on this controversial topic."

By 1985, ALA was ready to take a stronger stand on a case of actual rather than anticipated censorship. England's only gay/lesbian bookstore, Gay's the Word, had been raided in 1984 by British customs officers who arbitrarily seized as "obscene and indecent" quantities of books and periodicals imported from Giovanni's Room, one of the largest American gay bookstores and a major distributor of gay/lesbian materials to Great Britain and other countries. The manager and directors of Gay's the Word were up for trial for criminal conspiracy. In the resolution we proposed, we were asking ALA to criticize a foreign government. So we sought and got endorsements from no less than seven sub-groups of ALA, including two international-relations groups. After the resolution passed, ALA wrote to the British ambassador in Washington expressing "concern . . . about the restrictions on access to information in the United Kingdom" because of the raid on the London gay bookstore.[8]

The one section of ALA we could always count on to support our actions was our parent group, the SRRT. In addition, SRRT was as generous with money as it could be. Still, the few hundred dollars we got each year never covered our expenses for all our busy doings. So we cheerfully dipped into our own pockets, hustled donations, and became adept at doing things frugally but with flair.

For instance, our awards for the Gay Book Award were usually items that cost little or were donated, tokens of symbolic value or of personal interest for the author: hand-lettered scrolls, a lavender cape or commencement cap, mounted copies of gay art works, a butterfly kite, a movie poster.

At first, decisions about the title or titles for the Gay Book Award were made by consensus. When that became impractical, Frances Hanckel set up a committee to get nominations and make choices. By 1981 we had settled on formal guidelines and procedures for the award.

It was time to get our Gay Book Award inside the ALA tent. I applied to ALA's Awards Committee in 1982; the matter went on hold for a while, but finally I propelled it through. My last public act as coordinator of the GTF was to announce at our 1986 program that our Gay Book Award was now an official award of ALA.

I had fun in library land those sixteen years. I'm proud of our accomplishments. And I think it was more than chance that ALA was the first professional association to be liberated by gay activists. Librarians are after all committed to inquiry, the open mind, and dissemination of information. We worked in a truly civilized setting.

We got the gay tide rolling in ALA. Librarians: Run with it, get more and better gay materials in libraries. Library users: Do the same. Take a librarian to lunch, if you will, and enjoy yourself while making your pitch. After all, what is activism without fun? I can almost guarantee results!

NOTES

Author's Note: This chapter was originally intended to appear in *Gay and Lesbian Library Service*, edited by Cal Gough and Ellen Greenblatt (Jefferson, NC:McFarland, 1990). Unusual demands on my time kept me from meeting the deadline for the book.

1. By 1969 the gay rights movement was already two decades old and slowly growing. On June 28 that year in New York City, an ordinary police raid on a gay bar called Stonewall Inn sparked an extraordinary fight-back reaction that flared into three days of rioting in Greenwich Village. It was front-page news all across the country. In the afterglow of this spontaneous uprising, thousands of gay individuals who'd had little or no connection with the movement were inspired to join existing gay organizations or to start new ones—and within a year from Stonewall, the gay movement had expanded tenfold. A good brief account of the rebellion appears in *Sexual Politics, Sexual Communities: The Making of a Homosexual Minority in the United States,1940-1970* by John D'Emilio (Chicago: University of Chicago Press, 1983), 231-33.

2. Donald W. Cory, *The Homosexual in America: A Subjective Approach* (New York: Greenberg, 1951). This was the first American book to proclaim the radical idea that gay people are a minority group and should push for civil rights.

3. Some of this material can be found in the article by Steve Wolf, "Sex and the Single Cataloger," in *Revolting librarians*, ed. Celeste West, Elizabeth Katz, et al. (San Francisco: Booklegger Press, 1972).

4. "The American Library Association recognizes that there exist minorities which are not ethnic in nature but which suffer oppression. The association recommends that libraries and members strenuously combat discrimination in services to, and employment of, individuals from all minority groups, whether distinguishing characteristics of the minority be ethnic, sexual, religious, or any other kind." (Passed by ALA Council and ALA Membership, June 1971.)

5. Frances Hanckel and John Cunningham, "Can Young Gays Find Happiness in YA Books?" *Wilson Library Bulletin* 50 (March 1976). This article incorporated the "Guidelines for the Treatment of Gay Themes in Children's and Young Adult Literature," very slightly rephrased for librarians.

6. Dale C. Burke, "Homophobia in encyclopedias," *Interracial Books for Children Bulletin* 14, Nos. 3 and 4 (1983). This special issue of *IBCB* on "Homophobia and Education" also includes excellent articles on gay themes in teenage novels, the treatment of homosexuality in sex-education books, and access to gay/lesbian materials via cataloging.

7. Anita Bryant's crusade lent itself to being spoofed. GTF member Kay Lahusen wrote an ultra-short puppet play, "Flaming Fundamentalist Meets Football Faggot," in which gay football player Dave Kopay [*The David Kopay Story* (New York: Arbor House, 1977)] applies for a coaching job at Anita Bryant's Christian school—and worlds collide. The playlet was performed by puppet artist Jim Moyski at the 1977 ALA conference in Detroit.

8. In 1986 the British government finally got itself off the hook of international embarrassment by dropping all the charges.

7

A Personal Task Force Scrapbook:
"Incunabula," 1971–1972 and After

Photographs by Kay Tobin Lahusen
Captions by Barbara Gittings

I. The first Gay Book Award, Dallas, 1971. Barbara Gittings (left) and Isabel Miller (Alma Routsong).

II. Israel Fishman passes the crown of coordinator of TFGL to Barbara Gittings, 1971, who is wearing the only dress she owned.

III. Michael McConnell tells about losing a new library job after he and his lover, Jack Baker, applied for a marriage license in Minnesota in 1970, beginning a long job-discrimination battle within ALA and the courts. Dallas, 1971.

IV and V. Joan Marshall (above) and Steve Wolf (below) talking on "Sex and the Single Cataloger: New Thoughts on Some Unthinkable Subjects." Dallas, 1971. The TFGL got a reputation for provocative titles.

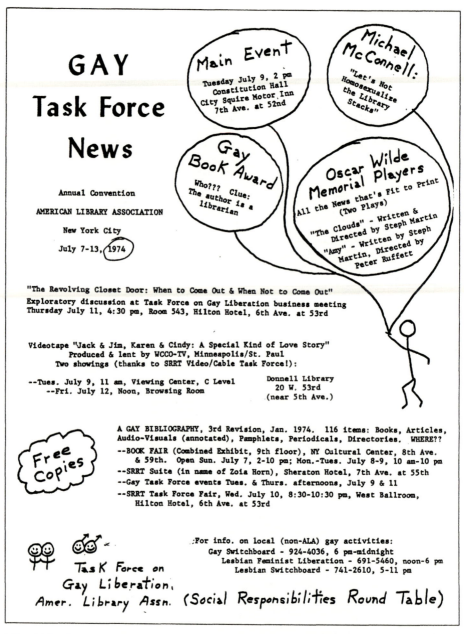

VI and VII. Two Task Force flyers from the 1974 New York City Conference and the 1984 Dallas conference (next page), with some evidence of graphic evolution. After the initial flurry of publicity surrounding the 1971 and 1972 conferences, coverage of Task Force events in the library press was

The Way We Were:
Gay Life Before
Gay Liberation

Come hear reminiscences by

- Dr. R.B. "Buzz" Tucker
- Mary X
- Phil Johnson

June 25, 1984, 11:30 a.m.
Dallas Convention Center
Room W-106

Charles Dana Gibson

Our 14 Years of Accomplishment

OUR CURRENTLY AVAILABLE PUBLICATIONS

Bibliography: A GAY BIBLIOGRAPHY, 6th edition 1980. Selective non-fiction list of over 500 items. One or two copies, $1 each; 3-9 copies, 80¢ each; 10 or more, 60¢ each.

Pamphlet: CENSORED, IGNORED, OVERLOOKED, TOO EXPENSIVE? HOW TO GET GAY MATERIALS INTO LIBRARIES. A GUIDE TO LIBRARY SELECTION POLICIES FOR THE NON-LIBRARIAN. 1979. $1 each.

Handy brief lists:
GAY RESOURCES FOR RELIGIOUS STUDY, revised March 1982
GAY AIDS FOR COUNSELORS, revised April 1983
GAY PARENTS: SOME HELPFUL MATERIALS, November 1983
PARENTS OF GAYS: SOME HELPFUL MATERIALS, January 1984
Two copies (same list or mixed), 50¢; 3-10 copies, 20¢ each; over 10 copies, 15¢ each; also special big-quantity rates.

All prices include mailing/shipping in USA & Canada. Orders under $25 must be prepaid. (Canada orders, pay in U.S. money.) Checks to "Barbara Gittings--GTF" at address below.

HIGHLIGHTS OF OUR PAST ALA CONFERENCE PROGRAMS

1971--Sex and the Single Cataloger: New Thoughts on Some Unthinkable Subjects
1972--Gay Poetry Readings
1975--The Children's Hour: Must Gay Be Grim for Jane and Jim? (gay themes in young adult novels)
1978--Gay Film Festival (18 documentary gay/lesbian films)
1979--An Evening with Gertrude Stein (featuring Pat Bond)
1980--Gay Materials in Schools: Out of the Closet and Onto the Shelves
1981--It's Safer To Be Gay on Another Planet (gay images in science fiction/fantasy)
1982--The Celluloid Closet: Lesbians and Gay Men in Hollywood Film
1983--Why Keep All Those Posters, Buttons, and Papers? The Problems and Rewards of Gay/Lesbian Archives

Our only money allocation is $300-$400 a year, a fair share of the small money pie of the Social Responsibilities Round Table, our parent division within ALA. To cover our actual expenses, we depend on donations. Please support our work. Every bit helps and is appreciated! Donation checks to "Barbara Gittings--GTF" at the address below. Thank you.

HISTORY OF OUR GAY BOOK AWARD

1971--PATIENCE AND SARAH by Isabel Miller

1972--LESBIAN/WOMAN by Del Martin and Phyllis Lyon
and
THE GAY MYSTIQUE by Peter Fisher

1973--No award

1974--SEX VARIANT WOMEN IN LITERATURE by Jeannette Foster

1975--HOMOSEXUALITY: LESBIANS AND GAY MEN IN SOCIETY, HISTORY AND LITERATURE edited by Jonathan Katz

1976--No award

1977--FAMILIAR FACES, HIDDEN LIVES: THE STORY OF HOMOSEXUAL MEN IN AMERICA TODAY by Howard Brown

1978--OUR RIGHT TO LOVE: A LESBIAN RESOURCE BOOK edited by Ginny Vida

1979--NOW THAT YOU KNOW: WHAT EVERY PARENT SHOULD KNOW ABOUT HOMOSEXUALITY by Betty Fairchild and Nancy Hayward

1980--NOW THE VOLCANO: AN ANTHOLOGY OF LATIN AMERICAN GAY LITERATURE edited by Winston Leyland

1981--CHRISTIANITY, SOCIAL TOLERANCE AND HOMOSEXUALITY by John Boswell
and
THE CANCER JOURNALS by Audre Lorde

1982--SURPASSING THE LOVE OF MEN: ROMANTIC FRIENDSHIP AND LOVE BETWEEN WOMEN FROM THE RENAISSANCE TO THE PRESENT by Lillian Faderman
and
THE CELLULOID CLOSET: HOMOSEXUALITY IN THE MOVIES by Vito Russo
and
The Jeannette Foster Memorial Award for Bibliography: BLACK LESBIANS: AN ANNOTATED BIBLIOGRAPHY by JR Roberts

1983--No award

1984--SEXUAL POLITICS, SEXUAL COMMUNITIES: THE MAKING OF A HOMOSEXUAL MINORITY IN THE UNITED STATES, 1940-1970 by John D'Emilio

Anyone wishing to serve on the Gay Book Award Committee should apply in writing to Gay Book Award Committee Chair, in care of the address below.

Gay Task Force, American Library Association (Social Responsibilities Round Table)
Box 2383, Philadelphia, PA 19103. Coordinator: Barbara Gittings (215) 471-3322.

ho-hum, in spite of witty program titles and big crowds. These flyers, along with the Task Force newsletter and word-of-mouth, were sometimes the only notice that conference goers received of upcoming events.

VIII. Our gang, Dallas, 1971. Front Row, Barbara Gittings, left, and Mary McKenney in spectacles near the end. Top row, Israel Fishman smiles at center while Jack Baker leans across Michael McConnell's knee. Baker was invaluable in teaching TFGL novices how to prepare press releases, arrange publicity stunts in such a way as to attract maximum media attention, and conduct their meetings with panache. Librarians, grass roots activists, and the general public mingled freely at the early meetings, setting a tone of common enterprise somewhat more informal than the later library-specific programs.

IX. The infamous kissing-booth, officially called "Hug-a-Homosexual." Barbara Gittings and Isabel Miller show the pop-eyed onlookers how it's done! Israel Fishman and the onlooking young man pictured here ran the "Men Only" side of the booth, but they did not have any customers either, and they confined themselves to hugging rather than this steamy type of smooch. Dallas, 1971.

X. Barbara Gittings and Michael McConnell make a library presence at the Gay Pride Rally in Chicago, 1972. The librarian contingent has been a presence at Gay Pride marches in the conference cities from the beginning of the gay liberation movement, although ALA members who protested a July/August 1992 *American Libraries* cover photograph of librarians in the San Francisco parade seemed unaware of this fact.

XI. Del Martin (left) and Phyllis Lyon (right) receive the Gay Book Award for *Lesbian/Woman*. The Gay Book Award also went to *The Gay Mystique* by Peter Fisher, seen at far right. Chicago, 1972.

XII. Barbara Gittings sits beside a full sized poster advertising Kay Tobin (Lahusen) and Randy Wicker's *The Gay Crusaders*. Chicago, 1972. The book was not considered for the Gay Book Award because Lahusen and Gittings are a couple, and Gittings was among the subjects of the book. This was the first collective biographical work on gay people.

XIII. In the front row (*L* to *R*), Frances Hanckel holds *Lesbian Woman*; an unidentified young man and Israel Fishman hold Dennis Altman's *Homosexual Oppression and Liberation*; Barbara Gittings displays Peter Fisher's *The Gay Mystique*; an unidentified man displays John Murphy's *Homosexual Liberation*. Back row, Kay Tobin (Lahusen) holds *The Gay Crusaders*; Michael McConnell shows off Lige Clark's *I Love You More Than Anybody*; an unidentified woman holds the McGraw-Hill version of *Patience and Sarah* by Isabel Miller (Alma Routsong's pseudonym), which won the first Gay Book Award in 1971 under the title *A Place For Us*; Phyllis Lyon and Del Martin display their own book and Kay and Randy's *The Gay Crusaders*. "Liberation" was the by-word in a quite democratic sense, and the Task Force opened its arms to all interested parties: one of the unidentified men worked for an airline and ran the hospitality suite, Hanckel was a medical technician, Lahusen worked for *Gay* newspaper, and Gittings was a freelance activist and editor.

XIV. Marie Kuda, Barbara Gittings, and John Cunningham celebrate Gittings's 50th birthday in 1982—the birthday coming after the ALA conference in Philadelphia where the Gay Task Force featured Vito Russo (author of *The Celluloid Closet: Homosexuality in the Movies*) and Kuda ("From 'Boston Marriage' to the Tell-All 1970s: 100 Years of the Lesbian in Biography"). Marie was a grass-roots (Chicago) activist who enlivened programs with images of gays and lesbians, which she collected and documented. It is fitting that she was a presenter at the 25th Anniversary Program of the GLBTF in Chicago (1995), "The Importance of Lesbigay Library History," because she compiled the first bibliography of lesbians in literature. Although she worked in libraries, she never received a library degree.

8

Reclaiming a Founding

Israel D. Fishman

Editor's Note: Barbara Gittings, whose history of the Task Force appears elsewhere in this volume, had in an early account of GLBTF history credited Janet Cooper as co-founder with Israel Fishman of the ALA Task Force on Gay Liberation.[1] As Fishman had already left the profession when her essay was published in 1974, he never had an opportunity to correct her account. Early on in my preliminary inquiries with Fishman, he confessed his embarrassment at asking for recognition as founder of the Task Force. When I asked Cooper direct questions about the founding of the Task Force, she seemed uncertain. Both Gittings and Cal Gough, whose contributions to the present collection concern the origins of the GLBTF, were anxious that the historical record be accurate. As Fishman himself stated, in an attempt to resolve this confusion, what may be at issue is a semantic difference, since obviously it takes more than just one person to sustain and further an organization. The ALA Archives at the University of Illinois at Champaign-Urbana confirm Fishman's recollections. There can be little doubt from the documentation I have examined and interviews I have conducted that Fishman provided the organizing genius for the Task Force.[2] It is also clear that in such a period of social and professional foment as that of the late 1960s and early 1970s, reconciling differences in the strands of individual stories and lives is complicated, that Fishman merely was the first to have the courage to do what others would perhaps eventually have done, and that many other now-forgotten pioneers made crucial contributions in the early meetings. In no way does the last statement minimize Fishman's contributions, which were substantial, brilliant, but short-lived. As for Janet Cooper, Joan Marshall, Jackie Eubanks, Bob Cookingham, Ed Bachus, Michael McConnell, Steve Wolf, and all of the other early Task Force members (over 100 people attended various meetings of the Task Force at the 1970 Detroit ALA meeting),[3] they were clearly organizing members. Lest the semantic argument seem trivial, I hasten to add that I have heard more casuistic historical distinctions made over lesser points. Moreover, how a person remembers historical events is often more telling than the specific facts themselves, and Fishman's account, along with Cooper's in the next chapter, suggest rather than enumerate the many betrayals encountered in professional life, the surviving volatility of incidents several decades old, the sometimes overwhelming cost of personal choices, and what ALA's statements of professional responsibility really mean. Certainly, no one was more attuned to these undercurrents than the young people who emerged in the profession in the 1960s and 1970s amid new revolutionary politics.

    The following account is excerpted and revised from an unpublished full-length biographical essay "Founding Father," which resulted from many months of transcribed letters, tapes, and phone calls to and from Fishman. I am deeply grateful to Betty Moore and Benjamin Lea for transcribing this material, and to Michael Norman for verifying the accuracy of factual data. —JVC

For years, I felt that my creation of the Task Force on Gay Liberation was something I had no right to own. Because I acted out of passion and personal feeling, and because I had been raised in a very rigid orthodox Jewish home, I had been trained to discount all such egotistical impulses as evil. Also, at times I suspected I had formed the Task Force only so that people would love me, and that reflected poorly upon me, because I lacked self-esteem, and felt that I could only be valued for my actions, rather than my essence.

    My most basic motivation in forming the Task Force was that I was lonely, and I wanted to meet other gay people—what could be more natural? I knew there were lots of gays in the profession, and I reasoned that if I formed a gay group, I would get to meet them. In my naivete, I imagined that the result of this activity would be an end to my loneliness. Also, because librarians tend to be self-effacing, because fame is an anomaly in librarianship, and because I had learned from watching other activist groups in the 1960s that infamy served as good a purpose as fame in promoting a cause, I acted on impulse in the direction of notoriety. This was a period in which revolutionary politics and outrageous behavior were fashionable among young people, and such ideas took many forms, from the seeming innocuous protest of "Flower Power" against the Vietnam War, to the very real threat that militant black nationalism seemed to pose to middle-class complacency. I imagined a Warhol-inspired scenario somewhat along the lines of "sleep with me, I'm famous." I now know, at least intellectually, that fame and approval don't work that way, and that neither necessarily results in an improved sense of self-worth. I also realize now that I was deeply ashamed of my baser instincts—what I imagined to be sexual aggression on the part of my conniving and manipulative ego—and eventually I became even more withdrawn than I had been when my activism began. Ultimately I felt that my actions that day represented bravado, exhibited for all the wrong reasons entirely. In short, I was ashamed of my role even though I was the founder of the Task Force. It was my idea, I got it started, and I carried the ball for over a year. I was the most visible, the most outrageous presence in the Task Force (or so I imagined), especially in the planning I did for the American Library Association's (ALA's) 1971 conference in Dallas. Looking back, I can say that the one activity which I did not formulate that first year was the Task Force's gay bibliography.

    Later, at one of the Task Force meetings at my apartment on East 11th Street in New York City, Jack Stafford (librarian at Queens Public Library, who was later murdered while cruising in a city park) turned to me after I had declined to assume yet another responsibility, and said, "but what have you done lately?" I felt so humiliated at that moment because I had been caught resting on my laurels, as if being my outrageous self were enough. Instead of the detailed drudgery of lobbying, stuffing envelopes, setting up chairs and tables for meetings—although I did plenty of those things too—I had been made to feel that I wanted to be the center of attention all the time, and that is not an admirable trait in anyone, especially in an upstart organization. Reflecting on these traits in my character, which were then unrecognized and unexposed, made me loath to set the record straight over what must seem to some people at least a very petty historical detail.

Janet Cooper and I have been friends for many years since the founding of the Task Force, and we share a highly volatile but always honest way of dealing with each other. She did not help at all with the *founding* of the Task Force in Detroit, although she was very active in early Task Force activities, did much of the grub work entailed in organizing and publicizing Task Force activities, and contributed some brilliant papers along the way. Other people who helped in similarly essential tasks such as distributing flyers, showing up for meetings, and volunteering for clean-up were Jackie Eubanks, Joan Marshall (a former classmate from Columbia School of Library Service), and Betty Carol Sellen, all from the Brooklyn College library staff, along with Ed Bachus from Skidmore College.

When I first came across reference to the statement that Janet and I had co-founded the Task Force in Barbara Gittings's essay "Combating the Lies in Libraries," I was hesitant to take Janet on about it, especially as she had worked closely with Barbara and Kay during the early years after I left. I didn't want to get in an argument about it lest she remembered it differently, and to be perfectly honest, I suppose I was still a bit afraid of Janet's ardent feminism, ruthless honesty, and emotionally direct way of dealing with me. During one period of my life, I had been through shock therapy, too (I still mix up names and places), and in the end, what difference did it make who founded the Task Force, so long as the group was still viable? The organization survives, no matter who gets the credit.

Naturally, over the years, a false impression has been created that Barbara Gittings was the founder of the Task Force because of her tremendous level of sustaining activity, although Barbara herself has always been very careful to give me credit for the founding. Actually, from the day she came on board in Dallas—a year after the founding—Barbara was the most visible presence in Task Force activities, especially after the Hug-a-Homosexual booth at Dallas in which she was one of the principals in *the* famous photograph (see p.101).

If one interprets the founding of the Task Force loosely, and if one considers Janet a co-founder, then everyone who was at any of the meetings that week in Detroit should also be co-founder: Jackie Eubanks, certainly, because she was the one who took me over to the Social Responsibilities Round Table section of the ALA office at the convention in Detroit so that I could type up the necessary paperwork and make it official. She would be the ideal person to verify this account, but she died of AIDS on November 19, 1995. In that very practical sense, Jackie could in some way be considered co-founder, and everyone who was there could to a lesser degree also be considered co-founder. Yet to be precise, anyone who was there that week really is a founding member perhaps, or one of the original members, but not a co-founder. In the strictest sense of definition, I did found it.

Janet came to a meeting later in the week, but she wasn't there the first couple of days. So strictly speaking she's not co-founder, although her later contributions to the Task Force and gay activism were considerable. If my feminist consciousness had been higher then and I had been more aware of social issues at the time, I probably would have made sure that a lesbian helped me to co-found it. I omitted to do that: *Mea culpa, mea maxima culpa.* Certainly Janet was not there that Sunday or Monday. She was on her way to another meeting to get an award when she was introduced to me.

At the same time (late June 1970) I was organizing and coordinating the Task Force in Detroit, I was looking for and found what turned out to be my last library job at Upsala College (no longer in existence). I was circulation and reference librarian. When the major library journals came out with my name, picture, and address, as founder of the Task Force, [4] a part-time librarian there set out to destroy my career. People still do such things occasionally, I believe. Every time anything about me appeared in the library press, this person would march back to technical services and "awfulize" about me. She became my nemesis, and she practiced subtle persecution.

We had an interesting dynamic there. The library director claimed to be a liberal but his liberalism was not very effective insofar as his being my advocate in library politics or in asserting himself over the "old timers" who ran the library. The reference librarian, who was my supervisor, was a Civil Liberties Union type, but I was too outrageous even for her tastes. And then there was the technical services librarian, who when I brought in gay publications to be cataloged, refused to catalog them, and returned them to me. Or, if I ordered any gay publications, they sat in the back office uncataloged. Yes, it hurt me, but these colleagues felt justified in pursuing their line of disapproval because I still had problems with basic work habits such as getting to work on time. Admittedly, I was not the model employee, but I believe I was a good reference librarian and had tremendous potential. I was smart, I was bright, I was intelligent, and I had good rapport with students. I lacked self-discipline and confidence.

The director had a bulletin board for suggestions and there were people who posted either explicit or indirect homophobic remarks about me from time to time. He would reply that such remarks were totally inappropriate, so he did support me in that sense, especially if you consider the social climate of the early 1970s. He did not provide good mentoring, however. He didn't point out to me that how I presented my gay identity might be a problem, or help resolve personality conflicts. I never guessed, for example, that having coffee with the rest of the faculty was *de rigueur* for maintaining good work relationships in that library, nor did I have any idea what specific steps I needed to ensure getting reappointed, such as seeking out committee assignments. The library paid for my ALA/Dallas 1971 air fare, and in that sense the library ostensibly contributed to my professional development, but that just fired up more resentment among the library staff because they suspected that my *entire* purpose in going was to be outrageously queer there.

Finally, in 1973 I was denied tenure. I was going to fight it and make a big stink, but it hardly seemed worth the trouble. The woman who was head of the college personnel committee was an orthodox Jew whose major interest was in black studies, yet who seemed to be relatively uniformed about gay issues. Then there was a faculty member who was gay, but very much in the closet. He was also on the personnel committee, and once came by the library to check out what I was really like: he was threatened by my flamboyance, I suppose, or just my being out, but at any rate, he was certainly no friend. I suppose the point of these anecdotes is to illustrate the fact that political/social ideology and sexual orientation do not guarantee like-mindedness among people of similar persuasions—in some cases, in fact, people find their most bitter opponents among fellow travelers.

It is perhaps rationalizing to state that many of my problems at work arose because I had no support as a gay person, and it is probably true that I caused some of my own problems due to ignorance and flaws in my own character. More accurately, I should state that the truth lies somewhere in between. I was not a happy person, and this was not a happy situation. I had no support system either in the college or outside it, the times being what they were, and, alas, not many gay people were then manifesting their love and concern for each other, or taking personal risks to relieve the suffering of fellow gays. For my part, I am not sure that I would have accepted such support even had it been available to me, because of the leftover rigidity of orthodox Judaism in which I had been raised, and my own deep discount of my personal feelings. The guilt just kicked in, and that was that for many years.

I did get along well with the students. My personal life wasn't the issue (i.e., whether I slept with the students). The issue was my gay identity. True, there was a list of technical reasons why I was not reappointed. I refused to go to graduation, for example, which was an obligatory function for all faculty. Instead, I went to the Church of the Beloved Disciple (a gay church) and because I had never missed a Sunday there, I played on the fact that Upsala was a Lutheran institution ostensibly in favor of gay rights. That didn't go over very well. I was not politically smart, I didn't get along well with the staff there, and I was lonely. I didn't have much of a social life, either, in spite of my sexual promiscuity, because I don't consider cruising Howard Johnson's on the Garden State Parkway, or going to the baths, much of a social life.

Actually, the director wasn't popular either because he had been an outside candidate for his job. I was another kind of outsider. The staff were very upset that I was there. Then when I appeared on the local radio station and at the state library association talking about the creation and purpose of the Task Force, some of them were incensed. When my mother died in 1971 the library staff wanted to know what to do, and I asked them to send money to Beloved Disciple, or have flowers at the altar, but they refused to do it because my mother "would not have wanted it." I tell this anecdote not to impugn these people, most of whom have long since died, but to give a sense of what gay isolation at the work place felt like. I can't imagine a similar request being denied to a straight colleague.

I didn't seriously apply for another position at a friendlier library because I was in very low spirits, and I just didn't think that I would be able to get a job. I felt that I would be known as a troublemaker. After all, my name had appeared in *Library*

Journal, American Libraries, and *Wilson Library Bulletin*—so much for brittle fame!—and with my growing sense of failure and shame, I implicated my sexuality and my personal choices: I had committed professional suicide!

Yet, now, a quarter century later I have no regrets and if given the chance, I would do it all over again. Owning up the founding of the Task Force is similar to owning up to my sloppy work habits at Upsala, not for the purpose of vaunting myself, but for the larger personal purpose of gaining a perspective on who I was, what happened, and what I became. Conditions have improved considerably for gay people in every walk of life, but there may be some souls in the backwaters who, like me in the 1970s, do not have the emotional resilience or intellectual maturity to realize their value as a person, and like me, they may confuse their own culpability in what some people still define as deviant sexual behavior with real existential crimes—self-hate, indifference to the sufferings of others, and the time and talents wasted in self-loathing. For any such oppressed individuals, all of these many years later, I now can assert that whatever disappointments and heartbreaks my career as a librarian entailed, the day I founded the Task Force—whether I acted as an instrument of blind fate, a prescient God, psychosexual impulses beyond my control, or my own lack of self-worth—my life and soul were partially redeemed.

NOTES

1. Barbara Gittings, "Combating the Lies in Libraries," in Louie Crew, ed. *The Gay Academic* (Palm Springs, FL: ETC Publications, 1978), 107–18.

2. See particularly Memorandum from Israel Fishman to SRRT Action Council re: "Task Force on Gay Lib.," June 30, 1970; also Minutes, Action Council Meeting, New York, October 3, 1970, p. 4, both in Record Series 49/1/5 SRRT Action Council Correspondence, ALA Archives, the University of Illinois, Urbana.

3. "Library Group Forms Gay Lib Task Force," *Advocate,* 2–15 September 1970, 19.

4. For example, "Of Note," *American Libraries* 1 (December 1970): 1013; "Gay is.*"Wilson Library Bulletin* 46 (September 1971): 12–13; Mary McKenney, "Gay Liberation," *School Library Journal* 18 (February 1972); and also in the local press, Alicia Marie Schudt, "Upsala Librarian Reflects on Gay Liberation," *Upsala Gazette*, September 28, 1971, clipping, Record Series 49/1/5 SRRT Action Council Correspondence, ALA Archives, the University of Illinois, Urbana.

9

Librarians as Cultural Enforcers

Janet Cooper

On June 18, 1953 the Board of Directors of the American Book Publishers Council and on June 24, 1953, the Council of the American Library Association (ALA) approved and endorsed "The Freedom to Read" statement:

We are aware, of course, that books are not alone in being subject to efforts at suppression. We are aware that these efforts are related to a larger pattern of pressures being brought against education, the press, films, radio, and television. The problem is not only one of actual censorship. The shadow of fear cast by these pressures leads, we suspect, to an even larger voluntary curtailment of expression by those who seek to avoid controversy.

Such pressure toward conformity is perhaps natural to a time of uneasy change and pervading fear. Especially when so many of our apprehensions are directed against an ideology, the expression of a dissident idea becomes a thing feared in itself, and we tend to move against it as against a hostile deed, with suppression.

And yet suppression is never more dangerous than in such a time of social tension. Freedom has given the United States the elasticity to endure strain. Freedom keeps open the path of novel and creative solutions, and enables change to come by choice. Every silencing of a heresy, every enforcement of an orthodoxy, diminishes the toughness and resilience of our society and leaves it the less able to deal with stress.

American librarianship's belief system, its *raison d'être*, its very foundation rests on this or some later edition of *The Library Bill of Rights* and "The Freedom to Read" documents. From this brief excerpt from the 1953 declaration, we librarians can take pride that our profession has been eloquently in the forefront in naming forms of social, intellectual, and economic oppression and suppression that leads to fear and the subsequent self-censorship we impose on ourselves in anticipation of social and economic ostracism. From another section of "The Freedom to Read" statement we read: "But no group has the right to take the law into its own hands, and to impose its own concept of politics or morality upon other members of a democratic society. Freedom is not freedom if it is accorded only to the accepted and inoffensive." This doctrine is not an Andrew Lang fairy tale.[1.] This principle is an essential part of being a librarian in the United States in any function of librarianship.

Most librarians can tell how well our local general reading and research libraries weathered the McCarthy years, the era of the origin of "The Freedom to Read" document, by how many of those libraries hold *We Are Your Sons* by Robert and Michael Meeropol, the sons of Ethel and Julius Rosenberg.[2] *We Are Your Sons* is one of the most forceful and moving books in American publishing history. How many of us found this title in our library catalogs? We librarians take pride in having *quality books* on our shelves.

To be a librarian usually means working in a bureaucratic institutional setting. Whatever initial enthusiasms one might have had upon becoming a librarian all too often evaporate in time spent serving to protect one's job, benefits, and pension. Bureaucracies and institutions do not reward their employees for having character or for having ethics. Bureaucracies and institutions reward employees for not bringing attention to themselves, not asking embarrassing questions, and not articulating long-range implications of silence about the major issues of our time.

As American culture changes, the ALA hierarchy eventually recognizes a trend. In 1970, for example, that hierarchy valued giving context to respectability, appearance, and platitudes when the tumultuous social and political events of the late 1960s were fresh in everyone's mind: Vietnam War protests, FBI abuses against such dissident groups as the Black Panthers, the Chicago Police and the National Guard brutality against unarmed demonstrators at the 1968 Democratic Convention at the Chicago International Theater some ten blocks away from ALA Headquarters, and the National Guard firing at unarmed students at Kent State University on May 4, 1970. To deflect the bizarre political and social interests of some of the younger librarians, the ALA hierarchy permitted a bureaucratic intermediary group to be founded—the Social Responsibilities Round Table (SRRT). The decision makers of the ALA gave the appearance of making room for the new political and social consciousness, but, in fact, the function of the SRRT was to gather political and social protests of all kind under its umbrella organization and to keep these issues from embarrassing, interfering with, and being integrated into the ALA itself. No librarian with a commitment to careerism needed to be concerned with contemporary issues such as democracy and civil rights that might challenge his or her own complacency. So the SRRT really functioned as a bureaucratic device for isolating dissidents.

Jackie Eubanks and Joan Marshall were the SRRT coordinators I remember who served with commitment, vitality, and enthusiasm. It was significant that they felt secure enough in their jobs at Brooklyn College Library to have worked so hard with such diverse groups supporting such controversial causes. Paranoid bureaucratic petty politics on the job did not distract them from engaging with the substantial issues of that time. Their personal patience and ability to listen enabled them to work with a great many mavericks whose personalities, willfulness, and eccentricities did not contribute easily to group cooperativeness and cohesiveness.

The ALA held its summer convention in Detroit, spanning the last weekend of June 1970. To us lesbigays, this weekend commemorated the first anniversary of the Stonewall riots. Stonewall had been the protest of mostly male street transvestites against New York City Police brutality and arrogance at a gay bar of that name in Greenwich Village. The first annual Gay Pride weekend in New York City honoring this action of protest and affirmation was about to take place all those miles away. Some of us in Detroit at the ALA convention wanted to be at that Gay Pride celebration, but we couldn't be in two places at once.

Israel Fishman, practical and visionary, identified first the bureaucratic procedure for establishing a Task Force for Gay Liberation under the SRRT rubric. Just before he signed the necessary document with Jackie Eubanks, someone pulled on my sleeve and said, "Come quickly and meet Israel Fishman. He's founding the first professional gay task force, the Task Force for Gay Liberation of the American Library Association. You'll want to be there." I did indeed want to be there, so I spoke with Israel very briefly to express my interest. We agreed he would include me when he convened a meeting in the New York City area in the fall.

By fall I had moved from the Haight-Ashbury district of Boston, the backside of Beacon Hill, to a town of 5,500 with a dominant white Fundamentalist Christian Church population in South Central Pennsylvania, about thirty miles north of the Mason-Dixon Line. The college where I taught had never hired an unmarried man over thirty lest he be gay, and interviewed men to scrutinize them in case they had an arch limp wrist. The walls on the college library's mens room had such graffiti as "Flush twice, the niggers are hungry." There was no conflict between town and gown.

My circumstances had changed. From a neighborhood and culture in which I had shared an affirmation of life, common causes, and values, I had come to work and live in a small Pennsylvannia valley for whose population the major questions, issues, and concerns of the twentieth century did not yet exist.

For me, the weekend four-hour drives to New York City, where I found people who shared my sense of reality, and some who shared my value system, and which validated that somewhere there was an intellectual community, was an open sesame trip. Therefore, for me, the first meetings of the Task Force were particularly important.

I probably know most about Israel Fishman and Barbara Gittings's contributions because Israel and I worked closely together, and still speak at least once a month on the phone. In Barbara's case, she certainly became the most visible among us after Israel left the Task Force. I remember some of the others who attended those first meetings, however, with particular vividness: Wayne Dynes, an art historian and professor who hosted our meetings in his apartment in Columbia faculty housing—he would be one of the founders of the Gay Academic Union three years later; Jack Stafford, a friend of Wayne's and a librarian at the Queensborough Public Library, who several years later chose to walk after dark through Rufus King Park in Queens, then near the library, and was killed; and Fred Haas, who finished high school in Richmond Hill, Queens, in the late 1950s and then hitchhiked across the country with a Sanskrit grammar and a stack of Sanskrit vocabulary flash cards. He then traveled to India and read and translated Sanskrit texts. Back in the States for a year to earn money to support his wife and child back in India, Fred was attempting to understand better the civil rights movements and the personal liberation movements that had gained momentum since he had left the United States before the 1960s.

While gay political activism had been burgeoning, none of the straight media would cover early gay activists' events of protest. "All the news that's fit to print," did not mean any news about lesbigay activities. Therefore, we didn't know what gay activism preceded us, or, just as important, what tactics and strategy gay activists had already pioneered.

Barbara Gittings, the first open political lesbian activist east of San Francisco and founder of the New York Chapter of the Daughters of Bilitis, and Kay Tobin, an openly gay former employee of the *Christian Science Monitor*, also attended these meetings. The number of open lesbigay activists was still so small that most of them knew each other and each other's political work, whether the population at large knew it or cared.

Israel understood that one of the primary powers of the ALA, in conjunction with the publishing industry, was to establish book awards. Over time, such accolades accumulate into bibliographies that have kept both worthy and unworthy books in print. Founding a Gay Book Award would create an audience, so that some day standard commercial publishers with wide distribution might publish lesbigay books. Every librarian understands the importance of purchasing award-receiving books.

Barbara's and Kay's contribution to Israel's idea was an example of the importance of having experienced gay activists with us. They understood how to penetrate the media blank-out on the lesbigay presence. After Israel suggested that we have a kissing booth, prominently marked "Hug-a-Homosexual," in the major public area of the 1971 ALA convention, Barbara joined Israel in staffing it, meanwhile leafletting vigorously. Most people viewing this outrage were aghast. One of the participants in the kissing booth was Alma Routsong, who, under the pseudonym of Isabel Miller, had written *A Place for Us*, later published as *Patience and Sarah*, the winner of the first Gay Book Award. Jack Baker, meanwhile, wrote a provocative news release that brought two TV stations and a *Life* magazine photographer to cover the event. The visuals of same-sex couples kissing remained in the minds of everyone who saw it. Discomfort, embarrassment, self-consciousness are not strong enough words to describe the effect of this event in the history of librarianship.

Ever after that celebration of our presence, the Task Force has met in one form or another at ALA conventions. One of our major contributions has been the distribution of Barbara's bibliography of books that portray lesbigays in positive ways—not in the pre-liberation fashion of suicides and evil characters, misery and despondency.

The fact that some of us most active in the founding of the Lesbigay Task Force of the ALA—especially Israel Fishman and I—never again worked as librarians, reflects the fallacy of intention between our foundation statement and the context we actually give to the practice of librarianship: the statement goes in one direction, the practice goes in another. Librarians might fight to put a book about our lives on the shelves but have been at best utterly indifferent, if not actively hostile, to employing us. I believe that the actual history of librarianship is not in "The Freedom to Read" statement, nor anywhere else in *The Library Bill of Rights*, but in the following quotation from Upton Sinclair: "It is difficult to get a man to understand something when his salary depends on his not understanding it."

Most of us live in the particulars and lose sight of the macrocosm. For many of us, how many billions more galaxies the Hubble space telescope reveals will never matter. Where our paycheck, title, benefits, and pension come from will be our center. Around such identity we will focus our lives and our value system.

Some of the founding members of the Task Force would make vital contributions wherever we worked. Israel was graduated at the very top of his class at City University and is fluent in Yiddish, Hebrew, and Italian. He became a masseur. For a number of years, many librarians around the world depended on Barbara's good gay books bibliography, but her activism and organizational talents were deployed in many other organizations as well, including the American Psychiatric Association, which honored her for her contributions. When will the ALA honor her? The Task Force nominated her twice for the Philip Immroth Award for Intellectual Freedom, and both times the ALA ignored her and awarded this honor collectively to trustees. Are we too absorbed in technobabble and library politics to notice social issues? Barbara's contributions to the Task Force and American librarianship are especially important because she acted as an individual, and because she was never a professional librarian. I became a cab driver.

Each of our new professions is as worthy as librarianship in personal challenges and discipline as well as frequently being more fun. These are not the reasons we are earning our livings other than as librarians. Israel and I trained as librarians, we still think as librarians, and we assumed we would be career librarians. No one will know what contributions the two of us might have made to library science, and apparently the ALA is reluctant to admit that a grass-roots advocate like Barbara has already accomplished a great deal on her own.

One lesson we learned, especially after we met people from other disciplines, was to ask how we can apply our *difference*—that is our lesbigay orientation—to our fields of study and practice, as complement to our respective experiences, backgrounds, vocational training, and educated sensibilities. Because there wasn't a forum for such questions within the ALA, we welcomed meeting people from other fields and feeling solidarity at the Gay Academic Union. I, for example, was able to present a paper on the purchasing power and influence as well as the cultural changes in early children's librarianship.

Our intellectual ancestors in other fields gave us examples of their experience and analysis when they encountered similar recalcitrant obstacles. Arthur Kinoy was a young lawyer who worked on the appeals to stay the execution of the Rosenbergs. As he recounts in his autobiography, *Rights on Trial*, with his colleagues Samuel Gruber and Mike Perlin, he raced to visit individual judges on the Court of Appeals for the Second Circuit. They had only a few hours to stop the executions. The chief judge of the Circuit, Judge Swan, a highly respected conservative judge, agreed to see them and listened to them argue a stay of execution. He agreed to grant a stay if they could get one other member of the Court to agree to sit on a panel and consider granting a stay. Jerome Frank, whom Kinoy describes as the intellectual leader of the New Deal, the architect of its most progressive legislation, and the model liberal when he taught law at Yale, was the other judge available. They raced to see him. Judge Jerome Frank listened to their case, urged them to develop their points and responded, "If I were as young as you are, I would be sitting where you are now and saying and arguing what you are arguing. You are right to do so. But when you are as old as I am, you will understand why I" —and he paused, and repeated—"why I cannot do what you ask. I cannot do it."[3]

Kinoy analyzes the implications of Jerome Frank's betrayal of his career and every principle he had ever advocated:

Jerome Frank might, in a profound sense, have changed the course of American history that afternoon. He could not do it. He was a prisoner of the system he served. As a liberal, as a progressive, he had risen to a position of leadership in society. He would jeopardize the usefulness of those labels and accordingly, the position they afforded him if he participated in the act of courage that Judge Swan, the conservative, was prepared to take. The labels themselves, Frank's "liberal" past imprisoned him—kept him from the course he would have taken if he were "as young as" we were. When we were "as old as" he was, he was telling us, we would understand that to preserve our position in society, we must compromise with those in control.[4]

On January 28, 1972, The American Library Association Council revised "The Freedom to Read" statement of 1953 concluding:

We believe rather that what people read is deeply important; that ideas can be dangerous; but that the suppression of ideas is fatal to a democratic society. Freedom itself is a dangerous way of life, but it is ours.

Those of us who never found employment as librarians again because we came out before coming out was fashionable and because our library colleagues, avowing "The Freedom to Read" statement, never saw a corollary with respecting our lives as they would the right to read a book about our lives, would like to state:

We believe that how each of us chooses to live is deeply important to all of us; that the ideas to which our lives give context can be dangerous; but that the economic and professional suppression of our lives is fatal to a democratic society. Freedom itself is a dangerous way of life, but it is ours.

NOTES

1. Andrew Lang (1844–1912), Scottish journalist, literary critic, historian and poet, author of a popular series of turn-of-the-century fairy tales, which, while they eschewed the references to bodily functions contained in the originals, were richer stories than

contemporary retellings.

2. Robert Meeropol and Michael Meeropol, *We are your sons: The legacy of Ethel and Julius Rosenberg* (Boston: Houghton Mifflin, 1975). Ethel and Julius Rosenberg were executed in 1953 for trading atomic secrets with the Soviets. Although the opening of Kremlin files to researchers since the fall of the Soviet Union has led to the release of evidence that would seem to implicate them, the federal government's prosecution did not apparently have such evidence available to it at the time, and acted mainly from political rather than patriotic motives. This case usually is used as an emblem of how repressive our culture became during this era. Every time the FBI paid a visit to anyone—willful visits of harassment, humiliation, and embarrassment— they provided an example of betrayal for all of us of our Constitution and civil liberties.

3. Arthur Kinoy, *Rights on trial: The odyssey of a people's lawyer* (Cambridge, MA: Harvard University Press, 1983), 123.

4. Ibid., 125.

10

The Gay, Lesbian, and Bisexual Task Force of the American Library Association: A Chronology of Activities, 1970–1995

Cal Gough

1970   The American Library Association (ALA) convenes its 90th Annual Conference in Detroit within the social context of the anti-Vietnam War movement, the civil rights movement, the women's liberation movement, and the wave of gay and lesbian activism sparked the previous year by the Stonewall Riots. One librarian attending the conference, Israel Fishman, at a session of the ALA's recently-formed Social Responsibilities Round Table (SRRT), has the idea for an official gay/lesbian caucus at ALA—the first in any nationwide professional organization. SRRT promptly endorses and funds a Task Force on Gay Liberation, and Israel is named its first coordinator. Preliminary meetings are held at Fishman's apartment in New York City. Barbara Gittings, an avid reader and gay activist living in Philadelphia, gets involved with the Task Force and helps put together a list of about three dozen gay-positive books, magazine articles, and pamphlets.

1971 At ALA's Midwinter Meeting, Task Force members distribute Barbara's list of gay/lesbian resources and continue their ambitious plans to make their presence known at the ALA Annual Conference planned that year for Dallas.

At the Dallas conference, the Task Force announces the first winner of its Gay Book Award and conducts its first formal program: "Sex and the Single Cataloger," featuring panelists Joan Marshall and Steve Wolf. After hearing gay library worker Michael McConnell describe the legal battle surrounding his employment at the University of Minnesota, Task Force members insist at ALA Council, ALA Membership, and Intellectual Freedom Committee (IFC) meetings that ALA respond to this clear instance of job discrimination, a case the IFC had earlier decided to ignore; persuade ALA Council to approve a resolution condemning discrimination against (among others) nonheterosexual library users or employees; leaflet several large conference meetings with their revised bibliography (now grown to forty-eight entries); staff a hospitality suite at the convention headquarters hotel; and stun conference-goers with a much-publicized Hug-a-Homosexual booth in the exhibit hall. Press releases about the Task Force's conference activities are hand-delivered to local media outlets and result in extensive publicity for the Task Force and its goals.

1972 Barbara Gittings joins ALA and becomes Task Force coordinator. (She also begins seven years of coordinating annual exhibits of gay materials at conventions of the American Psychiatric Association's conventions, whose gay/lesbian caucus she is instrumental in forming.)

In its February issue, *School Library Journal* publishes an article by Mary McKenney mentioning the Task Force's goal to get more gay-positive materials into the hands of young adult library users.

At the Annual Conference, Task Force program and social events are listed for the first time in ALA's official conference guide. Some 250 conference-goers attend the Task Force's second annual Book Award program, followed by Joan Marshall's presentation entitled "The Library of Congress Bows to Gay Liberation," and a public reading of poems by Sappho, Whitman, Cavafy, and Gertrude Stein. Local supporters help the Task Force staff a hospitality suite for twelve hours each day of the conference.

This is the year that authors of reference books begin listing the Task Force and its "Gay Bibliography" as information resources for lesbians and gay men.

1973 ALA meets in Las Vegas this year, but the Task Force does not participate with a formal conference program.

1974 Two volunteers blitz the Annual Conference in New York City with 8,000 copies of the updated "Gay Bibliography" and a flier announcing the Task Force conference activities. Approximately 300 people attend the Task Force conference program, a speech by Michael McConnell called "Let's Not Homosexualize the Library Stacks" and two plays by the "Oscar Wilde Memorial Players." In addition to the membership meeting where attendees discuss coming out at work, the Task Force sponsors two screenings of the Minneapolis/St. Paul public television program "Jack & Jim, Karen & Cindy: A Special Kind of Love Story." The Task Force also announces another Book Award winner. The ALA Council adopts an equal employment opportunity policy that condemns (among other things) discrimination against library workers with nontraditional lifestyles.

1975 Over 400 people attend "The Children's Hour: Must Gay Be Grim for Jane and Jim?" featuring speaker Donald B. Reynolds. This panel on gay and lesbian characters in young adult novels is planned by Frances Hanckel and John Cunningham, whose "Guidelines for the Treatment of Gay Themes in Children's and Young Adult Literature" (created in September 1975) are reprinted in a March 1976 article written by Hanckel and Cunningham for *Wilson Library Bulletin*. In cooperation with the Multi-Media Resource Center in San Francisco, the Task Force sponsors a film series featuring *A Gay View/Male*, *Dichotomy*, *Home Movie*, and *Sandy and Madeliene's Family*. During the ALA conference, the Task Force also begins distributing the fifth edition of "A Gay Bibliography."

The ALA's Task Force on Gay Liberation changes its name to the Gay Task Force.

1976 "The Children's Hour: Gayer Books Ahead" is this year's Task Force Chicago conference program; the panelists are Frances Hanckel, librarians John Cunningham and Dorothy Broderick, and publisher George M. Nicholson. The panel is followed by a series of skits illustrating common problems faced by lesbian and gay users of libraries.

In response to John Cunningham's pointing out that H. W. Wilson's *Public Library Catalog* recommended only two titles (one of them the gay-negative *Growing Up Straight*) under the heading "Homosexuality," the Task Force compiles and begins distributing its "Gay Materials Core Collection List" and updates it annually through 1980. In addition to distributing a supplement to "A Gay Bibliography," the Task Force compiles and begins distributing another specialized book list, "Gay Books in Special Format for the Blind and Physically Handicapped."

1977 The Task Force Book Award presentation at the Detroit Annual Conference is followed first by a speech entitled "It's Not OK to be Anti-Gay" by family specialist Sol Gordon and then by the only puppet show ever mounted for a Task Force conference program—a spoof based on the scenario of gay football player David Kopay applying for a teaching job at anti-gay crusader Anita Bryant's alma mater.

In the aftermath of Ms. Bryant's national crusade against legal and job protection of gay and lesbian citizens, the Task Force submits a successful resolution to the ALA Council reaffirming ALA's support of equal employment opportunity for gay library workers and reminding libraries of their obligation to provide information on all points of view on the topic of gay and lesbian rights.

1978 Repeated requests received by the Task Force coordinator for certain single-topic book lists result in the compiling and distributing of four new ones: "Gay Resources for Religious Study," "Gay Materials for Use in Schools," "Gay Aids for Counselors," and "A Short Lesbian Reading List."

At the Annual Conference in Chicago, the Task Force hosts a festival of eighteen gay/lesbian films. The Task Force also distributes several thousand questionnaires at the annual conference asking for information about discrimination against gay/lesbian library employees and censorship of gay/lesbian library materials. (135 people respond to the questionnaire, most of them reporting that discrimination and censorship were not major problems in their libraries.)

1979 The Task Force produces a booklet entitled "Censored, Ignored, Overlooked, Too Expensive? How to Get Gay Materials into Libraries," written by an eight-member committee chaired by Stuart Miller.

Lesbian comedienne Pat Bond's "An Evening with Gertrude Stein" is the Task Force's Dallas Annual Conference program.

1980 The Gay Teachers Association of New York City (GTANYC) co-sponsors the Task Force's Annual Conference program in New York. GTANYC members Phyllis Yuill and Joseph Zogby, and librarian and author John Cunningham, and librarian-author-activist Dorothy Broderick form a panel moderated by school administrator Walter Frankel, entitled "Gay Materials in Schools: Out of the Closet and Onto the Shelves." Also during the conference, the Task Force and the local gay synagogue co-sponsor screenings of Marita Simpson's film *World of Light: A Portrait of May Sarton* and Andrew Lee's film *Christopher Isherwood: Over There on a Visit.*

The final (sixth) edition of "A Gay Bibliography"—now grown to 600 items—is printed. Over 38,000 copies of the various editions of this book list are distributed between 1970 and 1986.

The Task Force approves written procedures for choosing the winner of its annual Gay Book Award.

1981 Lesbian and gay characters in science fiction are the focus of the Task Force's Annual Conference program in San Francisco, which follows the presentation of the book award. Author Robert Silverberg moderates a panel consisting of science fiction bibliographers Lyn Paleo and Eric Garber and author Elizabeth Lynn. ALA tapes the program to sell to ALA members who cannot attend.

1982 At ALA's Midwinter Meeting in Denver, two panelists from Colorado, Gerald A. Gerash and Carole Lease, address the Task Force about the likely consequences for libraries of the federal "Family Protection Act."

The Task Force's conference program at the Annual Conference, this year in Philadelphia, is "The Celluloid Closet," a lecture with film clips presented by Vito Russo, film historian and one of this year's winners of our book award. The Task Force business meeting is followed by a slide lecture by author/activist Marie Kuda, "From 'Boston Marriage' to the Tell-All 1970s: 100 Years of the Lesbian in Biography."

Giovanni's Room, at that time the country's largest gay/lesbian/feminist bookstore, hosts a reception for Task Force members.

1983 At the Midwinter Meeting in San Antonio, Edna Bogel, "Paul," Thomas M. Cain, and Travis Jordon (representing, respectively, teachers, students, the public, and librarians) address the topic "Out of the Closet and Onto the Shelves."

The Task Force welcomes to its Los Angeles conference business meeting a brief talk by Adele and Larry Starr, from Parents and Friends of Lesbians and Gays, and begins distributing "Parent of Gays: Some Helpful Materials," the latest in a series of special-topic book lists. Three longer program events also are held at this conference: "The Problems and Rewards of Gay/Lesbian Archives" presented by local gay archive coordinators Judith Schwartz and Jim Kepner; "The Troubadour as Archivist" (Leroy Dysart, singer); and a slide show presented by Judith Schwartz entitled "Radical Feminists of Heterodoxy: Greenwich Village, 1912–1940."

Task Force members are treated to two receptions at the Los Angeles conference, one at the local lesbian archive and another at A Different Light, the largest gay/lesbian bookstore in Southern California.

Interracial Books for Children publishes a special issue (vol. 14, nos. 3 & 4), "Homophobia and Education." It includes Task Force member Dale Burke's summary of the initial findings of the Task Force's "Encyclopedia Project." An examination of six major encyclopedias' articles on homosexuality show these supposedly "objective" articles to be riddled with sexism, heterosexism, debunked or questionable psychological theories, and negative stereotypes; their biographical sketches of selected famous lesbians and gay men are misleading or silent about the sexual orientation of those people.

1984 The Task Force's discussion topic for Midwinter this year (convened in Washington, DC) is "Gay/Lesbian Publishing and the Library of Congress: Coming Out and Going In." Panelists are Jacquelyn Reamy, Richard Anderson, Gary Huggens, and Lee Avdoyan, all from LC.

Librarians Charlotta Hensley and Robert Malinowsky follow the Gay/Lesbian Book Award presentation at the Dallas ALA Annual Conference with their talk "Closet Keys: Gay/Lesbian Periodicals." The next day, three older individuals from the local community share with Task Force members their pre-Stonewall reminiscences.

1985 "Gay Materials in Smalltown, USA?," a workshop led by Susan Bryson, is the Task Force's highlight of this year's Midwinter Meeting in Washington.

At the Task Force's program at ALA's Annual Conference in Chicago, indexers Clare Potter and Robert Ridinger focus on the indexing—or, rather, the lack of indexing—of most gay and lesbian periodicals. Four Task Force members at the program (Joseph Gregg, Dee Michel, Robert Ridinger, and Daniel Tsang) meet to brainstorm ideas for developing a thesaurus of subject terms that could be used to organize materials collected by the gay/lesbian–operated community libraries and archives that have begun to spring up around the world.

Other program events include a slide show by bibliographer/publisher/activist Marie Kuda entitled "Image/Artist: The Homosexual in the Visual Arts," and "Blind Lesbians and Gays: The Lavender Pen on Cassette and in Braille," with speakers Terry Gorman and John Feldman from Chicago's Lambda Resource Center for the Blind, joined by Womyn's Braille Press staffer Marj Schneider. Also, Chicago's gay/lesbian archives hosts a reception for us.

Task Force member Dee Michel moderates a scheduled open forum—"What Do We Want? from Each Other, from ALA, from the World?"—to discuss the future structure and direction of the Task Force. Among other things, it is clear that members want regularly scheduled business meetings as well as programs and discussion groups. Several attendees agree to serve as an ad hoc committee to draft a proposal for a new governance structure and to solicit candidates for elective offices.

After obtaining endorsements from seven other ALA groups, the Task Force submits a successful resolution directing ALA leaders to condemn a 1984 police raid on a gay bookstore in London.

1986 At the ALA Midwinter Meeting in Chicago, the Task Force and the Public Library Association co-sponsor the well-attended forum entitled "AIDS Awareness: The Library's Role," featuring speakers form local libraries and other providers of AIDS information.

In New York City at the Annual Conference, coordinator Barbara Gittings announces that, as a result of a process set in motion back in 1982, the Task Force's Gay Book Award has been recognized as an official ALA award. Following the presentation of the year's award winners, publishers Terry Helbing, Nancy Bereano, and Betty Powell join bookstore staffer Norman Laurila and record producer Sue Brown for a program entitled "Word is Out: Getting It into the Stacks and Used."

Having decided to march together in New York City's Gay Pride Parade as an identifiable contingent, Task Force members paint a banner to carry with them. Marching in the local Pride Parade becomes a part of the Task Force schedule whenever the Gay Pride Day occurs during ALA Annual Conferences.

At a business meeting, Task Force members endorse a slightly- revised proposal to revamp the Task Force governance structure developed earlier by an ad hoc committee. Another committee is formed to draft a set of by-laws. By mail ballot in November, members choose the group's first set of elected officers. Co-chairs Ellen Greenblatt and Dee Michel, and secretary/treasurer Roland Hansen head up what would eventually become a Task Force steering committee.

The Gay Task Force changes its name to the Gay and Lesbian Task Force.

1987 At the ALA Midwinter Conference in Chicago, the Task Force creates an information clearinghouse to coordinate the creation, updating, printing, and distribution of Task Force publications and other materials of use to gay and lesbian librarians and library users.

Back in San Francisco again for ALA's Annual Conference, our program features local authors Samuel Steward (Phil Andros), Monika Kehoe, Nancy Manahan, Mab Maher, and local educators/authors Jack Collins and "Midgett."

The Task Force also co-sponsors with the ALA's Intellectual Freedom Roundtable another conference program on providing AIDS information in libraries.

Over 600 people attend the Task Force's Annual Conference social event, this year a reception, co-sponsored by the local gay/lesbian archives, at the Harvey Milk Branch of the San Francisco Public Library.

Also at the Annual Conference, the Clearinghouse Committee begins distributing the first editions of its newest publications: directories of gay/lesbian/feminist bookstores, publishers, and community-based libraries and archives; a list of famous lesbians and gay men; and guidelines for efficiently selecting gay/lesbian materials for libraries.

Task Force member Rob Ridinger reports that the thesaurus of gay/lesbian terms undertaken in 1985 has been distributed to all originally contributing libraries and archives and to various other organizations.

The Library of Congress (LC) finally releases a set of currently-used gay- and lesbian-related terms for libraries around the world to use in classifying library materials. (Over the previous fifteen years various librarians—Sandy Berman, Joan Marshall, and Stephen Wolf among others—and, in 1974, the Task Force had repeatedly asked LC to replace various subject headings that were obsolete, misleading, or insulting to lesbians and gay men. What seems to have finally ended LC's stalling on this matter was the fact that earlier this year even the *New York Times* had reluctantly begun allowing its reporters to use the word *gay* in their news stories.)

In October during the weekend of the March on Washington for Lesbian and Gay Rights, the Task Force co-sponsors a second meeting of the International Association of Lesbian and Gay Archives.

1988 At the Midwinter Meeting in San Antonio, the ALA Council instructs the Executive Board to adopt a policy encouraging libraries nationwide to provide equal employment opportunity for gay and lesbian library workers and equal access to all library materials regardless of sexual orientation.

In New Orleans at the Annual Conference, an audience of about 200 participates in the Task Force program called "Positively Out: Gay and Lesbian Librarians in the Work Place." Librarians John Sandstrom, Mark Leggett, Bethany Lawton, and David Lewallen describe their personal experiences with being out of the closet in their various library settings. The panel is followed by a lively question-and-answer session.

Task Force members adopt a set of by-laws and begin receiving a quarterly newsletter, which also is distributed to other professional gay/lesbian caucuses, and to library schools around the country.

1989 The Clearinghouse begins distributing its newest publication, "Finding Gay and Lesbian Plays," and ALA finally begins listing the Task Force's publications in the official inventory of ALA publications distributed to all ALA members.

About 125 people attend the Task Force's Annual Conference program in Dallas, "Our Best-Kept Secret: Creating, Collecting, and Preserving Gay and Lesbian Materials," moderated by Carol Eyler and Lisa Fox, and featuring speakers Polly Thistlethwaite, Dan Tsang, Brenda Marston, Nancy Elkington, and Erich Kesse. The panelists talk about the various settings where gay and lesbian documents are being preserved and the various challenges faced by librarians working in those different settings.

The Task Force considers how to respond to ALA's 1986 publication of the *Disaster Preparedness Handbook*, which includes an outrageously subjective and indignant description of the problem of "Homosexual Loiterers" in libraries and that includes outrageous "solutions" ("Remove graffiti hourly," etc.).

A "Gay/Lesbian Read-Aloud," a celebration of gay writing first tried out at a conference program in 1972, is resurrected for the 1989 conference. It generates enough interest to convince the Task Force steering commmittee to schedule this event for every Annual Conference and Midwinter Meeting, just as it always schedules evening social gatherings.

The Task Force Co-Chairs appoint a liaison to ALA's Feminist Task Force.

1990 At the Midwinter Meeting, the Book Awards Committee announces that instead of continuing to give a single award each year, separate awards will be given for nonfiction and literary works.

The March/April issue of the *Lambda Book Report* lists the Task Force as one of the "literary forces" shaping the gay/lesbian literary situation of the 1980s.

At the Task Force program for the Annual Conference, AIDS activists Darrel Hildebrandt (Minneapolis AIDS Project), Anthony Shay (Los Angeles AIDS Project and AIDS Library of Philadelphia), and Nebraska Library Commission librarian Tim Lynch (among others) address the topic "AIDS Education: Meeting the Challenge."

The Task Force celebrates its twentieth anniversary at the ALA Annual Conference in Chicago with a commemorative T-shirt and a banquet attended by 140 people and featuring speaker Barbara Gittings. After the banquet, the Book Award Committee presents before an overflow crowd, along with the annual book awards, a special "Award for Exceptional Achievement in Literature" to Armistead Maupin.

The Task Force begins distributing a *Directory of Gay and Lesbian Library Workers* to facilitate social and professional networking. The Task Force newsletter begins publishing book reviews in each issue.

Task Force member Polly Thistlethwaite launches a letter-writing, petitioning, and telephoning campaign to persuade the country's major indexing services to begin indexing more gay/lesbian periodicals.

1991 The Task Force begins distributing two recently-created publications, "What One Librarian Can Do to Improve Services to Gay and Lesbian Library Users" and "A Reading List for Gay Men."

At the Annual Conference in Atlanta, *Gay and Lesbian Library Service* co-editors Cal Gough and Ellen Greenblatt examine stereotypes about gay and lesbian library users and materials in their presentation entitled "Gay and Lesbian Library Service: Exploding the Myths, Dismantling the Barriers." Approximately 175 people attend the program, which is combined with the annual presentation of the book awards.

The Task Force approves a new set of written selection guidelines for choosing its book awards.

The Task Force sends a letter to the Los Angeles City Librarian Elizabeth Martinez protesting her removal and destruction of a Gay/Lesbian History Month poster objected to by a local resident.

1992 The Task Force sponsors its first-ever preconference. Three dozen people attend the half-day session, entitled "When Sex is the Question, Who Answers?" Publisher Sherry Thomas and library educator Christine Jenkins respond to a speech by sexologist Estelle Friedman.

"Gay Media after Mapplethorpe" is the title of this year's conference program in San Francisco. Speakers are local university educators John DeCecco, Alfred Keilwasser, and Michelle Wolf, plus R. J. Curry from the Gay and Lesbian Press Association.

The Task Force approves for distribution the first edition of its newest publication, "Resources on Spirituality for Lesbians and Gay Men."

ALA members read about the Task Force in the July/August issue of *American Libraries* (*AL*), the association's official monthly publication. Judging from some of the letters-to-the-editor that appear for months afterward, not all ALA members are pleased with either the magazine's coverage of Task Force activities or *AL* editor Leonard Kniffel's cover photo of Task Force members marching in the annual San Francisco Gay Pride Parade behind the ALA/Task Force banner.

Task Force member Michael Montgomery asks other members to discuss whether the Task Force's name should be changed to explicitly acknowledge the importance of bisexuals to the Task Force's membership and to its goals.

The day after Colorado voters approve an anti-gay amendment to their state constitution, Task Force member Gary Klein creates a network of people interested in keeping each other informed via electronic mail about the amendment approval's aftermath. By the end of the year, the ad hoc network has evolved into a formal Internet discussion group, GAYLIBN-L, managed by Keith Trimmer.

1993 At ALA's Midwinter Meeting in Denver, approximately 150 Association members, including its president, join together to publicly protest Colorado's legalization of anti-gay discrimination. A march and rally at the capitol organized by Task Force Co-Chair Karen Whittlesey receives wide local media coverage.

In April, several Task Force members march behind our Pride banner along with dozens of other contingents representing professional associations at the National March on Washington, D. C.

"I Read You Loud and Queer: The Increasing Demand for Gay and Lesbian Literature" is the Task Force's program at the Annual Conference in New Orleans. Fifteen people attend a meeting scheduled to discuss whether the Task Force's name should be changed to acknowledge the existence of bisexuals in the Task Force's membership and their investment in the Task Force's goals. And despite the humidity and the heat, a boisterous group of Task Force members march in the city's annual Pride Parade through the French Quarter.

1994 The Task Force's combined program, "Beyond *Daddy's Roommate*: The Evolving Market in Gay/Lesbian Children's Books," and book awards presentation attracts over 300 attendees at ALA's Annual Conference in Miami. The Task Force also co-sponsors two other conference programs: "Women's Popular Literature," presented by the Women Studies Section of ALA's Association of College and Research Libraries (ACRL), plus "Rights, Legalities, and Compassion: AIDS Cases in the Workplace," presented by ACRL and the Library Administration and Management Association (LAMA).

1995 At ALA Midwinter in Philadelphia, Task Force members vote to change the group's name to the Gay, Lesbian, and Bisexual Task Force and to pursue all offers to add Task Force publications to Internet databases. Further plans are made for another preconference program (an all-day affair this time); and details are hammered out for the various festivities planned for the Task Force's twenty-fifth anniversary at ALA's Annual Conference in Chicago in 1995.

APPENDIX:
TASK FORCE OFFICERS, 1970–1995

Coordinators
Israel Fishman, 1970-72
Barbara Gittings, 1972-86

Elected and Appointed Officers
Female Co-Chairs:
Ellen Greenblatt, 1986-88
Helen Hill, 1988-90
Karen Whittlesey, 1992-93
Wendy Thomas, 1993-96
Male Co-Chairs:
Dee Michel, 1986-88
Vince Menotti, 1988-89
John Sandstrom, 1989-91
Roland Hansen, 1991-94
Leon Bey, 1994-95
Secretaries:
Lew Maurer, 1986
Roland Hansen, 1987-90
Joseph Eagan, 1990-94
Michael Nitz, 1994-96
Book Award Chairs:
Daniel Tsang, 1986-87
Leslie Kahn, 1987-88

K. T. Hornung, June-December 1988
Adam Schiff, 1989-91
Susan Hoffman, 1991-93
Ellen Greenblatt, 1993-95
John De Santis, 1995-97
Clearinghouse Coordinators:
  Cal Gough, 1987-89
  Ankha Shamin, 1989-91
  Ed SantaVicca, 1992-93
  Gail Defendorf and Dan Hodge, 1994-95
Newsletter Editors:
  Vince Menotti, 1988-89
  Steve Wooldridge, 1989-91
  Kathy Anderson, 1991-93
  Kart Fattig, 1993-95
Program Chairs:
  Leon Bey, 1986-90
  Timothy Lynch, 1990-92
  Terry Allison, 1992-94
  Michael Miller and Roland Hansen, 1994-96
Publicity Chairs:
  David Nieto, 1986-88
  Steve Murden, 1988-90
  Jim McPeak, 1990-91
  Leon Bey, 1991-93
  Mark Martin, 1993-95
Feminist Task Force Liaisons:
  Suzy Taraba, 1989-91
  Bonita Corliss, 1992-93

NOTE

The information from this chronology was compiled by Cal Gough from the following sources: "Gays in Library Land" by Barbara Gittings (June 1990); Ankha Shamin's "20 Years of the Gay and Lesbian Task Force: A Personal Reflection" (June 1990); Robert Ridinger's "Manual for [Task Force] Officers, Committee Chairs, and Committee Members" (June 1992); Task Force steering committee minutes and membership meeting minutes (after 1985); the Task Force's newsletter (Spring 1988–Spring 1995); and conversations and correspondence with current and previous Task Force officers.

Part Three

Saving Our Names: Lesbigay Library/Archival Collections

11

Archivists, Activists, and Scholars: Creating a Queer History

Brenda J. Marston

Like few other communities, the people with "the love that dare not speak its name" have poured attention into claiming a history (Duggan 1986).[1] As others in this volume describe in more detail, motivated lesbian and gay activists have played a crucial role in preserving the documents of our history. From Toronto to San Diego, community efforts produced volunteer-run archives to save records before professional archives were interested. Activists made themselves archivists.

Before there were academic jobs in the field, lesbian and gay activists, archivists, and scholars were also investigating the holdings of mainstream research libraries to uncover documents relevant to queer history. Results of such work are impressive by any standard (Katz 1976; Schwarz 1982; Bérubé 1990). The Lesbian Herstory Archives created a "found image" collection, copies of photos found in mainstream collections that are relevant to lesbian history though not identified as such by the mainstream repository. Through the 1980s, lesbians crowded into rooms at women's studies conferences to hear the stories of 1950s lesbian bar culture in Buffalo, New York that Madeline Davis and Elizabeth Lapovsky Kennedy were collecting for their book (Kennedy and Davis 1993). The 1985 "Sex and the State" conference in Toronto inspired a wave of research in lesbian and gay history. Independently, and now also as part of their professional work, lesbians and gay men have taken up the work of preserving and interpreting our own history. This work is important to us.

The archival profession, though not always right on the cutting edge, seeks to capture significant changes in society and the diversity of human endeavors. Through the 1970s, a number of mainstream archival repositories became enthusiastic about documenting labor, civil rights, and other social action movements, African Americans, and women, as historians increasingly asked for these sources (for example, The State Historical Society of Wisconsin started its Social Action Collection; Hinding 1979). By the 1980s, the notion of an "activist archivist" (Motley 1984) had emerged in the profession, and some archivists were considering how to document lesbian and gay communities and issues of sexuality. Now in the 1990s, it seems every other day another library announces a new archival program focused on some aspect of lesbian, bisexual, gay, or transgendered issues. The Lesbian and Gay Archives Roundtable (LAGAR) of the Society of American Archivists (SAA), founded in 1989, is a lively group that encourages archivists to preserve and make easily accessible the records of lesbian, bisexual, and gay lives. Today, queer history figures both in academia and with lesbian, gay, bisexual, and transgendered people. Lesbian, Bisexual, and Gay (LBG) Studies is a strong and growing interdisciplinary field on many campuses, enthusiastically embraced by English and literature departments and by cultural, media, and women's studies. Though history departments are lagging behind, the historical study of lesbian and gay issues coalesced in a conference, "Lesbian and Gay History: Defining a Field," organized by the City University of New York in October 1995. (Duggan 1995 constructively analyzes the lack of support for lesbian and gay historians and the continuing failure of history departments "to hire and train historians of sexuality, and lesbian and gay historians specifically.") The same year, the *Radical History Review* published "The Queer Issue." Community archives have continued to make great strides. The Lesbian Herstory Archives bought a brownstone in Brooklyn and re-opened there during the gay pride celebrations in June 1993. In June 1994, during the celebration of the twenty-fifth anniversary of the Stonewall riots, "queer public history projects were ubiquitous" (Murphy 1995, 195) in New York City, from walking tours to window displays to The New York Public Library's exhibit, "Becoming Visible." Hundreds of thousands of people participated in an event marking lesbian and gay history, an event created by archivists, historians, and activists, queer and nonqueer, professional and independent. The need to construct and preserve histories of sexuality and histories of lesbian, gay, bisexual, and transgendered people is resonating with a wider audience in the 1990s.

Since about 1982, I've been among those people pouring attention into the search for lesbian and gay history, first as a history graduate student and then as an archivist. Over time, I've learned more about how people produce a history and, in particular, how that process relies on effective interaction among archivists, activists, and scholars. In this chapter, I'll briefly describe my own odyssey into queer history and focus on the ways professional archivists and librarians can contribute to documenting a queer past. I encourage archivists and librarians committed to this work to engage with activists and scholars to take advantage of this time when academia is paying attention to lesbian and gay issues.

MY JOURNEY INTO QUEER HISTORY

The environment in Queer Studies today represents a big change from when I started graduate school. In the early 1980s, I became frustrated in my attempts to study lesbian history in the Women's History program at the University of Wisconsin-Madison. Having learned little queer history in high school or college, I planned to change that in graduate school. I wanted to find out more about how loving women was different for women in other times, in different situations. However, fifteen years ago, it was harder to find and get access to the sources for studying lesbian lives.

But it was possible. The Lesbian Herstory Archives was actively seeking and preserving documents. Mainstream archives had the papers of Eleanor Roosevelt, which Blanche Weisen Cook was studying. Judith Schwarz had found and studied the papers of members of the Heterodoxy Club, a diverse group of intellectual and artistic women in New York City at the beginning of this century, many of whom were lesbians, bisexuals, or had unconventional heterosexual relationships. Other collections awaited discovery, just as they do now, and academic libraries are full of books illustrating the medical, legal, sociological, and psychological professions' changing interpretations of women's sexuality. Moreover, historians have long relied on finding the sources they need in private hands, and research methods such as oral history don't depend on library sources.

Still, academic interest in lesbian and gay lives was just emerging in the early 1980s, the professional archival community was just starting to respond, and not all graduate advisors were enthusiastic about the idea. I heard "there are no sources" and "it will ruin your career."

Lucky for me, these obstacles changed the course of my life and led me to become a librarian. Without support for studying lesbian history and the history of sexuality, I completed a masters degree and then started to look for a job. I soon found myself engaged in the appraisal of state government records for the State Historical Society of Wisconsin. I discovered I liked archivists and I loved working in the archives. Eventually it dawned on me that I could do something about the lack of sources for studying lesbian history. I could become an archivist.

I don't know why I didn't make this connection before. I had worked in libraries the whole time I was in graduate school, for a long time with Sue Searing, then the University of Wisconsin Library system's Women's Studies Librarian. I couldn't have had a better role model. Still, I never imagined myself becoming a librarian until I saw archivists at work. Then I realized I could actually do something concrete to bring lesbian history out of the shadows. I could make things easier for future graduate students like me.

Excited by the idea of becoming an archivist who would help make our historical record more complete, I applied to library school. As a professional archivist, I planned to encourage the archival profession to do more to document sexuality and other overlooked subjects. I also planned to volunteer my newly acquired skills at a community-run queer archives. Just as I was finishing that degree, I saw a job announcement in the Society of American Archivists newsletter that stopped me in my tracks: Cornell University Library wanted someone to initiate a national collecting program on sexuality. I was stunned by the prospect of having my interest in the history of sexuality become central to my job. I was heartened to see that archivists had taken note of a serious gap in the historical record and that one institution had marshaled the resources to approach it in a substantial way. I ended up coming to Cornell to do that job.

Cornell's Human Sexuality Collection emerged from the early work of activists and their subsequent collaboration with scholars and academic librarians. The base of the Cornell collection is the 1988 gift of the archives of the Mariposa Education and Research Foundation.[2] Its members shared a concern that many professionals consulted about sexual matters—especially health professionals and the clergy—were not always knowledgeable enough to provide helpful answers. Mariposa believed that certain segments of the population—among them, lesbians and gay men—had been victims of the resulting misinformation, ignorance, and fear about sexuality. In addition to the development of its archives, another of Mariposa's major contributions was Bruce Voeller's study of the effectiveness of various kinds of condoms in preventing the transmission of sexually transmitted diseases. Appearing in *Consumer Reports*, the Mariposa condom study made information about safer sex widely accessible to the public.

Since 1978, Mariposa had worked to collect research material on the social and political aspects of sexuality. Bruce Voeller, Mariposa's president, enlisted a network of volunteers who assembled historical sources primarily on the U.S. lesbian and gay rights movement and culture back to the 1950s. Voeller, like other activist archivists at the time, understood that without prompt action, these unique materials would be lost forever. The resulting Mariposa Archive is a tremendous resource for looking at changes in forms and styles of gay erotica and at the development of gay and lesbian publishing, politics, and identity.

As this collection grew, Voeller began to consider how to ensure its preservation and professional care, make it accessible for scholarship, and increase its visibility. He was joined by a friend, David B. Goodstein, who was publisher of the *Advocate* and a 1954 Cornell graduate. They both believed that the time had come for a major research library to take up the project of documenting sexuality, and they envisioned the Mariposa archives attracting other collections and fostering the development of a major center for the study of sexuality. Goodstein brought the idea to his alma mater, and Cornell University Library eventually launched such a program—the Human Sexuality Collection.

Our goal at Cornell now is to continue Mariposa's work—to find and preserve documents on marginalized and controversial aspects of human sexuality. Further, we want to make these sources widely accessible and to promote research use of them. By gathering a more balanced historical record, we hope to allow greater understanding of the meanings of sexuality in our culture. We want to give people unique sources for studying the production and organization of sexualities and other interconnected identities.

After my graduate school frustration with hearing there were no sources for lesbian history, each addition to the Human Sexuality Collection makes me happy. Each extra box seems profoundly important, even those filled with old *Time* magazines I'll probably throw out. Along with the *Time* magazines come things that are the heart of queer history—things that can help us better understand individual queer lives and broad aspects of our society.

When I was looking for items to show Dana Luciano's class, English 289, "Body Politics: Medicine, Illness, and Representation," I found a letter from Gay Men's Health Crisis (GMHC) to New York City AIDS activist Robert Garcia saying that he had been put on a waiting list for a support group. When I showed this to the class, a mixed group of pre-med and humanities students, someone noticed that the letter had arrived just a few months before he died, so Robert Garcia probably never received the benefits of one of GMHC's support groups. However, his journals also show that he had tremendous support from his circle of friends. When he was seriously ill, a band of friends coordinated continual visits. When each person arrived, they made notes about Robert's condition. In different people's handwriting, you can trace what he ate, what symptoms he had, his weight, and how both Robert and the friend were feeling. Robert Garcia's journals, video tapes, and papers give details about his medical, financial, and emotional struggles as he dealt with HIV infection, the ways he came to terms with it, the political action he took, and the importance of his family and friends. They show how he articulated and acted from his sexual, gender, and ethnic identities. His vibrancy, courage, and humor shine through. The depth of these personal documents had an impact on the students in that class, people planning to be our future doctors, policy makers, and cultural analysts.[3]

Documents like these tell parts of the stories of our lives in ways nothing else can. They are individual and personal. They are real. With our library "filling up and spilling over" (to borrow the words of a 1980s lesbian anthem by songwriter Chris Williamson) with these kinds of queer primary sources, I see proof that there are sources to document our lives. I feel like I'm finding lesbian and gay history.

Locating the materials and getting them into appropriate archives is one of the key steps in constructing queer history. Since I've worked with the Human Sexuality Collection, the volume of manuscripts has tripled, but I didn't do this alone. I don't work in isolation, and, the truth be told, I don't really work only for the Human Sexuality Collection. I work every day (by e-mail, by phone, or in spirit) with the people at community-run archives, with other archivists and librarians at mainstream repositories, with lesbian and gay activists, and with scholars to find good homes for queer archival material.

How do people construct a history? Ordinarily, people live their lives, archivists collect records that reflect those lives, and historians come along, sift through all those papers, interpret them, and tell a story. However, I've found that the roles are never quite that neat or linear, especially not in the case of queer history. From my involvement in this work, I have been struck by the active interrelationships among lesbian and gay activists, archivists, and scholars. Each of these groups contributes to creating historical records, to finding materials that should be preserved, to placing them in an archival home, and to interpreting and telling the stories of our lives. Queer history is created by networks of people.

Some in the queer community worry that mainstream libraries' participation in this partnership will be short-lived, lasting only as long as LBG Studies is on the cutting edge in academia.[4] Certainly libraries strive to meet a great variety of demands and do respond to trends in scholars' needs. For those of us working in mainstream repositories, it's important that we try to make the most of the fact that LBG Studies is now a hot field in parts of the academy. This attention in academic circles brings the possibility of a concentration of resources that we can use to make serious plans for the permanent preservation of and access to our history. We can work to build stable institutional structures, develop cooperative professional networks, make a lasting impact on our profession, define collecting goals wisely, and establish a pattern of integrating input from scholars and members of the queer community. Careful work during this window of opportunity will have an enduring impact that we should be able to observe with satisfaction, even when new fields have captured the spotlight.

BUILDING INSTITUTIONS

Building a number of lasting institutions, both mainstream and community-run, that have a commitment to the ongoing maintenance and growth of lesbian and gay collections is one of our most important immediate priorities. As long as queer history is popular, many mainstream repositories will see the value in accepting new queer collections, encouraging their use, or creating an exhibit on a queer topic. During this surge of interest from the academy, we need to continue to nurture independent queer history projects. Continuing grass-roots efforts to mobilize queer people's interest in our own history and the mainstream institutions that are making an official commitment to the subject and building sizable, well-known queer collections now are the two guarantees that this kind of attention will endure fifty years from now. I believe that Cornell will be one of the mainstream libraries still devoted to acquiring and promoting the use of lesbian, gay, and bisexual historical sources fifty years from now because of what it has done so far. After Voeller and Goodstein proposed the idea in the early 1980s, people at Cornell who were committed to the idea of preserving historical sources for the study of sexuality started getting the approval of key players on campus. This was a slow and sometimes difficult process. Two faculty members, Isabel Hull and Sandra Bem, went to Mariposa's New York City apartment to review its archival holdings. They affirmed the material's interdisciplinary research value and the growing academic interest in the study of lesbian and gay lives and the social construction of sexuality. Staff, students, and alumni expressed support for the project. With diligence, people worked through the institution's many layers. They won the support of the University Librarian, and finally they obtained the official sanction of the University President and Board of Trustees for the establishment of an ongoing, national program to document and preserve the history of sexuality.

Cornell archivists were responsive to Voeller's and Goodstein's conviction that it was time for a research library to devote attention to this major and overlooked aspect of human life. At a time when many archives were scaling back their collecting efforts, however, they knew that embarking on an ambitious, new, national level collecting program depended on adequate funding. Goodstein's endowment made it possible to start. Cornell then had the resources to add a full-time archivist on the project, to pursue new collections, and to encourage research with them. Once all these pieces were in place, Cornell publicized its new commitment in academic and library journals, and I started speaking about it in a variety of venues: academic, political, and professional. We've made a public record of our respect for the activists who built the Mariposa Collection and our commitment to the continuing growth, care, and use of the collections. We've also sustained our fundraising efforts because we want to be able to expand the program over time. This has resulted in a critical mass of research materials that are visible and valued by researchers, lesbian, gay, bisexual, and transgendered people, and our institution alike.

Cornell's experience can give some direction to other archivists interested in documenting queer history and in establishing programs that will continue beyond the current set of players in institutional settings. Donors want to be confident that institutions have a long-term interest in their papers. The institution's reputation for caring for its other collections can help win that trust. A formal resolution from the governing board or top executives is another indication of long-term commitment. A defined interest in an aspect of queer history will further invite the donation of new papers and help you build a focused, coherent group of collections appropriate to your institution. Corporate, university, and religious archives and institutions with a subject or regional focus can all look at ways to incorporate queer perspectives into their pattern of collecting. If your institution's mission is to document the local region, try to add a paragraph or sentence in your brochure or collection development policy that specifically mentions the institution's interest in lesbian, gay male, bisexual, and transgendered people in the local community. Encourage efforts to institutionalize commitments in this area and then use a variety of ways to demonstrate the institution's interest.

Both Ginny Daley at Duke University's Special Collections Library and Mimi Bowling at The New York Public Library stress their belief that building strong and visible programs now is the key to continued success. Taking in many collections, publicizing them as they come in, describing them in on-line catalogs, interpreting and displaying them in exhibits and web sites, getting scholars to write books with them, and other methods of giving a high profile to the current flurry of queer collecting will help ensure that a repository values and maintains its collections over time. As Bowling said to me, "Their very existence and growth ensure more and better, not less and back in the closet." The momentum mainstream repositories create now will carry into the future.

The libraries and archives established by lesbians and gay men also will play a special role in keeping continuous attention on our history. It's important for the queer community to continue to build and nurture separate community-run history projects because they play a unique role in fostering both awareness and pride in our heritage. By their nature, they can be more successful than institutional archives in involving all segments of the queer community and in sharing the excitement of knowing our past. Librarians and archivists who have the opportunity to contribute to these community endeavors are helping ensure that our history survives.

Community-based lesbian and gay archives don't face the same issues of working within a larger institution and needing to convince that institution to commit long-term resources to queer history. They do need to focus on building a lasting organization and keeping the queer community's interest in history. Like mainstream archives, they build credibility through thoughtful planning, communicating and following their goals, reliably taking care of the materials entrusted to them, and securing adequate resources.

Funding always is a part of the process of building secure institutions. Archives caring for the primary sources of queer history need to secure funding for both preserving collections and enhancing access to them. To create a useable history, archives should be able to create guides that describe collections' organization and contents, publicize the material, make information available to remote users through the Internet or by mail, encourage use, and provide good reference service, as well as maintain a safe physical environment. The fundraising effort for San Francisco Public Library's new main library and its James C. Hormel Gay and Lesbian Center drew a big response from people convinced of the importance of saving our history and the importance of supporting a library that's doing it. Through the generous support of many individuals, San Francisco was able to create an endowment that should allow ongoing development of the collection. This kind of financial backing is important to all the archives working to preserve lesbian and gay history.

In addition to strong and enduring archival programs, the creation of lesbian, bisexual, gay, and transgendered history depends on institutional support for learning and research. Librarians and archivists need to lobby for increased funding for higher education generally, so more queer scholars can do graduate studies and then find jobs. We need to create more scholarships and travel grants to support research in LBG Studies. We need to defend the federal and state programs that have funded many innovative archival projects. It's our job, as archivists and librarians, to articulate both why these agencies are important and why the historical record needs to be inclusive and reflective of our society's complexity.

To consider giving their papers to an archives, people must believe their lives and history are important. The existence of numerous strong, stable, and visible archives, both mainstream and community-based, that are committed to queer history helps convey this importance. In whatever way you can, help create and preserve institutions with the authority, commitment, and resources to maintain and build queer collections into the future.

COLLECTING THE SOURCES

As librarians and archivists, we need to be conscious about our plans and approaches to building collections. Our goal as a profession should be to establish a full, complex, representative lesbian, gay, bisexual, transgendered archival record, making donors happy and proud in the process. We should get valuable collections into appropriate archives and connect donors with archives where they feel comfortable.

Archivists seeking these records should remember a general principle: there is no scarcity of queer sources. While a field is enjoying the popularity that queer studies is now, it would be easy for competition for collections, especially high profile ones, to develop. Many institutions may be eager to have the papers of a few national figures, but there are many lesbian, gay, bisexual, transgendered people doing many things, leading varied lives, many in the public light, many not. Our history also is made up of the ordinary and unusual people who are never in the limelight. Our history is tied to the history of every local community, of specific racial and ethnic groups, and of subjects such as work, religion, and music. We have so much queer history to document, in fact, that cooperation and coordination will serve our interests much better.

Faced with the wealth of queer documentation, we need reminders to look beyond popular people and safe subjects. Our history consists of the lives and work of lesbian and gay authors now celebrated in mainstream culture, as well as individuals, organizations, and issues controversial in and outside of gay communities, such as pornography, pedophilia, or gay nazi organizations. If we want to create a useful, complete historical record, we need to pay particular attention to issues that are controversial and unpopular.

Librarians and archivists should collectively keep an eye on what is being documented—and what isn't. We need to keep focused on preserving a diverse history. To do so we need to publicize our specific collecting goals, avoid duplicating other institutions' efforts, and always be open to new ideas. Activists and scholars play important roles in identifying important new areas to document. Once we become aware of new gaps in documentation, we should work collaboratively to develop collection strategies to address them. Since the 1970s, archivists have discussed both how to do a better job at documenting all aspects of our society and how to cope with the volume of late twentieth-century documents. The solutions that keep surfacing include coordinated, multi-institutional collecting approaches and an involvement of records creators, records users, and related professionals (librarians, rare book librarians, museum curators, folklorists, etc.) (Ham 1975,1981,1984; Samuels 1986; Hackman and Warnow-Blewett 1987; Alexander and Samuels 1987; Cox 1990; Krizack 1994).

I tried to keep these concepts in mind when I invited activists and scholars, as well as archivists and librarians, to join an advisory committee to shape Cornell's collecting policy. The committee agreed that to understand better the construction of sexuality, the Human Sexuality Collection should focus on preserving the perspectives of those outside the social and cultural majority. The collection should build on the strengths of Mariposa's holdings in the politics of pornography and lesbian and gay politics at a national level. The committee decided that Cornell could make a significant contribution by devoting the space and resources necessary for the often voluminous records of national organizations. The committee also wanted the Human Sexuality Collection to document a wide variety of individual lesbian, gay, bisexual, and transgendered people's lives. These goals fit with the needs of researchers and with the other holdings at Cornell, which are strong in personal and political papers. The existing strengths and concentrations of an institution can help direct what aspects of queer history it might take on. The synergy that develops between related collections encourages research and gives a focus to collecting.

Likewise, institutional weaknesses point to areas not to collect. With a national focus, Cornell considers papers from individuals across the country, but if they have a significant regional focus outside of New York, we encourage the donors to investigate local archives. Initially, we decided we wouldn't focus on religion or sex education because they weren't particular strengths of the Mariposa Collection, nor of the Cornell University Library. We also decided not to focus on reproductive rights or prostitution because other mainstream archives were already active in this area.

I've found it very helpful when other institutions have tried to clarify and publicize what they are collecting. To mention a few:

- The Gay and Lesbian Historical Society of Northern California is committed to preserving personal papers, organizational records, ephemera, periodicals, and artifacts from that region. (These records will now be housed at the main San Francisco Public Library.)
- Duke University is interested in lesbian and gay culture in the U.S. South, with a particular emphasis on writers and political activists.
- The Lesbian Herstory Archives in New York City defines its collection very broadly: anything related to lesbians. It's not a very narrow policy, but it's very clear and well publicized.

The LAGAR of the SAA is working this year to finish a directory of archives actively collecting lesbian and gay material. Having widespread access to the stated collecting goals of each repository will be immensely helpful and provide a way for more people to get involved in preserving queer history. Once you know what different archives are doing, you can help refer collections to the most appropriate place for them.

When you talk to people about why they should preserve their papers and where they could place them, you also have an opportunity to educate donors about archival principles. You can all do this in conversations anywhere—at a farmer's market, on the softball field, after committee meetings. The most basic message to get across to lesbians, gay men, bisexuals, and transgendered people is that their lives are historically important. Talk about why their diaries are important; why an archives would want their letters from their mom; why these personal things are important to historians and to the queer community; and why they should talk to an archivist before they throw anything out.

Once donors start thinking about placing their papers somewhere, many ask about putting parts of their papers in different places. Maybe they're thinking of giving their student papers to their alma mater, their files from their years as an activist in Philadelphia to the community archives there, their family correspondence to the state historical society that has their grandparents' papers, and their feminist materials to Radcliffe College's Arthur & Elizabeth Schlesinger Library on the History of Women in America.

When this happens, we should know how to explain why it's best to place all your papers in one institution. Researchers like to have people's papers intact in one place, and this is standard archival practice. One good solution to suggest is that the donor give the papers to one archives and ask that archives to provide information about the collection to the other archives the donor cares about. That way as many people as possible will know that the material exists, what is in it, and where to find it. Donors also have suggested that entire copies of their papers be placed at a number of archives. Again, I advise choosing one institution to take primary care for the originals, their arrangement, and description.

Finally, you can advise people that to make certain their wishes for their papers will be carried out, they should either deposit their material now or describe their intentions in a will. If there's reason to think any family members may want to destroy the material, people should also make sure their friends know what they want done and ask them to intervene in the event of their death.

In addition to what individual librarians and archivists can do, there are a number of organizations now that are playing a role in directing collections to appropriate archives. People have contacted the leaders of LAGAR for advice about donating their papers. Artists with AIDS can turn to the Estate Project for Artists with AIDS.[5] Organizations like these, not affiliated with any one archival repository, are positioned to play an increasing role in identifying important issues to document, communicating with records creators, and helping preserve important materials.

To summarize: archivists and librarians interested in queer history should all be involved in building queer archival networks. We need to know who's doing what, where, and how, so we can share this information and give helpful advice to potential donors, as we build strong and enduring archival programs. We must find ways to support mainstream and community archives that have laid the groundwork for permanent collections.

Still, no matter how well librarians and archivists build stable archival programs and coordinate collecting efforts, I've come to realize that it's a true miracle anything ever gets to an archives. I'm always amazed when and how it happens. Collections arrive at our doors because of a confluence of events largely beyond our control that connect people with the idea of an archives. We must keep in mind that as much as we cooperate with each other, develop very well-designed collection development policies, and work hard at national library and archives conferences, we are but one group of players in the whole picture.

Let me illustrate by looking at how closely Cornell's new collections match our collecting plan laid out in 1989–90. There are many areas where I haven't made as much progress as I would have liked. These include: the pornography business and porn debates; transgendered issues; lesbian lives; bisexual politics; and queer humor. We have, however, been able to enrich greatly our documentation about the lives of gay men. We've added personal collections from many different individuals, materials that reflect their work lives and much about their friendships and relationships, as well as the place of both racial and sexual identity in their lives.

Why have we done particularly well in this area and not others? First, there's the snowball effect; we started with the Mariposa archives,which was weighted heavily with gay men's collections. That influences what else comes our way.

Also, what you see is not all we have. The time from the first conversation until an organization actually sends its records to an archives is very unpredictable. Often it involves a large number of people reaching consensus, and we know how long that can take. Personal papers often don't come until people are in their sixties or seventies—or after they die. There are many collections on a variety of subjects that are promised to us, but won't actually arrive for some time.

The final reason our collections don't exactly match our collecting policy is that archives get what people think is important and what they are determined to save. One reason we have such strong documentation of the personal impact of AIDS is the determination of people to get these collections into archives. Because of AIDS activism, people who are HIV positive are more likely to know that their lives and experiences are important. They know AIDS is historically monumental. Symbols like the NAMES Project Quilt have reinforced the message that individual lives count—that remembering individual lives is important. That makes it easier for people to understand what we're doing in the archives now. When we preserve someone's personal papers, we provide a way to remember an individual's life.

We have found that many of our collections come to us through the careful shepherding of friends. People who have lost a friend to AIDS play active roles in getting their friend's papers to an archives. They do so out of a determination to create a memorial of some kind, to make sure another story isn't lost. In the age of AIDS, friends know that their personal tragedy also is a communal one.

We also are finding that an increased awareness of mortality and of the impact of AIDS on lesbian and gay communities influences the content of the collections we receive. Many of the collections from gay and bisexual men who are HIV positive reflect an unusual self-awareness and sense of history. That consciousness now shapes what kinds of records people create, what they note in their diaries, what they save, and what they eventually give to an archives. When Robert Lynch taped into his diary a hot pink plastic warning and precaution sign that had hung outside his hospital door, he captured the indignity and isolation that many other gay men have experienced. In creating the diary, he acted both as a unique individual and also as someone who shared the experience of AIDS with thousands of others (Robert Lynch Papers).

We find this same self-awareness in people's coming-out stories. At the same time people relish telling their own personal tale, they are aware that it is part of a larger story. A Cornell student set up a Web site for people to share their coming out stories, and people contribute their stories because they recognize that they're important to other people as well as themselves. The historical record will be largely made of what people know is important to them and to others—important enough to create and then to save.

Polly Thistlethwaite, a reference librarian and volunteer at the Lesbian Herstory Archives for over a decade, has pointed out the pivotal role lesbians and gay men have had and will continue to have in preserving their own history. She states that "gay and lesbian history is tangible today because lesbians and gays had the will and determination to constitute and reclaim histories by writing books and building presses, and by establishing community-based archives and history projects"

(Thistlethwaite 1995, 10, 24) . This was happening while mainstream libraries were just starting to use the subject headings "Homosexuality" and "Lesbianism" instead of "Sexual perversion" (Greenblatt 1990). Libraries have indeed lagged behind lesbian and gay activists in understanding lesbian and gay issues. What we can hope for in the future, I think, is libraries and archives shortening that lag time and becoming more responsive to activists, both in and outside of the profession. "Professional activists" involved in the ALA's GLBTF and the SAA's LAGAR have done a lot to raise the profession's awareness of historical problems with access to queer materials.

Continued collaboration between archivists in mainstream repositories, people in community-based history projects and repositories, activists, and scholars will provide for the best possible documentation of queer history. I urge mainstream archives to continually incorporate new ideas from these other sources. Mainstream archives can't make collection development decisions in a vacuum and shouldn't pretend to. In the future, activists and scholars, in and outside of the academy, will continue to play vital roles in identifying and communicating important aspects of lesbian, bisexual, gay, and transgendered culture as it shifts over time. Organizations such as the Estate Project and professional groups such as LAGAR also will contribute to interpreting and preserving our history. It's up to mainstream archivists to hear their ideas, give them due credit, and respond to them. This collaboration should produce a more secure and rich body of resources that will be available to researchers.

Finally, I come back to researchers—people like the history graduate student I was years ago. I now recognize more clearly the vital role researchers play in building these collections. In the course of their work, they both find and create the sources that make it possible to study queer history. They not only interpret archival material, they help it get there in the first place.

When a woman researching the development of modern dance from 1920 to 1960 and perceptions of dance as a "gay space" asked what we had on that, I said to her something I often have to say: "You know, at this point you can help me more than I can help you. You are going to do the kind of painstaking research that will uncover the gay men involved in dance in this period. When you talk to them, you can find out whether they've saved their correspondence over the years. You can encourage them to leave their papers to an archives. And if they'd like to consider giving them to Cornell, I'd be more than glad to talk to them." Many of our collections come exactly this way, by way of researchers.

One of the most important things I've been able to do as an archivist is to provide some funding for transcribing tapes from oral history projects. Researchers who conduct these projects give us incredible documents about the lives of people who would ordinarily remain unknown and invisible. One study by historian Roey Thorpe includes extensive discussions with African American lesbians in Detroit from the 1940s to the 1970s. She has captured the life stories of women who otherwise would be unheard. She talked to women who met in bars in the 1950s and referred to each other as fish, fem, bulldagger, and butch. She's finding out about differences in the ways white families and African American families incorporated their lesbian daughters into their world. She's finding out how life was different for lesbians from different backgrounds. Not only has Roey Thorpe started to write about her research, she also has given all the tapes and transcripts from her conversations with these women to the Human Sexuality Collection for others to go through in detail and interpret for themselves (Thorpe 1996; Roey Thorpe Files). Through our joint efforts we're preserving parts of lesbian history a lone archivist could never have done on her own.

My point is that developing networks is essential to creating the archival record of queer history. We don't want just one archivist's view, or even just the views of a bunch of archivists and librarians. Archivists need to be open to ideas and input from lesbians, bisexuals, gay men, and transgendered people, as well as from independent scholars and academics working to interpret our history. We can all shape what we will know as our queer history, and working together has great results. Please share your ideas about people or organizations with interesting records and how to contact them.

USING THE SOURCES

In my consideration of how to document a queer past, I've focused on institution building and collection development. Because we create lesbian and gay history by using these collections, let me add a few words about outreach and reference work. We really don't have a history until people start telling it. For us to know our history, we need droves of people to come into the archives, roll up their shirt sleeves, and start sifting through the contents of box after box. We need them to bring their knowledge, theories, and experience creatively to bear on what they see and then to communicate what they find.

I work in a variety of ways to encourage researchers to interpret our collections and write queer history. I publicize our holdings and new acquisitions on our web site, through mailings and press releases, and through speeches and exhibits at academic, political, and professional conferences. At Cornell, I go to the Women's Studies brunch at the beginning of the academic year, to LBG Studies meetings, and to orientation sessions for new graduate students and invite people to visit and make use of the Human Sexuality Collection. When new undergraduates come for library orientation tours, they hear about the collection. As Ginny Daley, Women's Studies Archivist at Duke University, has found too, a job title also can play a role in encouraging research. When students see there is someone in the library with the title Curator of the Human Sexuality Collection, some bypass the general reference desk and come right to me with their questions. The title tells them there's at least one person in the library who is prepared to help them with their paper topic.

I've been deeply involved in introducing novice scholars to our collections. This has not been as easy as I thought it would be, and the unforeseen challenges have made it especially rewarding. (For another perspective on the challenges of presenting lesbian, gay, and queer history in classrooms of the 1990s, see Abelove 1995.) Kevin Ohi, who was teaching English 165, "Literatures of Fantasy," at

Cornell, thought that as a librarian, I could talk to his class about cataloging. "The idea behind this would perhaps be," he e-mailed me, "to suggest the strange way in which fantasy becomes not only knowledge but also fantasy through the effort of cataloging itself."[6]

We didn't talk about this in my cataloging course in library school. I asked him to explain this a little more for me, and he wrote back: "A discussion of cataloging would be useful for my class because they are reading James' *The Turn of the Screw* next week, and I am trying to get them to think about the connections in this text among knowledge, cataloging, cataloging knowledge, ghost stories, seduction, 'frames,' visuality, and 'closets.'" [7]

Oh. After some further discussion between us, I wrote back: "OK, I think we can do this. I need to emphasize, though, that from my experience, the more BASIC and directed, the more successful these archives assignments for freshman are. It's really a big leap to consider how to use primary sources, and I've seen many students left to flounder. Here are my recommendations to avoid floundering."[8]

I went on for a whole page with practical things I thought would help the students —like knowing to bring pencils. All of it seemed hopelessly mundane compared to what the instructor was thinking about. While I was talking about pencils and paging slips, he was talking about "frames" and "visuality." But together, we ended up really doing a great job with the students. They read twenty pages of a lesbian or gay pulp novel published between 1950 and 1965 and answered a number of questions such as:

- What in the text indicates its time period? How can you tell that the book wasn't written, say, yesterday? Do the "fantasies" in the book seem outdated? Why? What separates them from fantasies you might read today?
- Would you call your text "pornographic"? What does pornographic mean?
- How does the text build suspense or sustain interest? How would you contrast the way it builds suspense to say, the opening of the The Turn of the Screw?[9]

With a concrete and directed assignment and with some direction about how to navigate the archives, the students were able to discover the joys of primary sources. They found the project both challenging and manageable. About the library visit, the instructor wrote afterwards: "I think also that my students were engaged—at least several of them forbore wearing baseball hats, which I think is a good sign."

At times like this I see the power of education. When students come in and handle another person's diary or a 1954 gay novel, they have a concrete way to begin to see all the current rhetoric about sexuality in another light: through the personal notes of another man or woman, through an artifact from a time before they were born. It's much different from reading about or being lectured to about gay history. For me, as an archivist, it is immensely rewarding to give people the chance to have such experiences looking at the past and coming face-to-face with people's private lives and to play a role in encouraging them to think critically about sexuality.

SUMMARY

Archivists documenting queer history need to take advantage of this period of relative popularity. We should focus on building lasting structures: well-supported community archives and history projects, academic programs, and well-endowed institutional archives with the permanent authority and commitment to build queer history collections. We should continue building strong networks among librarians and archivists so we can educate donors about the historical importance of their material and about basic archival principles, refer collections to appropriate archives, thoughtfully look for gaps in our documentation, and encourage archival institutions to address those gaps. Instead of competing for the same archival material, we can diversify and strengthen our documentation of queer lives. Through coordinated efforts, we can preserve and make accessible materials that fully represent queer people's lives, at the same time making donors proud of their choices.

Lastly, we need to understand the important roles scholars as well as lesbian, bisexual, gay, and transgendered people have in shaping our history and work in concert with them. Activists and scholars are important partners in creating, preserving, and interpreting our queer history. If we do all this, no one will be able to say there are no sources for lesbian and gay history.

NOTES

1. Polly Thistlethwaite (see Chapter 12), a longtime volunteer at the Lesbian Herstory Archives, frequently refers to the strong "self-documenting" tendencies of lesbians.

2. Founded in 1978 by Bruce Voeller (former executive director of the National Gay and Lesbian Task Force), Karen DeCrow (former president of the National Organization of Women), Aryeh Neier (former executive director of the American Civil Liberties Union), and others, Mariposa promoted scholarship and the distribution of information about human sexuality. The Mariposa Education and Research Foundation worked for seventeen years to change negative cultural attitudes toward sexuality in general and homosexuality in particular.

3. Robert Garcia Papers, #7574, Division of Rare and Manuscript Collections, Cornell University Library.

4. You find similar concerns expressed by other marginalized groups. For instance, concerns about libraries' trustworthiness with documents of science fiction fandom surfaced on a listserve called the "Discussion of Popular Culture Resources in Libraries," (POPCULIB@LISTSERV.KENT.EDU). The parallels with conversations about preserving queer history merit sharing a couple of the messages. On Feb. 18, 1997, Billie Aul, Senior Librarian, Manuscripts and Special Collections, New York State Library, wrote "Re: Librarians and Fans":

While you folks were at ALA, I was at . . . Fanhistoricon, a gathering of fan scholars and collectors to discuss the preservation of fan history [. . .]Several people at the session I attended had had very bad experiences with libraries, including being told by one library that a major collection of fanzines, which the library had held, had been thrown out. One of the scholars was recommending that fans no longer donate their collections to libraries, that they are in better hands if kept within the fan community itself.

While I believe that it is better that materials go to libraries and archives, it is difficult to assure donors that their material will be respected forever. Archives follow trends like everything else and one archivist's very important collection is the next generations junk. Also, most important collections are brought in by individual librarians who are knowledgable in a certain area.

So my question to the list is, how do we inculcate in the people who follow us the value of certain collections, so that they don't get thrown out or otherwise lost in the shuffle? Also, how do we maintain connections with the community we're documenting after the librarian who made the contacts leaves?

On Feb. 20, 1997, in "Re: Librarians and Fans," Paul Camp responded:

One basic problem we might work on is educating fans/collectors to differentiate between types of libraries. To many collectors, a library is a library, regardless of whether it is a local public library, a teaching-focused college library, or a research institution.

I have heard numerous horror stories about how someone donated his/her complete run of "Argosy" [or whatever], the product of many years of labor, to their local general purpose library . . . which of course had no use for it and trashed it. The public library in Poohaw Valley [population 1,500] probably has no need for a unique collection of rare late 19th century bindlestumps, even though it's the first library the local would-be donor happens to think of [my apologies if there really is a Poohaw Valley Library]. The International Bindlestump Archive [est. 1904], on the other hand, would committ nameless crimes for that many pristine specimens. The fan/collector needs to know the difference, which he/she all too often doesn't.

We need to educate fans to get their materials to the right type of library in the first place . . . a stable research institution with a demonstrated long term interest in the field in question. Admittedly, even these undergo change of collection focus, etc., but at least there's an orders of magnitude better chance material will survive if it goes to a suitable institution in the first place.

5. LAGAR can be contacted through the Society of American Archivists, 600 S. Federal, Suite 504, Chicago, IL 60605, (312)922–0140, or at its web site: http://www.archivists.org/. The Estate Project is at 330 West Street, New York, New York 10036 or web site: http://www.artistswithaids.org/estate.html (April 15, 1997). The web site explains that the Estate Project for Artists with AIDS, created in 1991, "has evolved into an initiative with a unique purpose: to encourage artists with HIV/AIDS (and other life-threatening diseases) to continue their creative output for as long as possible and to make the necessary legal provisions that will protect their work from being compromised following their deaths. The premise of the Estate Project is that planning their estates is an act by these artists of self-respect and self-empowerment in the face of death, not a capitulation to death. In this way, the Estate Project helps ensure that as much as possible of the art being created by people with HIV/AIDS survives." (http://www.artistswithaids.org/estate.html, April 15, 1997)

6. Kevin J. H. Ohi, "Literature of fantasy visit," Personal e-mail (Sept. 18, 1995).

7. Kevin J. H. Ohi, "Re: Literature of fantasy visit," Personal e-mail (Sept. 19, 1995).

8. Brenda J. Marston, "Re: Literature of fantasy visit," Personal e-mail (Sept. 20, 1995).

9. Kevin J. H. Ohi, "Re: Literature of fantasy visit," Personal e-mail (Sept. 23, 1995).

REFERENCES

Abelove, Henry. 1995. "The queering of lesbian/gay history." *Radical History Review* 62: 44–57.

Alexander, Philip N. and Samuels, Helen W. 1987. "The roots of 128: A hypothetical documentation strategy." *American Archivist* 50 (Fall): 518–31.

Bérubé, Allan. 1990. *Coming out under fire: The history of gay men and women in World*

War Two. New York: Free Press.

Cox, Richard J. 1990. "Archivists confront a changing world: Documentation strategies, the reformulation of archival appraisal, and the possibilities of multi-disciplinary cooperation." In *American archival analysis: The recent development of the archival profession in the United States*, Richard J. Cox, ed., 291–303. Metuchen, NJ: Scarecrow Press.

Duggan, Lisa. 1995. "The discipline problem. Queer theory meets lesbian and gay history." In *Sex wars: Sexual dissent and political culture*, Lisa Duggan and Nan D.Hunter, ed. New York: Routledge.

Duggan, Lisa. 1986. "History's gay ghetto: The contradictions of growth in lesbian and gay history." In *Presenting the past: Essays on history and the public*, Susan P. Benson, Steven Brier, and Roy Rosenzweig, eds., 281–90. Philadelphia: Temple University Press.

Garcia, Robert. Papers, #7574. Division of Rare Books and Manuscript Collections. Cornell University Library.

Greenblatt, Ellen. 1990. "Homosexuality: The evolution of a concept in the Library of Congress Subject Headings." In *Gay and lesbian library service*, Cal Gough and Ellen Greenblatt, eds., 75–101. Jefferson, NC: McFarland.

Hackman, Larry and Joan Warnow-Blewett. 1987. "The documentation strategy process: A model and a case study." *American Archivist* 50 (Winter): 12–47.

Ham, F. Gerald. 1984. "Archival choice: Managing the archival record in an age of abundance." *American Archivist* 47 (Winter): 11–22.

Ham, F. Gerald. 1975. "The archival edge." *American Archivist* 38 (January): 5–13.

Ham, F. Gerald. 1981. "Archival strategies for the post-custodial era." *American Archivist* 44 (Summer): 207–16.

Hinding, Andrea. 1979. *Women's history sources: A guide to archives and manuscript collections in the United States*. New York: Bowker.

Katz, Jonathan. 1976. *Gay American history: Lesbians and gay men in the U.S.A.: A documentary*. New York: Crowell.

Kennedy, Elizabeth L., and Davis, Madeleine D. 1993. *Boots of leather, slippers of gold: The history of a lesbian community*. New York: Routledge.

Krizack, Joan D. 1994. *Documentation planning for the U. S. health care system*. Baltimore: Johns Hopkins University Press.

Lynch, Robert. Papers. #7320. Division of Rare Books and Manuscript Collections. Cornell University Library.

Motley, Archie. 1984. "Out of the Hollinger box: The archivist as advocate." *Midwestern Archivist* 9, no. 2, 65.

Murphy, Kevin. 1995. "Walking the queer city." *Radical History Review* 62: 195.

Samuels, Helen W. 1986. "Who controls the past." *American Archivist* 49 (Spring): 109–24.

Schwarz, Judith. 1982. *Radical feminists of heterodoxy: Greenwich Village, 1912–1940*. Lebanon, NH: New Victoria Publishers.

Thistlethwaite, Polly. 1995. "The lesbian and gay past: An interpretive background." *Gay Community News* (Winter): 10–11, 24.

Thorpe, Rochella. 1996. "'A house where queers go': African-American lesbian nightlife in Detroit, 1940–1975." In *Inventing lesbian cultures in America*, Ellen Lewin, ed., 40–61. Boston: Beacon Press.

Thorpe, Roey. Oral history project files. #7607. Division of Rare Books and Manuscript Collections. Cornell University Library.

12

Building "A Home of Our Own": The Construction of the Lesbian Herstory Archives

Polly J. Thistlethwaite

A PRESENCE IN OUR OWN LAND

April 1975

Dear Sisters,

We are a group of women who met initially at the first conference of the Gay Academic Union in the fall of 1973. Some of us formed a C[onsciousness]-R[aising] group, and as we grew closer to each other we began to focus on our need to collect and preserve our own voices, the voices of our Lesbian Community. As our contribution to our community, we decided to undertake the collecting, preserving, and making available to our sisters all the prints of our existence. We undertook the Archives, not as a short-term project, but as a commitment to rediscover our past, control our present, and speak to our future . . . Sahli Cavallaro, Deborah Edel, Joan Nestle, Pamela Oline, Julia Stanley.[1]

So began the first newsletter of the Lesbian Herstory Archives (LHA). The first Gay Academic Union (GAU) conference was held during the 1973 Thanksgiving weekend at John Jay College in New York City, attended by independent scholars, activists, college faculty, and graduate students. The project was conceived in a lesbian-feminist consciousness-raising group, which had begun to meet separately from the men in GAU.

Reflecting the emerging politics of both lesbian-feminism and gay liberation, LHA was founded to nourish the idea of community through the strategy of institution-building. LHA founders saw lesbians* as a people and sought to congeal a lesbian identity and community, distinguishing lesbians both historically and culturally from straight women and gay men. It was formed to identify,

---

* I spell "Lesbian" with a capital "L" in this chapter when published that way in original texts, following the use of activists in the 1970s and 1980s to reflect assertions of nationalism, unified culture, or confederate identities.

chronicle, rescue, preserve, and share the historically suppressed silences, continuities, and invisibilities about sex and love between women. LHA was a project designed to redress the monopoly on lesbian representation held by colonizing mainstream interests and to create a multidimensional lesbian historical record, useful in tracing and advancing the political struggles of lesbians. Informed by lesbian-feminism and gay liberation, LHA founders believed that a collectively assembled, authentic, accessible, and celebrated lesbian history would work to unite lesbian people and empower resistance to oppression in its many forms. The principles of the LHA were published in 1979 by Joan Nestle, the best-known founder and spokeswoman for the project.

NOTES ON RADICAL ARCHIVING FROM A LESBIAN FEMINIST PERSPECTIVE

1. The archives must serve the needs of the Lesbian people.

a. All lesbian women must have access to the archives; no credentials for usage or inclusion, race and class must be no barrier.

b. The archives should be housed within the community, not on an academic campus that is by definition closed to many women. The archives should share the political and cultural world of its people and not be located in an isolated building that continues to exist while the community dies. If necessary, the archives will go underground with its people to be cherished in hidden places until the community is safe.

c. The archives should be involved in the political struggles of the Lesbian people, a place where ideas and experiences from the past interact with the living issues of the Lesbian community.

d. The archives should be staffed by Lesbians so the collection will always have a living cultural context. Archival skills shall be taught, one generation of Lesbians to another, breaking elitism of traditional archives.

e. The community should share in the work of the archives; contributing material, indexing, mailings, creating bibliographies and other forms of information sharing.

f. The archives will collect the prints of all our lives, not just preserve the records of the famous or the published.

g. Its atmosphere must be nourishing, entry into our archives should be entry into a caring home.

h. The works of all our artists must be preserved—our photographers, our graphic designers, our scribblers, our card makers, our silversmiths.

i. The lesbian feminist archives must refuse cooption from the patriarchal society around it even if it comes in the name of a "women's college."

j. The collection must be kept intact and never be bartered or sold.

k. The archives is an act of mothering, of passing along to our daughters the energies, the actions, the words we lived by. It is a first step in reclaiming a place in time; our response to the colonizer who makes us live on the periphery or not at all.

2. There should be regional Lesbian Herstory Archives, preserving and gathering the records of each Lesbian community. A network can then be set up (Nestle 1979, 11).

With this radical set of motives, the LHA began to amass records and evidence of lesbianism from sources both conventional and bizarre by mainstream archival standards. The LHA opened for "community use" in 1976 in Joan Nestle's apartment (an apartment she then shared with Deborah Edel and subsequently with

Judith Schwarz, Mabel Hampton, and Lee Hudson) on Manhattan's Upper West Side, and remained there until it reopened in 1992 in a Brooklyn townhouse. Uncompromisingly lesbian-focused, LHA rejected traditional, elitist collection development practices outright in favor of an open call, welcoming donations of all things lesbian. LHA collected lesbian and womyn's books and periodicals published by alternative presses then uncollected by all but specialized archives in a few academic institutions. The archives collected mainstream works about homosexuality and lesbianism written by doctors, sociologists, psychologists, pornographers, and clergy—called "enemy literature"—reflecting the politic of understanding the philosophies and mechanisms of lesbian oppression to combat them. Lesbian donors and volunteers rescued or appropriated material from the mainstream press and other archival collections, material often unidentified as lesbian-relevant in original contexts, re-establishing it within LHA as lesbian-relevant found texts and images. The founding philosophy of the LHA, "maintained by and about Lesbians and our communities" (*Lesbian Herstory Archives Guide* 1993) assumed that a self-identified community of class- and race-conscious lesbians could together identify, assemble, and organically construct a lesbian history with political integrity and meaning that would serve to inform and empower resistance to lesbian oppression and the destruction of herstory.

The LHA's liberationist, institution-building strategy of grass-roots archiving has not been uniformly embraced by gay activists. Jim Monahan of Chicago's Gay Academic union criticized "ghettoized," "separatist" grass-roots lesbian and gay institutions as not only wrong-headed, but divisive and dangerous. Jim Monahan and Joan Nestle both published articles about grass-roots archiving in the spring 1979 issue of *Gay Insurgent*. Monahan wrote:

A collection of resources in an archive established to serve the interests of the gay community and available mainly for those interested individuals who wish to document what has been diminishes the vision of gay history to not much more than antiquarianism. . . . To remain separate, both physically and intellectually from general history is to cultivate parochialism. . . . Separatist tendencies and factional politics are odd luxuries to be suffered only until they militate against this goal, and that they seem to be doing. . . . If archives remain precariously preserved in the ghettos, their preservation is next to pointless. (Monohan 1979, 9)

Monahan asserted that academic institutions were the best place for gay and lesbian archival collections because recognition by academic experts offered gays and lesbians acceptance and assimilation into mainstream culture. He argued that lesbian and gay lives would be unignorably present and more readily studied by mainstream authorities in academic settings. Monahan neither romanticized nor valued the organic construction and lay use of gay and lesbian archival collections. Instead, he argued that only qualified activists, academics, and students should have access to archival collections:

Gay archives should go into repositories located within academic institutions [because] research is better facilitated; the economic burden of a researcher is lessened; the historical profession is faced with a body of rich material that cannot be ignored.

Access to the materials cannot be accorded every curiosity seeker or individual not pursuing serious research.

The researcher should give evidence of one of the following: 1. membership in a gay organization 2. appointment at an academic institution 3. student status at an accredited institution [with] a letter of support from an instructor. (Monohan 1979, 9)

Nestle's womyn's-languaged response to Monahan articulated the case for establishing independent lesbian and gay archives outside academic settings. Her words reflect mistrust of a patriarchal world and mainstream institutions where lesbians exist, yet mask themselves. She advocated investing in institutions "in our own land" where an otherwise diminished lesbian presence is realized:

Radical lesbian feminism is a challenge to do things differently, to recreate the energy of hags and form a world reflective of an age old spirit reborn. We cannot trust "historical understandings" or "academic institutions." Both of these terms are failures.

The Lesbian Herstory Archives must stay in its community, not out of parochialism but out of herstorical vision. We do not exist in historical understanding or academic institutions, though we travel incognito. We live in our homes, on the streets, in the bars, at our desks, at our jobs, with our children, in our groups, and we create our herstory every day. It is this story the archives wants to preserve and share. Once Lesbians have generations of herstory to experience, they will change history by the force of their presence.

When a people transform a world, that can never be parochial; it is the other world that must question its ways. Our concept of an archives must be different; we are different. But difference is not invisibility; it is presence in our own land. (Nestle 1979, 10)

Monahan raised issues of archival security, which he answers with re-commendations for credentialed, professional handling of archival materials. Nonexperts were likely threats to the physical security as well as the political usefulness of archival material, aggravating the potential for government intrusion and inappropriate storage: "Security is the major problem; it is compounded by an unqualified policy of access to the material. . . . While no site can guarantee 100% security, an established repository is in a better position to stave off police incursions, deal with the matter of subpoenaed materials, and provide the appropriate storage facilities" (Monohan 1979, 9).

Given the frequent arson attacks on lesbian and gay bars, publishing offices, and community centers which continue from the 1970s to this day, most grass-roots archivists shared Monahan's concern. Nestle addressed Monahan's concerns for security and his call for a regimented archival professionalism by emphasizing different notions of safety, a political safety, at the heart of LHA archival philosophy. In words mirroring the sentiment of Audre Lorde's oft-quoted phrase, "the master's tools will never dismantle the master's house" (Lorde 1984, 110), the 39-year-old Nestle argued that to secure lesbian history, lesbians must forge and safeguard it in new territory: "To ask the patriarchal destroyer to preserve is a suicidal act. It does not express our sinister wisdom. We would be surviving in their context, in an ongoing world dedicated to power, elitism, and survival of the patriarchal fittest" (Nestle 1979, 10).

Notions about the mission, constituency, and safety of lesbian and gay archival collections hold entirely different meanings for Monahan and Nestle when grounded in their differing political strategies. For Monahan, the research institution provided more safety with better locks and alarms, environmental control, professional assurances of privacy and protection, and an unavoidable and potentially empowering presence in a respectable, academic world. For Nestle, the community-based setting —in this case her home in an apartment building with a doorman, advertised by word-of-mouth and community-based publications—was the better guarantor of safety, integrity, growth, and lesbian ownership of the collection.

The differences between Monahan and Nestle reflect strategies drawn in the 1970s black, feminist, and gay political movements. The tensions established then between the political strategies of liberation and reform, separatism and assimilation still structure divisions within lesbian and gay political communities today. These competing political ideas continue to inform the institutional placement, content, and structure of lesbian and gay history, criss-crossing discussions about the content and safety of queer history.

The language articulating the early work of community-based history projects, the LHA in particular, celebrates the imparting, discovery, and possession of personal histories and collective memory as healing, recuperative, empowering individual acts fostered by a "safe space," a nourishing home of a community-based archive. "Always there was the incredulity at our assertion that her life was the important one. But I had known this deprivation so searingly in my own life that it was a question that brought out all my fire and love—yes, yes, you are the Lesbian the archives exists for, to tell and share your story" (Nestle 1979, 90).

LHA provided a physical and historical space for women to transform themselves, to come out—first to recognize and understand themselves as lesbians, then to come out into a community—a grass-roots public that stationed itself between isolated private and mainstream public spheres. This community-based archival space transcended the physical geography of bars, social groups, and political meetings in that it promised lesbians temporal endurance, a lasting place in lesbian history. LHA and grass-roots archives did not promise individuals fame or a position in mainstream history. But grass-roots lesbian and gay archives, LHA in particular, campaigned and allowed for lesbian and gay lives to be held in esteem by their own community, the members of which would in turn benefit from knowledge of other lives and protect them from danger and dishonor.

Activists since the 1970s have celebrated coming out as an individual's liberation from the psychological deprivation and solitude of the closet, which gay liberationists vilify as a primary structure of lesbian and gay social and self-oppression. A lesbian's coming out into the community is embraced by that community as a courageous, politically relevant, mentally healthy act. Gay historians D'Emilio (1979) and Chauncey (1994) both describe coming out post-Stonewall as an act performed in a mainstream context—with family, friends, or employers. LHA, though, has assumed that a lesbian's coming out is relevant primarily to her community, not necessarily to her nonlesbian public of friends and family. LHA considers coming out to be a personal step taken with considered risk, over which the out individual is likely to desire and deserve control. LHA recognizes that individuals are often differently out in different social venues, that being out bears tremendous variety and nuance, and that coming out generally is not a wholesale surrender of a private life to the scrutiny of a mainstream public. Therefore, LHA guards against exposure of lesbian lives and archival records to the noncommunity public, particularly when that exposure involves inclusion in the mainstream press or media. Many collections donated in the 1970s and 1980s came with explicit agreements granting the widest public access, but in the absence of explicit agreements only a community-based public is assumed permissible. LHA positions the noncommunity public as a sphere separate from and potentially hostile to lesbians. This assumption is buttressed by a knowledge and stories of disasters, even annihilations of identity, that befall lesbians exposed to family, friends, employers, doctors, clergy, or government. During the 1990s, with growing mainstream interest in lesbian and gay archival collections and lives coinciding with activists' continuing challenges to the closet, (that is, the advent of the queer political strategy of involuntarily outing closeted individuals), LHA developed explicit donor agreement forms making clear terms of access to individual collections, given the plethora of understandings about privacy, the closet, and coming out.

With its formation in the 1970s, LHA welcomed every lesbian to come out in a new community-based historical venue not only for personal but also for political reasons. Gay liberationists theorized that a political movement would be fueled by individual acts of coming out. Greater public visibility would not only beget greater tolerance for lesbian and gay lives, it would also force the destruction of social and political oppression while strengthening a lesbian and gay community. A 1978 LHA newsletter proclaimed, "It is our responsibility to validate the lesbian experience for each other because it is through our collective rejoicing, reclaiming and renewing that our survival as a Lesbian community will be determined."[2] Suggesting an evolving vision of LHA's future public, the LHA Spring 1979 newsletter included *A Plea for Coming Out*, "We need women to tell us if they should be part of the Archives. Help us end silences if not for now at least for the future."[3] LHA founders believed the future would hold in store another kind of end to silences, with lesbian voices announcing themselves in a mainstream arena from positions of strength forged by the construction of a lesbian community base.

LHA sought to establish itself as a project providing safe space, protecting its constituency and its collection against particular hostilities infringing on lesbian lives, history, and culture. Violent attacks on gay and lesbian public spaces fed the perception that the world is precarious harbor for an individual and institutional lesbian presence. Several LHA founders, lesbians in their twenties and thirties in the 1970s, had immediate experiences with police and criminally-regulated queer spaces—the New York City bars of the 1950s through 1970s. The desire for safe or self-regulated, uninfiltrated lesbian space was informed by these experiences as well as a radical feminism that positioned patriarchy in general, and men in particular, as primary oppressors of women. Police violence against Civil Rights,

Black Nationalist, and anti-war demonstrators, the Stonewall riots, and the 1950s excesses of McCarthyism all positioned the government as an aggressive enemy of the people and their political movements. The prospect of government siege or systematic persecution of lesbians and gays was a trepidation widely shared in liberationist circles, reflected in the third LHA principle, asserting that the community-based collection might be harbored and protected by its people under siege. The specter of the Holocaust and Nazi book-burning loomed large in grass-roots archival lore—the first gay archive, Germany's Institute for Sexual Science established in 1918 by Magnus Hirshfeld, was destroyed in 1933 in this manner (Lauritsen and Thorstad 1974, 40–43). LHA's self-protection was informed against a historical backdrop of lesbian persecution and oppression.

The metaphor of LHA as home took hold as LHA functioned and grew within Nestle's own apartment. Nestle and Edel's warm hospitality, reflected and enhanced the homeyness of the project. That there was no money available for any other archival home was, initially at least, a secondary reason for embedding LHA in Nestle's life and apartment as it was. Founders sought to provide a safe, nourishing context for lesbian history. (For a critique of the feminist use of the concept of home, see Martin and Mohanty 1986).

The LHA was not constructed for a mainstream and academic public, but for a lesbian constituency coming out in the 1970s, believed to be deprived of and hungry for access to lesbian history, culture, and community. LHA's politic was shaped by lesbian-feminists and gay liberationists opposed to an assimilationist politic, attempting to combat and remedy the invisibility of lesbians in the historical mainstream. The legal status of archival collections (whether they were legally secured by the institution and legally ready for publishing researchers) was of secondary importance. LHA's primary concerns were to build the collection for lesbian visitors to share, to garner reciprocal trust and ownership, to protect the privacy of individuals named in the collection (from the dangerous public sphere outside the community), and to guarantee a political and financial future for the institution.

Upon its opening, the LHA collective began to explore the possibilities for situating itself within mainstream legal frameworks, primarily to obtain tax-exempt status to garner financial contributions for the project. The obvious first option considered was incorporation as an official archive and educational institution, sanctioned by the New York State Board of Regents. This option was rejected, however, because it risked too much state intervention, inspection, and control. Many fledgling lesbian and gay cultural projects had been denied, scrutinized, and challenged as they attempted to incorporate, mainly for advocating radical political positions.[4] But in 1979, the group successfully incorporated the project as an educational corporation with the New York State Division of Corporations and State Records which, unlike the Board of Regents, has no authority to inspect the collection and no explicit legal provisions for confiscating the property of organizations under their purview. So the Lesbian Herstory Archives became legally recognized as the Lesbian Herstory Educational Foundation (LHEF). The collective strategized to position LHA outside the legal definition of libraries and archives given the high degree of state regulation required, yet fit itself inside the legal definition of a tax-exempt organization to allow it to gain financial strength.

Throughout the 1970s, LHEF built its collection and constituency through slide shows and presentations in community-based venues—meeting in bars, homes, festivals, conferences, churches, and synagogues. In 1980 LHEF began to sponsor "women welcome" events called At Homes, first in Nestle's apartment and later in the larger Women's Coffee House room in New York City's Gay and Lesbian Community Services Center. Members of the LHEF collective staffed information tables at local and national lesbian gatherings, soliciting volunteers with flirtatious invitations to "help file, stamp, stuff, and lick" at the archives every Thursday evening, with the promise of sisterhood or sexual attention. The archives also staged itself in the most public of community-based spectacles, New York City's annual Lesbian and Gay Pride March, with a popular, photogenic contingent. All women have always been welcome to march with LHEF in the front section of the march reserved for women's groups, with marchers carrying poster-sized images of lesbians and "word signs" bearing multi-lingual slang and formal names for "lesbian" (dyke, fem, bulldagger, tortillera, marimacha, uranian). In 1975, LHEF began an annual-or-so newsletter free to individuals and organizations on the mailing list, and in 1978 the lesbian, gay, and feminist press began to carry articles about the project. LHEF listed its mailing address—but never the project's street address—in lesbian, gay, and women's directories. These community-based activities, services, events, and publicity brought LHEF into the lives of lesbians who donated archival collections and money to the project, sustaining it to this day.

Upon its inception, LHEF assumed a politic of anti-racism and sought to achieve class and ethnic inclusivity (see the LHA principle 1a on page 158). Throughout its history, LHEF has made frequent efforts to represent and incorporate the lives and collections of lesbians of color, featuring racial and ethnic inclusion in its descriptions and representations of the collection. This politic of diversity, practiced by many post-Stonewall lesbian and gay political groups, inevitably situates its proponents as self-consciously lacking yet accountable for the racial and ethnic diversity it idealizes. The backdrop of whiteness of LHEF in particular and lesbian culture in general is revealed both by its fundamental politic of inclusivity as well as by the predominance of white women among its proponents and participants. (For more about the whiteness of lesbian culture, see Boyd 1996). The language of multi-culturalism (for example, the terms "outreach," "difference," and "inclusion") works to highlight and embrace diversity ("others") against a body self-conscious about its own whiteness and about the potential racism realized by that too homogenous composition. The LHEF, a cornerstone of lesbian culture, represents a predominantly white, Jewish, and self-consciously anti-racist leadership, constituency, and collection, which reflects and desires ethnic and racial variety in all aspects of its operation.

Collections donated to LHEF in the 1970s represented a predominantly white group of lesbians participating in New York City lesbian life, culture, and politics.

Early LHEF collective members Joan Nestle, Deborah Edel, and Judith Schwarz and other LHEF volunteers offered up their own selected papers, hoping to build an archive and inspire community trust by offering up their own collections as example. Lesbian activists Frances Doughty, Bettye Lane, Janet Cooper, Karla Jay, Joan E. Biren, Julie Lee, and Naomi Holoch donated collections early in LHEF's history. Writers Adrienne Rich and Elsa Gidlow contributed personal material soon after LHEF opened, as did J.R. Roberts, a white lesbian librarian who used LHEF's collection to construct the first published bibliography on black lesbians (Roberts 1981). Lesbian organizations and cultural projects donating records in the 1970s included the Lesbian Cultural Festival, the Lesbian Front, and the Lesbian History Exploration group.

Several lesbians of color have joined LHEF's governing collective over the years, crossing lines drawn around participation in lesbian identity-based groups by both white racism and ethnic nationalism. In LHEF's early years, Georgia Brooks, Irare Sabasu, Rota Silverstrini, Mabel Hampton, and Paula Grant made significant contributions in shaping the collection and the institution, establishing a New York City lesbian community prominently manifest with women of color. LHEF collective member Georgia Brooks (who was also among the founding collective of New York City's Salsa Soul Sisters in 1976) organized a discussion and study group for black lesbians that met weekly during the spring of 1980 in the Archives, Nestle's apartment. The first black lesbian writing group that met formally in New York City (The Jemima Collective) donated work and records to LHEF in 1977, and the group producing the black lesbian journal *The Echo of Sappho* donated the project's original artwork and paste-ups to LHEF in 1979. Prominent and influential among the black lesbians who donated collections and labor to LHEF were the writer Becky Birtha who donated poems, stories, and articles in 1979, and Audre Lorde who donated many of her early manuscripts and correspondence to LHEF in 1983. Mabel Hampton (1902–1989), an African American butch elder, was a consistent presence at LHA until her death, in great part because of her life-long friendship with Nestle. Hampton was crucial to LHEF's politic embracing racial diversity and to LHEF's mission to offer heroines to a community in short supply of accessible elders, and LHEF provided Hampton with a home filled with friends and admirers and a platform for her community-based renown. Through her willingness to be out in her work with the archives and SAGE (Senior Action in a Gay Environment), and with her appearance in the 1986 film *Before Stonewall: The Making of a Gay and Lesbian Community*, Hampton came to be a lesbian celebrity and role model, unique for someone of her generation and social standing. (For more background on Mabel Hampton, see *Not Just Passing Through* 1994.)

In New York City during the late 1970s and early 1980s, ethnic identity-based lesbian groups formed independently to assemble historical images and narratives. Asian Lesbians of the East Coast (ALOEC) co-founder Katherine Hall, wrote a letter published in the 1984 LHEF Newsletter:

ALOEC started organizing in August of 1983. In our formation we began to realize that
we needed a history. Without a history, we had no past from which to identify ourselves.
. . . so we ventured up to the Lesbian Herstory Archives where we found a fine collection
of Asian Lesbian and gay books, periodicals, photographs, letters, etc. all on us Asians.
. . . That's when we decided to start an Asian Lesbian History Project. . . . Many thank
you's to the Lesbian Herstory Archives for your support and assistance in helping Asian
Lesbians of the East Coast in finding their roots.[5]

Though Hall's review of LHEF's assistance was gracious, ALOEC did not
intend to combine its work with LHEF, but instead formed its own Asian Lesbian
History project. June Chan, who along with Hall co-founded ALOEC, popularized
this work with a slide show of Asian lesbian images and historical tales, which
screened in mostly Asian lesbian venues during the 1980s.[6]

The whiteness of the archives often signaled and justified the need for and
value of ethnic-based lesbian history projects. In her preface to *Compañeras*, the
first published anthology of latina lesbian writing, Juanita Ramos noted:
"Although the Lesbian Herstory Archives has always been very supportive of the
project, the journals and books we researched confirmed what we already
suspected: only a handful of Latina lesbians had ever been included in any of these
publications" (Ramos 1987, xv). Upon completion of the project, LHEF
sponsored an At Home reading from *Compañeras* (June 21, 1983) to benefit
Latina Lesbian History Project members. Over the years, LHEF has co-sponsored
readings, performances, and events showcasing the ethnic diversity of lesbians in
New York City. LHEF has generally neither underwritten nor appropriated the
work of independent scholars and lesbian history projects, but rather assisted,
promoted, and supported independent projects designed by and for lesbians and
particular communities of lesbians. With the participation of some dedicated
lesbians of color in the archives' collective and by the LHEF extending support
and valuing a range of ethnic- and identity-based historical work, LHEF
positioned itself in a multi-cultural milieu reflecting a lesbian community that is
predominantly white, while overtly inclusive and ostensibly open to lesbians of all
ethnicities.

Joan Nestle's writing, particularly her political stance around butch-fem and
the lesbian-feminist sex wars of the 1980s, has shaped the scope and popularity of
the LHA collection, and expanded understandings of what a lesbian might be.
Nestle, whose writing became best known with the 1987 publication of *A
Restricted Country*, broke with dominant lesbian-feminist politics by defending and
honoring working class butch-fem identities, S and M practices, and the
possibilities of intergenerational sex. Though winding up on many a lesbian-
feminist enemy list (see Nestle 1987, 144–150, for details), Nestle and the Lesbian
Herstory Educational Foundation explicitly welcomed the presence and solicited
the records of lesbians marginalized by other lesbians for their class standing and
sexual practices.

Still, the LHEF has firmly stationed "lesbian" within the category "woman."
While recognizing the instabilities of lesbian identities and fluidity of genders and
sexualities, the organization continues to affirm itself as lesbian and feminist.[7]

With the lesbian-feminist traditional "all women welcome" policy for most LHEF-sponsored events, LHEF continues to embrace the mission of providing "safe," "comfortable," "connectivist" social space for lesbians who prefer the absence of any kind of man. All women's events are staged to honor and celebrate lesbians and to enact, represent, and inspire the political ideal of a cohesive movement or community of lesbian women. The archives continues to welcome men (and women) to use the collection, however, by appointment outside of the hours reserved for welcoming women only.

In the early- to mid-1990s, with the rise of a transgendered movement in general, and particularly with the presence of openly male-identified butches and male-to-female lesbians as volunteers, LHEF's collection and constituency expanded to include transgendered lesbians. LHEF welcomes material relevant to all self-identified lesbian lives, including former or current lesbians living female-to-male or male-to-female. However, former butches who have become transgendered self-identified men are presently unwelcome at LHEF's "women welcome" hours or now sometimes "dykes welcome" events. Straight and gay men are unwelcome as well at most LHEF-sponsored events designed to forge and strengthen communities of women, dykes, and lesbians. (For more about how lesbians and female-to-male transsexuals distinguish themselves and their territory from each other, see Boyd 1997.)

In the late 1970s, LHEF began to obtain grants from women's, lesbian, and radical funding sources for special projects such as publication of the newsletter and purchase of archival supplies and electronic equipment. Into the 1990s, LHEF persisted in building a funding base of mostly individual lesbians, true to the vision of an organization by and for lesbians. The organization has never pursued funding from government sources given both the invasive nature of state oversight and the capriciousness of government funding for lesbian and gay projects. In the 1980s, LHEF organizers started a fund that enabled the purchase of its own building in 1990. With the final payment on its commercial loan in 1996, the four-story town house becomes the first building in the New York City metropolitan area owned by a lesbian organization, the culmination of Nestle's vision for lesbians to possess a history "in our own land."

In both the tradition of feminist collectivity and as a condition of the loan obtained for the purchase of the building, LHEF has remained an all-volunteer organization. Staffing for visitors and researchers is currently available by appointment nearly every Saturday or Sunday, as well as a few evenings and afternoons during the week. A group of from ten to fifteen self-appointed volunteer lesbian coordinators meets about every three weeks, deciding political and practical issues through the process of discussion and consensus. This practice is based on the notion that lesbians who do the everyday work of the archives are entitled to govern the organization, not a board of directors or advisory group assembled to raise money or window-dress a constituency with race, class, ethnic, age, gender, or geographic parity. LHEF's governing practice resembles the styles of contemporary direct action groups such as ACTUP and the Lesbian Avengers. This politic assumes that a people working together can best manifest an organization and collection with political integrity, cultural authenticity, and an unwavering mission to represent its constituency.

The building now housing the Lesbian Herstory Educational Foundation is located in Park Slope, Brooklyn, a well-known lesbian neighborhood (Rothenberg 1995).   LHEF continues to position itself as a community-based institution guarded against a mainstream public. The building is unmarked except for a small plaque beneath the doorbell and a rainbow flag on the front door. The archive's street address is unpublished except on occasional handbills advertising events to the community. A caretaker lives on the top floor of the building to provide the best possible security for the collection. However, because the archives is not staffed and open everyday and because there is lack of consensus among LHA coordinators about the gravity of risk should the building be public beyond the community-based venue of its origin, the archives remains publicly unmarked as a lesbian institution. (For evidence of LHEF's low mainstream profile, see Cohen 1996.)[8] The LHEF phone number and post office box mailing address are listed on LHEF publicity, in national and local lesbian and gay directories, and in New York City's Yellow Pages.

Over the 1970s and 1980s, the Lesbian Herstory Educational Foundation and other grass-roots archival projects pioneered and popularized a lesbian and gay history unprecedented and unimaginable in mainstream institutions. Lesbian and gay archival projects established new space—historical, psychological, and physical—that worked to promote the value of lesbian and gay self-representation and to diminish the power of scientific, religious, legal, and academic professions to pathologize and oppress. Born of and sustained by feminist and liberationist politics, the Lesbian Herstory Educational Foundation has functioned to define lesbian identities and to coalesce a lesbian community featuring class, ethnic, and sexual diversity. This community, as reflected and represented by LHEF, positioned itself in opposition to the state, mainstream institutions, and the noncommunity public, all which were understood to be exploitative of individual lesbian lives and hostile to the lesbian community.

OUTLAW MATERIAL IN MAINSTREAM SETTINGS

In the recent body of professional archival literature pertaining to gay and lesbian material, the terms "headaches," "vexing," and "problems" appear frequently. Lesbian and queer archival material presents "special needs" to mainstream archivists, requiring the application of extra sensitivity and discretion. The language archivists use to talk about the trouble with queer material is the language the heterosexual world uses to talk about the trouble with queers.

Ruthann Robson wrote, "We call each other lovers, friends, sisters, compañeras. We are coupled or not, sexual or not, co-habitating or not. But whatever we are, we are not legal" (Robson 1992, 117). The legal system, she explains, works against queers to separate parents from children, to trivialize queer lives and relationships. Similarly, the legal system works to detach queer people from ownership and inheritance of archival material. By privileging biological or heterosexual family structure, the laws of inheritance interrupt the impulse for lesbians, gays, and others with nonnormative families to bequeath their property to loved ones and to make their private lives public after their death. There is ample archival literature providing harrowing tales of how lesbian, gay, and sexually suggestive archival material in mainstream institutions has been disguised from or denied to researchers, removed from collections, or destroyed by biological family or family executors entitled by law to do just that.[9]

Even with the absence of legal privacy protection for dead people, mainstream archival institutions often invest in garnering the goodwill and financial support of the presumed-to-be homophobic executors of a collection by restricting or more subtly discouraging its use. Historian and LHEF archivist Judith Schwarz points out that, "while individual privacy and confidentiality may be of paramount concern while the individual lives, a full disclosure of deceased individuals' history can do little harm and yet add much to the lives of others" (Schwarz 1992, 189). While mainstream institutions most often govern themselves in a legalistic fashion around acquisition and use of archival material, grass-roots archival concerns are not those involving homophobic relatives or executors fearing the revelation of sexual activity or identity of a deceased relative. LHEF's practice, for example, reflects the desire to provide the broadest possible on-site, community-based access to the collections of deceased and living lesbians, unless the collections are specifically restricted by the donor or unless they threaten to expose another lesbian to mainstream scrutiny against her will.

Researchers and publishers using grass-roots archives are sometimes frustrated to find that a good amount of the material is not legally sanctioned for use or display in a mainstream public. This is because of the outlawed, extra-legal status of queer lives and families. When a lesbian brings her deceased lover's collection to the Lesbian Herstory Educational Foundation, for example, she is not recognized as the legal owner of copyright to the collection unless there is a will or other legal document that makes it so. Instead, homophobic next-of-kin may be the legal bearers of property rights or copyright to her collection. In many cases, their legal reckoning with the collection may threaten its very existence. Much of the time, the risks of publicizing a lesbian or gay life in any venue are few. "Lesbian history is made up of other people's garbage," Nestle offers, and most homophobic heirs to lesbian collections do not care much if or where it exists, as long as it remains out of the range of their attention. But lesbian history is in large part an outlawed history, meaning its existence is contested by the state. Queer archival material, particularly that reflecting closeted lives, might only survive if it remains outside legal boundaries, away from the attention of a mainstream public.

Queer archival material constitutes a precarious historical record. Mainstream archival collections are formed and designed to serve researchers and publishers who generally operate within legalistic frameworks—and the content of mainstream archives reflects that. Mainstream archival practice prescribes explicit, legal deeds of ownership for any collection of papers accepted by a mainstream institution. The Society of American Archivists recommends, for example, that "before entering into a gift agreement, the archival institution should make sure that the prospective donor is competent and has clear title to the materials" (Peterson and Peterson 1985, 24). This professional tenant poses an impossible standard for lesbian and gay people seeking to control either public or private history. If a lover or friend of a deceased person offers a collection up to an archive, he or she must be legally sanctioned to give it away, or else present an archive with a legal conundrum. Nonbiological queer families are not, without legal maneuvering, holders of "clear title" to the documents of deceased loved ones. In the 1990s, more lesbians and gays are out in the most public of spheres, and some are both inclined and wealthy enough to make legalistic arrangements regarding the inheritance of their property. But this is true for only a fraction of the population. Queers without traditionally valued property are less likely to make those arrangements. If queer archival material is not properly willed or deeded by legally recognized executors, it may never find its way into historical record except through private or community-based collections or through professionals resisting or ignoring professional archival standards.

Contrary to Monahan's 1979 prediction about the "security" of mainstream archives, even collections that are the legally recognized property of an archive and restricted from public access are not protected from outside, particularly government, intrusion.[10] Lesbians and gays have a history strewn with instances of state surveillance and regulation. The professional ethic of librarians and archivists assures the privacy of donors and researchers; however, the state is routinely successful in undermining that assurance (Robins 1988, 481; "Police subpoena library records" 1990).[11]

Aside from under-valuing queer archival material and failing to collect legal and extra-legal archival material, perhaps the most prevalent state of compromise mainstream libraries and archives exhibit around queer material is in the description and classification of those records. Ellen Greenblatt has outlined the Library of Congress' (LC) history of classification of "homosexual" material, detailing how subject headings have failed to reflect changes in both popular nomenclature and self-definition (Greenblatt 1990).[12] Subject headings applied to gay literature are perpetually clumsy and out-of-date.[13] Mainstream library catalogs and periodical indexes are plagued with deficiencies in description, foiling computer subject and keyword searches. A world of lesbian, gay, transgendered, and queer-relevant material languishes unidentified and even uncataloged in libraries and archives (Taylor 1994). While it would be an impossible task for archivists to ferret out contemporary research interests and assign relevant headings to every piece of archival material(for example, Sedgewick 1990, suggests that a great part of the Western literary canon can be understood as homo-relevant in a most essential way, and is therefore inadequately indexed), mainstream archivists too often fail to assign relevant subject headings to queer archival material because of their own queer-phobic concerns.

Much archival material relevant to homosexuality is found in the collections of individuals who were either closeted, or who did not self-identify as queer, homosexual, lesbian, gay, or transgendered. So, what's an archivist to do? In a

1992 talk at the Society of American Archivist's (SAA) convention, Eva Moseley of the Schlesinger Library suggested that archivists use of language "obviously tentative" in the narrative of archival finding aids to suggest to the researcher "that someone may have been bisexual or indigent or polygamous." She discouraged archivists from using subject headings, a researcher's primary finding tool, because it "makes a rather bald statement and there is no room for explanations" (Moseley 1992). Moseley's primary concern then is not about the accuracy or helpfulness of a description, but rather the library's social or legal liability vis-à-vis that description. Susan VonSalis, another Schlesinger archivist at another SAA convention offered a story about a researcher looking for archival material on friendships between women. The researcher, perplexed, commented to her, "All these collections on 'friendship' seem to be about lesbians" (VonSalis 1994). This practice of coding or softening the language used to describe archival collections is at the root of queer invisibility in historical record. It is this tradition of closeting by mainstream archivists that leaves lesbians present, yet incognito in mainstream historical record. When archives fail to name or explicitly identify collections with established or even speculated queer content, they construct a veiled, closeted history—a silent, unannounced inheritance no more apparent in the mainstream public than it was in the pre-Stonewall era.

Professional archival standards must evolve to reflect regard for the historical value of archival records, with secondary concern for the legal issues pertaining to use and publication. Archivists and librarians must devise their own non-LC subject headings, or pressure the LC to change theirs, to provide meaningful access to queer archival records (see Berman 1971). Brenda Marston at Cornell's human sexuality archive, for example, routinely uses the nonstandard heading "Gays and Lesbians" instead of the LC heading "Gays" so that a catalog keyword search on "lesbians" will retrieve records relevant to lesbians when gay men are involved as well. The presence, longevity, and integrity, then, of queer archival records, like other aspects of queer lives, can be endangered and compromised by mainstream institutions in ways grass-roots and private archives are positioned to safeguard.

THE MAINSTREAMING OF LESBIAN AND GAY HISTORY

Twenty years after activists began grass-roots lesbian and gay archives, mainstream institutions are beginning to value lesbian and gay archival material and to solicit holdings to fortify their collections. With the embrace of multiculturalism by the liberal mainstream and the rise of queer studies in the academy, libraries are finding it appropriate and beneficial to create gay and lesbian archival collections, often by acquiring or conjoining the collections of grass-roots projects. Mainstream research institutions are poised to colonize queer archival material in new, problematic ways.

San Francisco's Gay and Lesbian Historical Society (GLHS), founded in 1985, is a successful, well-known grass-roots archive that now houses an impressive collection of well-indexed materials stored in a climate-controlled space on Market

Street. Begun by community-based activists and historians, GLHS is now governed by a board elected by its dues-paying members. The collection is administered by a full-time professional archivist and a fleet of volunteers. In 1996, the board of GLHS, announcing an end to lengthy negotiations with the San Francisco Public Library (SFPL) regarding partial deposit of their collections in SFPL's new James C. Hormel Gay and Lesbian Center, assured their constituency:

The Library will be open to provide research access six days a week, and its facilities will be able to accommodate more users than the reading room at GLHS. However, we have been concerned with the long-term protection of our collections. The Library is, after all, a government agency and subject to ever-changing political winds and city-budget priorities. While gay, lesbian, transgender and bisexual people currently enjoy a degree of "normalcy" and protection unavailable in many other places or times, history has taught us that such conditions can change. The agreement GLHS has negotiated with the Library has been designed to meet these concerns. In other words, as a deposit agreement, this contract provides GLHS with the means to remove our collections from the Library should they ever be jeopardized.[14]

The June L. Mazer Lesbian Collection was founded in Oakland in 1981 and moved six years later to Los Angeles with the support of the Connexxus Women's Center. Named for it's early donor and benefactor, the collection has now established itself in West Hollywood. After initially agreeing to accept the University of Southern California's (USC) 1995 invitation to provide housing and financial support, the Mazer collection reversed that decision given the small space, increasing costs, and lack of long-term security USC was willing to offer. The Mazer collection's letter to its constituency explains that the collection has always represented an effort "where all lesbians come first," and that "the future preservation and accessibility of our lesbian life-stories will be best protected by lesbians ourselves."[15]

In the summer of 1994, coinciding with the wider-spread mainstream recognition of a lesbian and gay market, the New York Public Library (NYPL) mounted the grand exhibit *Becoming Visible: The Legacy of Stonewall*. The exhibit featured a history of the city's lesbian and gay citizenry and trumpeted the arrival of lesbian and gay history to New York's cultural mainstream. It was a significant political marker for lesbian and gay history, a coming out in new territory. The exhibit portrayed the NYPL's historical relationship with lesbian and gay material as one of happy inclusion. For example, the research guide published to coincide with the *Becoming Visible* exhibit states: "The Research Libraries of the New York Public Library have managed since their beginnings to collect materials relating to this large, but submerged, population. Although the subject entries in the Dictionary Catalog of the Research Libraries, 1911–1971, employ terms that appear today to be abstruse or arcane, the very presence of these works, some quite rare, attests to the Library's interest in acquiring in this field" ("Gay and lesbian studies" 1994).

Becoming Visible provided the NYPL with the platform to present itself as having "long been a friendly place for queers," implying that lesbians and gay men have always been welcome, recognized, and well-represented as one of the many parts of its diverse collection. (For a laudatory account of NYPL and *Becoming Visible*, see Duggan 1995, 188–94.) This institutional fluffing or face-saving masks a history of cloaking lesbian and gay books and archival collections. To point to these texts, both those with and others without subject headings, as the NYPL does in its research guide, proclaiming them evidence for a long-lived interest in collecting lesbian and gay history, plays on the duplicity of the closet the library has imposed on lesbian and gay titles. Material that has languished in the stacks unnamed or ineffectively named for years is only in 1994 highlighted in a research guide to coincide with the timely *Becoming Visible* exhibit. The library more appropriately might have been reflective about its problematic relationship with lesbian and gay material, perhaps by offering plans for correction and reclassification.

A "Donors and Lenders" panel bearing the names of eighty-two individuals and organizations contributing to *Becoming Visible* was erected only days before the exhibit opened, and then only at the insistence of the Lesbian Herstory Educational Foundation. LHEF had offered several display items for the exhibit and provided curators with indicators to lesbian-relevant material unmarked and unacknowledged as such in several archival collections, including NYPL's very own. Tucked to the left of the exhibit entrance (in striking contrast to the "Financial Contributors" panel prominently displayed to the right), the panel represented a break with NYPL's policy, in that it was the first time that the library recognized outside lenders in such a "prominent" fashion in any curated exhibit.[16] Stretched to the limits of their courtesy by this unprecedented gesture, NYPL officials refused to include information about how exhibit-viewers could contact any contributing archive or organization. There was no significant information about the history of the NYPL's International Gay Information Center collection, the folded grass-roots archive donated to NYPL in 1988, which provided the bulk of original artifacts for the exhibit. The *Becoming Visible* exhibit was willfully framed to appear as though it had been berthed from the stacks, archives, native savvy, and magnanimous goodwill of the NYPL, doing a magnificent honor for gays and lesbians, deprived yet deserving of mainstream recognition. For this service, NYPL expected immense gratitude and humility. Riding the wave of queer culture chic, the library was eager, upon the twenty-fifth anniversary of the Stonewall Rebellion, to represent itself as the largest, most accomplished, major repository of lesbian and gay history.

Becoming Visible, as it turns out, was one of the largest money-making exhibits in the NYPL's history.[17] Shortly after the exhibit opened, the library issued a fund-raising appeal written by gay marketeer Sean Strub, signed by gay playwright Tony Kushner, and mailed to potential lesbian- and gay-friendly donors. It incited a size war and invited a gay market to "become a Friend of the New York Public Library," boasting that "the Library's gay holdings are the world's largest" and added, inexplicably, that the NYPL "receives no public funding to build and maintain its great research collections, like its gay and lesbian archives."[18] The NYPL may have boasting rights to the largest gay collection in a mainstream institution only if you interpret "gay" to mean only gay men, not lesbians. But even this is questionable given the size of Cornell University's Human Sexuality Collection.

For the library to misrepresent the contributions of non-NYPL history projects while failing to address its own tangled relationships with the lesbian and gay history secreted in its stacks is not only less than gracious, it is a self-serving betrayal of the processes and institutions that have constructed the history it sought to exhibit. Queer people are starved for historical recognition, not only from community-based organizations but also by major mainstream institutions. Institutions building the legacies of marginalized people will position themselves with respect to that content with various political agendas. It is important to consider how each institution is vested in accommodating archival records, how individuals and organizations will be represented in them, and how these institutions will selectively preserve historical evidence.

CONCLUSION

Both mainstream and grass-roots archives, like all social institutions, are shaped and reflected by individuals and communities bearing both shared and conflicting political beliefs, goals, fears, and ideologies. The Lesbian Herstory Educational Foundation was shaped by 1970s lesbian-feminist political ideals and strategies of institution and community building. LHEF is a resource created to honor, heal, and inspire individual lesbian lives, to provide a protected social and historical, community-based space for woman-identified lesbians to come out to each other, to make themselves known to each other, present and future. This project was designed to remedy the personal and historical deprivation lesbian and gay liberationists identified in the post-Stonewall 1970s, embracing the ideal of lesbian community while pointing to mainstream social institutions as sites of colonization incapable of generating a liberating remedy. LHEF was designed to ensure that, in a community-based context, authentic, inclusive notions about lesbian identity, history, community, and history could form and sustain themselves, fortifying the people it sought to represent by forming a tangible historical presence "in our own land." LHEF has, into the 1990s, refrained from forging a high-profile position in a mainstream public experienced and theorized as hostile to lesbians, assigning itself instead to function within the community-based home of its origin.

The advent of a multi-cultural mainstream interest in lesbian and gay archival records has expanded and positioned queer history in the most public of venues and institutions. Reflecting the success of a grass-roots archival movement, this development is welcomed by community-based activists, but it is also greeted with as much suspicion. The construction of an archival record offers it up for a number of political uses. Mainstream institutions, hopping on a multi-cultural bandwagon, may now present themselves as wonderlands to their newly recognized gay and lesbian constituencies and markets, but in doing so threaten to appropriate the work, recognition, and funding of grass-roots institutions.

The outlaw status of queer collections and the near impossibilities of guaranteeing legal, safe space for those collections, continues to regulate the acquisition, availability, description, and use of queer archival material by all constituencies. When applied to a lesbian or gay archival record, issues of safety transcend commonplace professional understandings of security and preservation. Institutions complacent within legalistic frameworks are severely circumscribed in their ability to construct a viable queer historical record. Institutions that can work outside legalistic frameworks in some sense, mirroring the complexity and subversiveness of the people that history represents, are more successful in constructing a multi-faceted archival record. Queer archival record is loaded with conflicting political meanings for its public and community-based constituencies, and it is likely to remain highly contested for some time to come.

NOTES

Author's note: Thanks to the women of the Lesbian Herstory Archives—especially Amy Beth, Deborah Edel, Joan Nestle, and Maxine Wolfe—for their comraderie and significant contributions to this article. Thanks also to Nan Alamilla Boyd for her critical insight and other generosities.

1. *Lesbian Herstory Archives News*, April 1975, 1.
2. *Lesbian Herstory Archives News* 4, February 1978, 3.
3. "A Plea for Coming Out," *LHA Newsletter*, Spring 1979, 3.
4. In 1967, the New York State Attorney General unsuccessfully challenged the incorporation of the Daughters of Bilitis as a group "contrary to public policy or injurious to the community." (In the Matter of Daughters of Bilitis of New York, Inc., Supreme Court of New York, Special Term, New York County, 52 Misc. 2d 1075; 277 NYS 2d 709, 28 February 1967.) In 1973, both the Gay Activists Alliance and the Lambda Legal Defense Fund encountered legal resistance to incorporation in New York State, though both groups eventually won the battle to incorporate (Harvard Law Review, eds.1990, 156). In 1974, the lesbian feminist publication *Big Mama Rag* was denied federal tax exempt status by the IRS, though Colorado had granted it the requisite non-profit status. The publication finally won the right to incorporate in 1980, when the Court of Appeals for the District of Columbia Circuit reversed a rule that allowed the IRS to withhold tax exemption based on the "content and quality of an applicant's views and goals" (*Big Mama Rag, Inc. v. United States*, 631 F2d, quoted in Harvard Law Review, eds. 1990, 157).
5. "Announcements," *Lesbian Herstory Archives News* 8, Winter 1984, 3.
6. *Not Just Passing Through* contains a 10-minute segment on ALOEC, including some of Chan's slide show.
7. The New Alexandria Archive, in contrast, has transitioned from a collection with a lesbian focus to one embracing a variety of queer identities. For more information see Hemmings 1996, 35–59.
8. The New York Public Library coded the banner advertising its 1994 exhibition on lesbian and gay history, ironically titled *Becoming Visible: The Legacy of Stonewall*. The arrival of lesbian and gay history to New York's cultural mainstream was thus announced subtly, "in code" to those clued-in to queer history and iconography. The banner bore only a pink triangle and the exhibit title, not the words "gay" or "lesbian."

9. Lesbian Herstory archivist Judith Schwarz documents an incident in which the descendants of Margaret Sanger refused historian Jonathan Katz access to love letters written by Marie Equi to Sanger, housed in Sanger's collection at Smith College (Schwarz 1992, 184). Elena Danielson describes similar incidents in which the families of such influential figures as Sigmund Freud and Ludwig Wittgenstein refused a biographer access to papers (Danielson 1989, 52–62). Martin Duberman describes a library staff's refusal to grant permission to publish the homoerotic letters between antebellum politicians James H. Hammond and Jeff Withers housed in the South Caroliniana Library (Duberman 1991). Roz Baxandall notes in her acknowledgements (1987, ix) that party members staffing the American Institute of Marxist Studies library in New York somehow "lost" intimate letters between Flynn and Marie Equi (the same Equi involved with Sanger) as they were transferred to the Tamiment Library at New York University.

10. For example, the Anne and Carl Braden papers at the State Historical Society of Wisconsin were subpoenaed in 1986 by the FBI, over the restrictions placed on the collection by Anne Braden. The court ruled that the archival restriction did not protect Braden's collection from subpoena, and the Historical Society granted the FBI access. See Knowlton 1993.

11. The Reagan administration's "Library Awareness Program," 1986–1987, recruited library staff to identify people with foreign names or accents (allegedly potential spies) who spend time in science libraries reading technology journals. In 1991 the New York City police department subpoenaed and readily obtained circulation records from the New York Public Library bearing the names of patrons who had recently requested Aleister Crowley's *Book of Law*, a text with which the media-hyped "Zodiac Killer" was evidently familiar. The NYPD's dull-witted investigation led to the questioning of a Wall Street executive who was quickly determined not to be a suspect, unfortunately for him not before he was pictured in police custody on the front page of the *New York Post*.

12. Greenblatt explains that "Homosexuality" did not become an authorized subject heading until 1946, however, and "Lesbianism" was not recognized by LC until 1954. LC continued the "see also" reference from these terms to "sexual perversion" until 1972. It was not until 1976 that LC denoted "Lesbians" and "Homosexuals, male" as classes of persons, and "Gay" was only sanctioned as a subject heading in 1987.

13. "Gays," for example is used as an umbrella term instead of "Lesbians and Gays." In addition, LC subject headings do not exist for crucial, let alone nuanced elements of lesbian lives and culture. The addition of subject headings such as "Butch-Fem," "Lesbian feminism," and "Lesbian separatism" would be useful. In addition, there are few headings to describe the literature pertaining to the varieties of nonnormative sexual identity that are not necessarily lesbian or gay. There is no heading for "Transgender," for example, or "Queer," for that matter. There is one for "Transsexuals," but nothing yet to distinguish works on male-to-female from female-to-male transsexuals. In addition, there are no headings for "American Literature—lesbian authors" or "American Literature—gay authors" equivalent to "American literature—Asian American authors" or "American literature—women authors."

14. February 15, 1996 letter to GLHS Members.

15. March 15, 1996 letter to June L. Mazer Collection supporters.

16. Telephone conversation with Mimi Bowling, Curator of Manuscripts, New York Public Library, June 1994.

17. Telephone conversation with NYPL public relations office representative, January 12, 1996.

18. "Discover the Legacy of Stonewall . . . At the New York Public Library," fund-raising letter of the New York Public Library, 1994. Special collections, Lesbian Herstory Archives, New York.

REFERENCES

Baxandall, Roz. 1987. *Words on fire: The life and writing of Elizabeth Gurley Flynn*. New Brunswick, NJ: Rutgers University Press.

Berman, Sanford. 1971. *Prejudices and antipathies: A tract on the LC subject heads concerning people*. Metuchen, NJ: Scarecrow.

Boyd, Nan A.1997. "Bodies in motion: Lesbian and transexual histories." In *A queer world: The Center for Lesbian and Gay Studies reader*, edited by Martin Dubberman. New York: New York University Press.

Boyd, Nan A. 1996. "Beyond lesbian bodies: Lesbian nationalism in the 1970s." Paper presented at the American Studies Association Conference, Kansas City, Missouri. (May).

Chauncey, George. 1994. *Gay New York, 1890–1940*. New York: BasicBooks.

Cohen, Martin F. 1996. "Neighborhood report: Park Slope; in lesbian archive, education and sanctuary." *New York Times*, April 7, sec. B, 9.

Danielson, Elena. 1989. "The ethics of access." *American Archivist* 52 (Winter): 52–62.

D'Emilio, John. 1979. *Sexual politics, sexual communities: The making of a homosexual community in the United States, 1940–1970*. Chicago: The University of Chicago Press.

Duberman, Martin. 1991. "Writhing bedfellows in antebellum South Carolina: Historical interpretation and the politics of evidence." In *About time: Exploring the gay past*. New York: Meridian.

Duggan, Lisa. 1995. "Becoming visible: The legacy of Stonewall, New York Public Library, June 18–September 24, 1994." *Radical History Review* (Spring): 188–94.

"Gay and lesbian studies." 1994. Research guide 29, New York Public Library General Research Division (June).

Greenblatt, Ellen. 1990. "Homosexuality: The evolution of a concept in the Library of Congress subject headings." In *Gay and lesbian library service*, edited by Cal Gough and Ellen Greenblatt, 75–101. Jefferson, NC:McFarland.

Harvard Law Review, eds. 1990. *Sexual orientation and the law*. Cambridge, MA: Harvard University Press.

Hemmings, Claire. 1996. "From lesbian nation to transgender liberation: A bisexual feminist perspective." *Journal of Gay, Lesbian and Bisexual Identity* 1 (January): 35–59.

Knowlton, Elizabeth. 1993. "Researcher access to records documenting human sexuality vs. Donor privacy concerns." Paper, Society of American Archivists (September).

Lauritsen, John and Thorstad, David. 1974. *The early homosexual rights movement (1864–1935)*. New York: Times Change Press.

Lesbian Herstory Archives Guide to the Collection. 1993. New York: Lesbian Herstory Archives.

Lorde, Audre, ed. 1984. *Sister outsider*. Trumansburg, NY: Crossing Press.

Martin, Biddy and Mohanty, Chandra T. 1986. "Feminist politics: What's home got to do with it?" In *Feminist studies, critical studies*, edited by Teresa de Lauretis, 191–212. Bloomington: Indiana University Press.

Monahan, Jim. 1979. "Considerations in the organization of gay archives." *Gay Insurgent* 4/5 (Spring): 9.

Moseley, Eva. 1992. "Describing sex and gender in historical collections." Paper, Society of American Archivists Meeting, September. St. Petersburg, FL: Conventions

Recordings International.

Nestle, Joan. 1987. "My history with censorship." In *A restricted country: Essays and short stories*. New York: Firebrand Books.

Nestle, Joan. 1979. "Notes on radical archiving from a lesbian feminist standpoint." *Gay Insurgent* 4/5 (Spring): 11.

New York Public Library. 1994. "Discover the legacy of Stonewall . . . At the New York Public Library." [Fund-raising letter]. June. Special Collections, Lesbian Herstory Archives, New York City, NY.

Not just passing through. 1994. Produced and directed by Jean Carlomusto, Dolores Perez, Catherine Saalfield, and Polly Thistlethwaite. 51 minutes. Women Make Movies. Videocassette.

Peterson, Gary M. and Peterson, Trudy H. 1985. *Archives and manuscripts: Law*. Chicago: Society of American Archivists.

"Police subpoena library records in hunt for NYC's zodiac killer." 1990. *American Libraries* 21 (September): 703.

Ramos, Juanita, ed. 1987. *Compañeras: Latina lesbians, an anthology*. New York: Latina Lesbian History Project.

Roberts, J. R. 1981. *Black lesbians: An annotated bibliography*. Tallahassee, FL: Naiad Press.

Robins, Natalie S. 1988. "The FBI's invasion of libraries." *The Nation* 246 (April 9): 481, 498–502.

Robson, Ruthann. 1992. *Lesbian (out)law: Survival under the rule of law*. Ithaca, NY: Firebrand Books.

Rothenberg, Tamar. 1995. "And she told two friends: Lesbians creating urban social space. In *Geographies of desires: Mapping sexualities*, edited by David Bell and Gill Valentine, 165–81. New York: Routledge.

Schwarz, Judith. 1992. "The archivist's balancing act: Helping researchers while protecting individual privacy." *The Journal of American History* 79 (June): 179–89.

Sedgewick, Eve. 1990. *Epistemology of the closet*. Berkeley: University of California Press.

Taylor, Marvin. 1994. "A queer point of view: Looking askance at library collections." Paper presented at New York American College and Research Libraries Diversity Committee Conference, John Jay College, New York City, October.

VonSalis, Susan. 1994. [Speech]. Society of American Archivists Meeting, Cincinnati, OH. St Petersburg, FL: Convention Recordings International.

13

An Accidental Institution: How and Why a Gay and Lesbian Archives?

Jim Kepner

What impelled me to collect over 20,000 books and a larger mass of periodicals, loose papers, art, and other memorabilia relating directly or indirectly to Gay/Lesbian concerns, sexuality, and morals, starting at a time when such materials were very hard to find and sometimes dangerous to possess, and to make that collection a public institution? One Gay French visitor, seeing the "Gay Archives" sign on our door, sniffed, "Whatever for?" as if the idea was pointless and gauche.

Growing up religious but in Texas darkness with regard to "The Love That Dared Not Speak Its Name," I nonetheless knew by age four that certain of my feelings were not what people around me expected. I found those feelings reflected in the Biblical stories of Ruth and Naomi, David and Jonathan, and later in Greek special friendship stories. I quickly realized that others did not see what I saw in them, or in the subtly homoerotic Horatio Alger, Jr. novels (virtuous poor boy makes good with kindly older gentleman's aid) sent by Aunt Ida each birthday and Christmas for my moral edification. I longed for such a kindly older gentle-man-guide, and flirted timidly with Momma's boyfriends—got a few hugs but nothing more. If I dared mention my feelings, I was told I'd grow out of it, that the right girl would someday come along and ZAP! Housekeeping! In church, which I left before finding a name for my Gayness, I heard none of what's now called homophobia, beyond some sissy teasing.

Despite high school years heavy on Latin, English, Science, History, Math, and ROTC, alliances with a succession of tomboys, and a few unrequited crushes, I remained uninformed until age nineteen, when friends began talking about homosexuals. I didn't know the word. They defined it revoltingly. My dictionary was more kind, and explicit enough. By luck, the *Galveston Daily News* that week advertised 1,728 freethinking Little Blue Books at five cents each—including "What Is Homosexuality?" and "Homosexuality in the Lives of the Great." I virtually sat on our mailbox for two weeks so my parents wouldn't intercept these.

One was my first encounter with depressing Freudian theory. The other told me that Socrates, Caesar, and Virgil (both of whom I'd read in Latin), Michelangelo, Leonardo, Bacon, Shakespeare, George Washington, Florence Nightingale, Oscar Wilde, Walt Whitman, Radcliffe Hall, and others were homosexual. I was elated. I had a name—one worn by highly admired men and women. But in four high school years I'd heard not one word of that. Resenting those years in ignorance, I set out to learn all I could.

With my father and sister, I moved to San Francisco in 1942, searching the city's public library (long marble halls and no books in sight) for books on homosexuality. The card catalogue listed only Krafft-Ebing's study, a waxworks museum of sexual monstrosities, long since checked out. Like many inquisitive Gays stifled by the straight world view, I'd developed peripheral interests (we often found our identity in the unswept corners of life). San Francisco's library was less helpful than Galveston's on those interests—but Field's, MacDonald's, and McDevitt's used bookstores were goldmines—though it took long hours of hunting. I soon filled three shelves with books and little magazines at very little cost. My father never looked at books, still I hoped he wouldn't notice the titles—*Strange Brother, The Well of Loneliness, Leaves of Grass, Intermediate Types Among Primitive Folks, A Study in Greek Ethics, The Homosexual Neurosis, Bisexual Love, We Too Are Drifting, The Gay Year, This Is My Beloved*—in between the little magazines and science fiction. He complained about the space and cost, and later threw out books and periodicals I've never been able to replace.

But my pack-rat habit had been solidly established, and as I moved during the next eight years to Los Angeles, New York, briefly to Miami, and back to San Francisco and Los Angeles, my collection grew, and my interests widened—with books on freethought and religion, science and philosophy, history, linguistics, astronomy, political philosophy, and the problems and progress of Blacks—all focused on fitting my Gayness into a world context. I viewed the conditions and struggles of ethnic minorities and of women as analogous to and instructive for those of homosexuals or Gays. (I use both terms as Gay women and men used them then, to include both genders.)

Gayness does not exist in a vacuum. It is variously interrelated to most world concerns. From childhood, I'd compared the way Blacks and Latins were treated to the treatment of sissies, while also recognizing important differences. When my Sunday school teacher told a sweet story about racial equality and denied it had anything to do with Blacks not coming to "our" church, I'd already noticed that peculiar blindness that lets "normal" people miss the meaning of David's love for Jonathan, or Jesus' for John.

Once I found a word for my feelings, and knew I wasn't "the only one in the world," I felt that discrimination against Gays was a social problem that we needed to do something about. I also wanted to find out all I could about the subject. It took me awhile just to find other Gays, most of whom considered organizing dangerous and doomed to failure. They accepted the need to slink in dark corners as the best of an unhappy situation. Few of them cared about the books I was accumulating. In truth, most of the books then were pretty depressing.

So I went back to science fiction fandom, where we could fantasize about more adventuresome or kinder worlds. "Normal" people considered America's few hundred "overt" sci-fi fans queers. *Saturday Review* and *Time* magazine used the same shrinks who pontificated about homosexuals to explain this "pathology" of rejecting paternal authority and Mother Earth's bosom to imagine flying off in a penis-shaped rocket ship, with a penis-shaped rocket gun in a homosocial camaraderie of outer space. Sci-fi fans, many of them repressed Gays, were nervous about this. Of the writers, only Olaf Stapledon and Theodore Sturgeon touched directly on homosexuality, though most 1940s stories were homosocial, all-male adventures. Women writers or fans were still rare.

I felt that the seeds of Gayness were close to what makes a sci-fi fan: a tendency to question what others take for granted, a yearning to fly off to places where life is different. I felt that most straights (a term sci-fi and jazz fans shared with us) were basically satisfied with things as they are, or if dissatisfied, they didn't approach the problem with much imagination.

In 1945, four friends and I, hoping to do more than dream about a better world, became communists—a choice that seemed reasonable to us then. Despairing of being able to campaign for Gay rights any time soon, I worked for peace, progress, the rights of workers, Blacks, and other minorities—hoping, as many closeted Gays did in those days, that "comes the Revolution," some of the freedom and respect we'd won for others would rub off on us. We idealized the Soviet Union, but learned how to debate, picket, and organize where it was dangerous, while hoping to build that Shining Tomorrow.

Kinsey's first volume came out just before the Communist Party booted me for being Gay (a guy who'd joined when I did turned out to be an FBI spy). I moved back to San Francisco, opened a bookstore in North Beach with a friend who later came out. I was digging up more gay history, often written between the lines, building an extensive honors list, detecting a homophilic leaning in writers who were never explicit, and refining my ideas about how Gayness related to other social, political, and cultural concerns. I became sensitive to homophobic slams in the press.

I discovered the overwhelming role that Gays played in avant garde arts, pacifist, civil rights, or metaphysical groups, in ballet, railroad hobbying, tennis, antique collecting, and many other areas. Without going out of my way to collect books and papers in these areas, unless they had specific Gay references, I felt that they deserved a place in the Gay Studies that were yet to be.

I was finding more of the older, obscure Gay literature, a vast resource that was long hidden. Better Gay novels were coming out, and Donald Webster Cory's *The Homosexual in America,* the first widely sold broad survey of the subject from a homosexual viewpoint. Like James Barr's novel *Quatrefoil,* Cory suggested the need to organize, and during gatherings at my hillside house, I often proposed that idea to a select few. No takers. I didn't know that Mattachine Society had already started, or that its founders lived not far from me.

Word about Mattachine spread quickly. I worked the midnight shift in a factory and used public transportation, so I didn't get to a discussion group until December

1952 when Betty Perdue, a longtime sci-fi friend and neighbor took me. Few people there had read any Gay books. I was asked to discuss *The Well of Loneliness* at the next meeting. A month earlier, independent plans had been laid for *ONE* magazine, America's first openly-sold magazine by and for homosexuals. And the publication started feistily during the most conformist, witch-hunting period in American history.

Mattachine soon ripped itself apart, as neither the old leaders nor the new members could deal with our great diversity. "We all want the same thing, don't we?" they bleated when disagreements arose. I knew we differed enormously on goals and strategy. I felt Mattachine had taken a wrong turn, so I followed some Mattachine founders to *ONE*, and began writing for and working with the magazine early in 1954. Anti-Gay witchhunts had erupted in Congress, in England and Miami, and later in other places, and I began collecting newspaper clippings and correspondence. I covered worldwide Gay news for *ONE* and other publications for seven years, returning frequently to that line of work in later years.

My cache of Gay-related history, art, philosophy and psychology books outgrew the capacity of my house, so I donated 400 of them to *ONE*'s newly-formed library, now under the protective corporate aegis of ONE, Inc. The librarian sold some of them off as irrelevant. In a *ONE* schism later in 1965, that librarian took most of those books for what became the Homosexual Information Center, which still insists that the right of privacy is our only concern. By then, I'd built new shelves, adding more books than ever. More biographies and histories were mentioning the subject, though not yet in great or explicit detail. More novels had minor gay characters. And more shrinks were claiming to cure homosexuals—I wrote scathing criticisms of a couple of those.

In the summer of 1956, members of ONE, Inc. decided to collectively explore what we knew and what we needed to know about the whole subject. In a nine week class in September, we surveyed the information, misinformation, and methodology of biology, anthropology, sociology, religion, law, history, literature, philosophy, and what we called programmatics—i.e., how to correlate this information to benefit the growing gay community and movement. Of four ONE, Inc. faculty members, I alone lacked a college degree. So I worked harder.

In Spring of 1957, we expanded this to a 36-week course and added a 36-week course in World Homophile History. (The term Homophile, like Gay, included our sexuality, but much more.) Dorr Legg (who held ONE rigidly on course for forty-one years) and I explored various cultures and countries. We did a heavy search for who we had been in the past, and I gathered many additional books on Classical, Near Eastern, German, Scandinavian, Japanese, British, and American history—finding far more material, between the lines or explicit, than I'd expected. Stories about kings, queens, generals, writers, and artists were easier to find than social history that included us in the picture, but as we repeated the courses, and offered others, information filled in—though nothing like the explosion of Gay and feminist history since 1970. ONE's classes continued, with sometime university or state accreditation, until 1994, and we gave brief extension classes in several cities. Many in the homophile movement jeered, "What's to study? I've been to college, and besides, I know all the positions." They regarded Gay life as just so many sexual positions.

I left ONE in December 1960, returning during the 1970s. By then I was also active in the Council on Religion and the Homophile, the North American Conference of Homophile Organizations, the Gay Liberation Front, SPREE (a Gay theatre and film club), the Gay Community Services Center, the Los Angeles parade committee, and so forth, and wrote for or edited several periodicals—all of which fed my growing collection of meeting notes, newsletters, fliers, posters, photos, correspondence, audio tapes, and buttons.

In 1977, while acting as ONE librarian, I offered the organization my private collection, asking only that ONE, whose prime leader sniffed at new trends in the movement and in Gay writing, try to be more complete in its collecting. I also asked that they open the library to non-credentialed students and readers, not just to certified scholars (Dorr Legg often refused to help even those if their approach was gay liberationist rather than sexological.) ONE spurned my offer, so I decided to concentrate on making my collection public. Others had been contributing to it and using it since 1956. I hadn't started with the idea of making my personal library a public institution, but other private collections were not being used by the movement and mine was larger and broader in scope than ONE's.

Earlier, in 1972, I'd opened the Western Gay Archives in my Torrance, Calif., apartment to students one afternoon a week. I later moved to a Hollywood cottage behind a hotel supposedly once used by Rudolph Valentino for Gay parties. The Gay Community Services Center provided the first full-time Comprehensive Employment and Training Act (CETA) worker. In 1979, under a second Board of Directors (the first had played out), we incorporated The Gay Archives, and moved, with Clark Polak's help, into a 21,500 square foot-storefront plus basement just off Hollywood Boulevard. We expanded our name to The International Gay & Lesbian Archives: Natalie Barney/Edward Carpenter Library. It took all my fund-raising ability to meet the rent, which rose from $600 a month to $1,300 by 1987, plus utilities and a bit more for operating expenses. I upset image-conscious board members by crying wolf too often, but while they met once a month to make rules, I had to keep the place open from fifty to seventy hours a week with untrained Service Center volunteers and a few dedicated ones, raise funds, prepare and mail newsletters, do advertising and public relations, arrange twice-a-week programs and six art shows a year, move things around when the roof leaked or the ground shook, and listen to endless complaints of: "Why are you keeping this?" "Why can't you find things the moment I ask for them?" "Why did you tell a volunteer to do one thing one day and something else the next?" "Why do you waste time with students who aren't paying for your time?"

With my first computer, a Kay-Pro II, I began working on our mailing list and announcements as well as a worldwide chronology of Gay history, "Becoming a People"; a story-board display on "Our Movement Before Stonewall"; a massive descriptive name list of Gays and Lesbians, contemporary and historical that I'd been building since 1942 (when I got that twenty-six-page booklet, "Homosexuality in the Lives of the Great"); and autobiographical-movement history notes, which have expanded to thousands of pages.

In 1986, artist Olaf Odegaard mounted our display of 400 pieces of Gay male art by 100 artists—on a rainy weekend, and Jean-Nicholas Tretter, our St. Paul, Minn., board member, later displayed eighty of those for a month in the Twin Cities. The artists donated many of these works to our collection. We have since done art and history displays at Pride Festivals in Los Angeles, Long Beach, the Twin Cities, Milwaukee, New York, and Washington, DC.

Among our prize holdings: a hardbound copy of the 1906 German Gay culture magazine, *Der Eigene*—220 pages with tipped-in tinted illustrations—revealing youthful correspondence from 1900 of Merritt Thompson, Dean Emeritus of the USC School of Education, who helped us set up ONE, Inc.; 1940s correspondence between Henry Gerber, Manual Boyfrank (later secretary of ONE, Inc.), and others who hoped to organize homosexuals; copies of the New York gossip paper, *Broadway Brevities*, with lurid reports on Gay life in the early 1930s; hundreds of mounted photos of Los Angeles Black men taken over five decades; first editions of Amy Lowell's poems; intimate records of hundreds of Gay and Lesbian organizations; a museum-quality collection of movement buttons—many 150 years old; several personal journals; complete files of scores of Gay, Lesbian, and feminist periodicals, including editorial files of some.

By late 1987, with the collection overflowing our quarters, we got behind in the rent and went into storage until the city of West Hollywood gave us space (smaller than what we'd outgrown.) Sudden and unexpected deadlines made the move more hectic than it should have been, and as new materials came in since, many publications were microfilmed, and two-thirds then four-fifths of our collection, properly catalogued, went into storage nearby. I no longer live near the archives, where skilled volunteers are cataloguing, rearranging, and seeing to long-term preservation. Because I'm a natural pack-rat, I've again built a private collection for my immediate use in writing. About as large as the Archives was when it was incorporated, it will go to ONE/International Gay and Lesbian Archives (IGLA) later, after agreement is reached on what is relevant enough to keep.

Relevance has been a matter of debate over the years. Those now doing the cataloguing don't see some of the books I collected as relevant. I've collected writings and biographies, for example, of Tolstoy and Hemingway, each of whom projected a super heterosexual public image, but research indicated that their heterosexuality was a sham. Simon Karlinsky analyzed that with Tolstoy, and a long *New York Times* magazine story reported that the first draft of most Hemingway novels centered on a homosexual or transvestite scene. Two early biographies of Oscar Wilde denied that he was really homosexual, as did many of Whitman. Only right-wing gossip columnists had suggested a lesbian leaning in Eleanor Roosevelt until her love letters to Lorena Hickman were revealed. Arnold Rampersad's two-volume biography of Langston Hughes argued in detail that the Black poet couldn't have been Gay because (1) he wasn't effeminate, (2) he didn't hate women, (3) he didn't have sex with his openly Gay friends, and (4) when white sailors gang raped a pair of native boys on the coast of Africa, Hughes reprimanded them, instead of joining the fun as any "Gay" would have done!

I always tried to balance male and female materials, out of genuine interest in my sisters, and a feeling that our lives and problems were at least partly shared. I collected books and periodicals on feminist theory even if lesbianism was not mentioned, and books by and about independent women even when there was no evidence they'd had sex with other women (few left such evidence around.) I felt it was enough if unmarried women had lived with or were especially affectionate with other women, or if their marriage seemed "convenient."

Many books that contained no explicit references to homosexuality or Gayness provided needed background. I'd written a long account for *ONE*'s, October-December 1956 issue, of the forgotten 1907-09 trials on homosexual charges of intimate friends of Kaiser Wilhelm II—which in effect removed most moderates from the government and set Germany on the tragic road to world wars and the Nazi horror. To research this story I'd used every book I could find that covered the background or described principals in the case, though few such books discussed the trials or Prince Eulenburg explicitly. So were these books relevant? I say yes, like early sociology or psychology texts which treated homosexuality peripherally or with extreme prejudice. That cover-up and misinterpretation is essential to history.

Are novels and poetry books by writers who were Gay or Lesbian to be kept only if they have explicit homosexual references—or if the writers came out publicly? Readers now expect everything to be on the surface. In earlier times we learned how to read between the lines, how to detect the little traces and special flavors of the closet. Those also are parts of our heritage we ought not lose, even if Gays today need to resort far less often to subterfuge.

Ultimately more important, or at least more used, than the archives' books were our periodicals and loose papers, a massive record of the post-1940s Gay community and movement, with a few much older clippings, letters, photos and such. Others have joined in the collecting. Large collections are coming in from everywhere, and I've retired from actively processing all this and preparing it to move to the new building being readied for us just off the University of Southern California campus. Some universities had suggested we give them "the material and good-bye. We'll keep what we want, and process it when and if we get around to it." Others were willing to take the collection if we came up with $1,000,000 or so to cover operating costs.

The merger in late 1994 of the ONE, Inc. library and the archives, already the world's two largest known Gay collections, under the name ONE/International Gay & Lesbian Archives, has gone smoothly with the combined collection more than doubling in size during the last year. We have a strong working Board of Directors; several major art, AIDS, theatre and music projects in the works; and improved finances.

My crying wolf several years ago, which seemed necessary then, had left us a reputation for instability. We wanted the umbrella and facilities of a larger institution, while ownership, management and control of what to keep and how to use it stayed within the Gay community. The University of Southern California offered such a generous arrangement, even if the initial steps have been frustratingly slow. We must do fundraising on a scale far beyond what we've done before. The large new building planned for the center will be crowded by the time we move in, and we have architectural plans to construct additional buildings on that and an adjoining property, expanding hopefully to a museum, theatre, and cultural center.

I'm happy to see other major collections developing around the country and world, to preserve information about Gay life and make it available to people who aren't on-line and can't afford long distance travel, and to guard against the record of our history and culture being burned on one site and long forgotten, as happened outside the Hirschfeld Institute in Berlin, May 6, 1933.

Still at issue for us is the balance between security and over-protection of the collection, as opposed to accessibility and how much will be available to non-USC students and noncertified researchers. I built the two collections not just for the use of researchers—many of course have used it—but in hopes it would play a major role in developing the consciousness and directions of the Gay community and movement. Such decisions now lie with our Board of Directors.

I have spent thousands of hours with researchers, liberally giving away information that might have gone into my own writing, but my greatest joy has been opening up the subject to young Gays or Lesbians who are just coming out and asking "Who am I?" "How do I live?" If they don't pay cash for the time I spend with them and the articles I give them, neither do most researchers. But helping modestly by my writing, my activism, and teaching to shepherd this movement from obscurity, shame, vilification, and persecution to its present open and proud state has been an enormous compensation.

Editor's Note: Jim Kepner died on Novermber 15, 1997 at Midway Hospital in Los Angeles after an intestinal operation. He was 74. At the time of his death, the collection that he founded in 1942 consisted of 22,000 books, 100,000 newspaper and magazine articles dating back to 1906, and hundreds of multi-media materials, ephemera, and artifacts.

14

Safe Harbour: The Origin and Growth of the Lesbian and Gay Archives of New Zealand

Phil Parkinson and Chris Parkin

As we strive for full recognition of our rights, our culture and our spirituality, we are creating documents that demonstrate this remarkable process. But these will benefit no one in the future unless they are preserved . . . in a way that makes them accessible to future researchers.

—Phil Nash[1]

The Lesbian and Gay Archives of New Zealand is a national heritage research collection of manuscripts, archives, audiotapes and videotapes, photographs, ephemera, books, serials, and miscellanea. It is permanently housed as a research collection in the Alexander Turnbull Library, which is the research library within the National Library of New Zealand. This large and diverse body of materials is formally owned by a charitable trust, which appoints one or more curators of its collections. It is emphasized that the collections do not belong to the State. For all practical purposes the National Library is housing and providing access to the documentary history of gay and lesbian communities, individuals, and movements in New Zealand, and has been doing so for almost a decade without any problems.

This is, so far as we are aware, a unique situation in the world, but it is one that other major gay and lesbian archives and libraries should seriously consider as a way of safeguarding and securing the future for such collections. The costs of maintaining them in private hands are high and dependent upon a flow of community funds, which can easily dry up. Their continued existence often relies on small numbers of volunteers, and may be as vulnerable to malice as to misfortune. In this chapter we describe how an outcome was achieved that ensures better access, greater security, and a safer physical environment than the community could ever have managed from its resources alone.

THE LESBIAN AND GAY RIGHTS RESOURCE CENTRE

What was to become the Lesbian and Gay Rights Resource Centre (LGRRC) was established in 1978, under the auspices of the National Gay Rights Coalition (NGRC), as the NGRC Resource Centre. The purpose of the resource centre was to look after the papers of the NGRC, and to collect and disseminate educational materials. The centre's administrator, from 1981, was Phil Parkinson, and it was run by a collective of interested individuals within the NGRC. The NGRC Resource Centre was at first a desk in a private household, but from 1980, it was housed in the Wellington Gay Community Centre at 6 Boulcott Street in central Wellington. The NGRC was restructured in 1981, and its resource centre became an autonomous collective, LGRRC. The LGRRC retained links with the NGRC, and also developed a strong relationship with the Pink Triangle Publishing Collective through the decade covering its relocation from Christchurch in 1980 and 1981 until its winding up in 1991.

The purpose of the LGRRC was, as the choice of name indicates, to provide resources that could support activities on a number of fronts including law reform, censorship, human rights and associated legislation, lesbian and gay health, and many more. The centre accumulated material about gay and lesbian sexuality, identity, and culture—and history. It acted as the archival repository of the NGRC and its various member groups. It became increasingly obvious that huge amounts of invaluable material might be lost for all time if active efforts were not made to preserve it, and to encourage awareness in individuals and groups alike of the need to do so.

The archival role of the LGRRC demanded that careful attention be given to striking a balance between access and confidentiality. The criminal status of all male homosexual acts, coupled with social hostility to all gay men and lesbians, made our group records and personal material much more sensitive than most and, for this reason, access to unpublished material was carefully supervised. Subject to such restrictions on account of privacy, the collections were available for research and study by seriously interested members of the lesbian and gay community, and by other bona fide researchers. The Pink Triangle Publishing Collective was a major user of the information held by the LGRRC. The Gay Switchboard counselling service worked with the LGRRC in selecting and presenting information. Documentation was provided for the Human Rights Commission, and background material for the newspaper press. The LGRRC serviced the information needs of the Lesbian Radio and Gay Broadcasting Corporation radio programs broadcast on the 2YB Access Radio wavelength. The premises were used for small meetings, and out of town reference inquiries were answered. The LGRRC also was heavily involved in law reform efforts, and in the collection and dissemination of information for the AIDS Support Network.

In mid-1983 the LGRRC began gathering and assimilating current material on AIDS prevention strategies alongside relevant medical information. At the end of that year, it wrote and distributed the first New Zealand AIDS leaflet *AIDS: Choices and Chances*. The Resource Centre hosted the meeting in 1984 at which the AIDS Support Network, later to become The New Zealand AIDS Foundation (NZAF), was set up. The NZAF and other agencies, governmental and nongovernmental, benefited from the valuable coverage of AIDS in gay community papers, most of which were not held anywhere else in New Zealand. The LGRRC developed a substantial collection of AIDS education and prevention leaflets, and a filing system of medical information. Both have been widely used.[2]

Membership of the LGRRC was open to anyone who supported its objectives: "To recover and preserve the resource materials (both the factual record and the work of lesbian/gay imagination) which document the activity of lesbian/gay history and society. To work for the rights, interests and well-being of lesbians and gay men everywhere, and to assist concerned people to work for the rights, interests and well-being of lesbians and gay men." The LGRRC never incorporated and saw no need to do so, because it did not handle any substantial funds and was not liable to register for GST, New Zealand's goods and services tax regime.

The LGRRC had ceased to operate as a collective by 1983; administrative responsibility for the collections fell to the administrator with some assistance from a small informal group of LGRRC members appointed trustees, of whom the adminstrator was one. At about this time the Wellington Gay Community Centre was reorganized and refurbished. The LGRRC contributed a portion of the rent, paying for its own operating expenses. Its relatively low expenses were met in part from NGRC funds and, increasingly, from *Pink Triangle* newsletter revenue, from donations, and from gay student dances and other fund-raising activities. Income was small and irregular, but sufficient for the time being and furnished by the community.

This situation continued until 1986. The building was sold before site redevelopment, and the groups housed there were already looking for other premises. The LGRRC trustees were facing potentially huge problems in safeguarding the future of the archives. And we were in good company. In the mid-1980s it seemed that lesbian and gay archives everywhere were struggling: the Australian Gay Archives were to go into storage; the Hall-Carpenter archives in England lost their premises; in Dublin the Hirshfeld Centre would be burned; the Canadian Gay Archives were under threat; the International Gay & Lesbian Archives in Los Angeles ran out of money. In New Zealand, finding an alternative to the Boulcott Street premises, which was both accessible to, and affordable by, gay and lesbian communities, promised to become a major headache.

Before we address the efforts made to find a solution to the problems just outlined, we point out that 1986 saw the culmination in New Zealand of a turbulent and long drawn out sixteen-month campaign for law reform with the passage into law of the Homosexual Law Reform Act. We have already touched on the LGRRC's commitment to law reform efforts. Our next task is to set the reform in historical context and assess some of its social significance.[3]

HOMOSEXUALITY AND THE LAW, 1840–1961

The land of the long white cloud, Aotearoa, was settled by Polynesian people in about the eleventh century. There was some contact between European explorers and indigenous Maori in the seventeenth and eighteenth centuries, and European settlement began from about 1814. The territory was annexed to the British Crown on February 6, 1840, by the Treaty of Waitangi; there has been division and debate ever since about the beliefs and intentions of those devising and signing the treaty.

New Zealand, Aotearoa, was subject to English law, initially through the laws of New South Wales, under which buggery (the term did not drop out of New Zealand legal parlance until the Crimes Act 1961) was a capital offence. The death sentence for buggery was finally abolished in England under Sir Robert Peel's government, which enacted the Offences Against The Person Act 1861, but that legislation also introduced a new statutory offence: indecent assault upon a male; hitherto sodomy alone had been criminally proscribed. The New Zealand Offences Against the Person Act 1867 copied its English predecessor in both respects, and formed the basis of subsequent legislation in this country relating to homosexuals. It was repealed upon enactment of the Criminal Code Act 1893, which nonetheless retained the substance of the earlier act's provisions. The only apparent influence of Westminster's infamous Labouchere amendment, which made every sexual act between males a criminal offence, was in the final clause of Section 137, which reproduced the "consent is no defence" provision of the 1885 English legislation. Sections 136 and 137 of the Criminal Code Act 1893 were re-worked as Sections 153 and 154 of the Crimes Act 1908, which remained in force until 1961, save that the provision for flogging or whipping was removed in 1941 and that for hard labour in 1954.

A major consolidation and amendment of the Crimes Act was introduced in 1957 and no significant modification of the provisions concerning homosexual acts was envisaged. But when the bill was reintroduced in 1959 following a change in government, the Minister of Justice, the Hon. H.G.R. Mason, influenced by the suicide of a talented Auckland friend, sought—acting independently of the Department of Justice—to diminish the penalties for indecency between consenting adults. He personally instructed the Law Draftsman to remove consensual acts from the scope of the sodomy clause, on the mistaken assumption that they would remain punishable as the lesser offence of indecency between males. A howl of protest was raised, which eventually caused Mr. Mason, fed up with the bother, to direct a reversion to the existing law. Perhaps the two most notable features of the Crimes Act 1961 are that the maximum penalty for indecency between males, whether consensual or not, was two and a half times greater than that in England during the entire eighty-two years that the offence existed; and that Sections 135 and 139 introduced the concept that a woman could commit a sexual offence against another female, consent being no defence.

UNSUCCESSFUL ATTEMPTS AT LAW REFORM: 1961–1983

Before 1961 was out, calls were made for law reform, primarily as a civil liberties issue, led, perhaps unexpectedly, by the New Zealand Methodist Conference.[4] The New Zealand Howard League for Penal Reform added a secular voice, endeavouring to promote the recommendations of the Wolfenden Report[5] by direct pressure on the Minister of Justice through 1963 and 1964,[6] and successfully recruiting the support of the National Council of Women.[7] But then a more sinister note was sounded.

On January 24, 1964, six youths had, by their own later admission, queerbashed Charles Aberhart in Hagley Park in Christchurch, resulting in his death. On May 11 all six youths were found not guilty of the manslaughter charge, a verdict that passed almost without comment in the press.[8] The murder led to the first attempt by gay people to work for law reform, through the formation in 1964 of a Legal Subcommittee of the first gay club, the Dorian Society, founded the previous year. Its members joined forces with churchmen, professional people, and academics to promote a Wolfenden-style[9] reform. This informal group called a public meeting in Wellington in April 1967 to launch a Wolfenden Association, though what emerged was the New Zealand Homosexual Law Reform Society (NZHLRS). By July, a constitution had been approved and the first officers elected, in an atmosphere of some optimism just a week or so after the British reform.

The first political move made by the NZHLRS was a petition to Parliament, signed by a bevy of prominent and respectable citizens and presented in October 1968. The petition failed, and when the Chairman of the Petitions Committee, Mr. G. G. Grieve, reported its No Recommendation back to Parliament on November 8, he concluded with a personal outburst: "Speaking personally, I believe the practice of homosexuality is revolting. We all stand for certain moral principles, and the legalizing of homosexuality would indicate to society that we do not really condemn homosexual behaviour."[10]

Following the failure of the petition, a period of lobbying and political consciousness-raising ensued. By mid-1971 the annual conferences of both the National and the Labour parties had passed remits favouring reform, encouraging the NZHLRS to believe that pressure for a government reform measure was now politically possible. Its approaches to the Minister, Sir Roy Jack, were, however, roundly rejected.[11]

Progress had to wait until the election of another Labour government in 1972. The new Minister of Justice, Dr. Martin Finlay, personally favoured reform but made it clear to an NZHLRS deputation in April 1973 that a government measure was unlikely and that a private member's Bill, subject to a free vote in accord with conscience not party lines, offered the most promising avenue of progress. Even here there were problems as Prime Minister Norman Kirk, strongly opposed to reform, effectively blocked introduction of such a Bill from any member of the Labour Government. Eventually, opposition member, Venn Young, introduced a Bill on Wolfenden lines in 1974.

The procedure with Bills in the New Zealand Parliament, which is unicameral, is that they are debated at introduction (First Reading) and then referred to a Parliamentary Select Committee for study. The Committee can amend the Bill, but generally does not do so where matters of conscience are concerned. The Bill is then reported back to the House, and goes to a Second Reading debate which deals with the principles of the Bill. If it survives the critical vote at the end of the Second Reading debate it goes to the Committee Stages, where a Committee of the whole House analyses it clause by clause. There is a further vote when the Bill as amended is reported back to the House from the Committee, and if it survives that, it goes to a Third Reading debate. If it passes a final vote, it becomes law. There are a number of fences at which it can fall.

Venn Young's Crimes Amendment Bill survived the First Reading and went to Select Committee where the age of consent was reduced from twenty-one to twenty. At the Second Reading on July 4 1975, with over a quarter of the MPs absent from the debating chamber, the Bill was lost by 34 to 29.[12]

The early 1970s saw important changes.[13] Gay liberation groups sprang up, mainly on university campuses, starting with Auckland in March 1972. They, and other lesbian and gay groups, questioned, at times vociferously, the validity of the NZHLRS commitment to the simple Wolfenden reform, and of its willingness to compromise to some extent on the age of consent to make progress. The growing strength and confidence of the movement manifested itself in many ways. In 1977, a number of groups joined forces as the NGRC. The NGRC included the NZHLRS, which was not a gay organization but had had and would continue to have a significant gay membership. It was in an environment following a decade of frustrated law reform effort, witnessing a powerful burgeoning of lesbian and gay political initiative, and in which a radical NGRC and a civil libertarian NZHLRS co-existed in varying degrees of unease, that the Resource Centre, in time the LGRRC, was founded.

Late in 1979 a retiring Labour MP, Warren Freer, indicated his interest in introducing a reform Bill, and held consultations with the NZHLRS and the NGRC. He initially agreed an age of consent at sixteen but later opted for twenty as what he thought Parliament was likely to accept. His refusal to adopt an equal age of consent led to opposition from the gay community and the Freer Bill (version 1) was scuttled. It surfaced again in 1980 with a suggested age of eighteen, Freer having continued negotiations with NZHLRS, ignoring the NGRC, which had the previous year declared two criteria for the acceptability of new legislation: equality in the age of consent and protection against discrimination. NGRC opposition to Freer's Bill renewed once it was known what was afoot. On June 20, 1980, Freer announced in Parliament that he was abandoning the Bill.

Meanwhile the NGRC had asked a group of gay lawyers in Auckland to draw up a law reform measure. The Equality Bill was devised by the first Auckland Gay Task Force (later the Equality Bill Campaign independent of the NGRC, which broke up in 1983) and was worked on between 1980 and 1983. However, the small group of men who drafted this promising initiative had not obtained the support of the lesbian community, who found grave deficiencies in the Bill, and the intending sponsor, Labour MP Fran Wilde, dropped the Bill in late 1983.

THE WILDE BILL CAMPAIGN, 1985–1986

The election of July 4, 1984, returned Labour to power. Fran Wilde became junior government whip. Still interested in promoting a homosexual law reform measure, she began discussion with gay community leaders late in 1984. After going through some sixteen drafts to secure wide support from the lesbian and gay community, her Homosexual Law Reform Bill was introduced on March 8, 1985, by a healthy margin of 51 to 23. The Bill met the objectives of the political gay movement; it gave an equal age of consent (sixteen) and provided for the Human Rights Commission to deal with complaints of discrimination on the grounds of sexual orientation in areas of employment, accommodation, and access to goods and services. It was generally assumed that the Bill would go through with only minor fuss in a few months.

A bipartisan group of MPs immediately launched a campaign against the Bill, forming an uneasy alliance with the religious right. They began to tour the country whipping up sectarian hatred and religious bigotry. The opponents' principal strategy was a national petition against reform, whose administration was in the hands of the Salvation Army and an organization founded by millionaire business-man Keith Hay. One of his prominent visiting "experts" was the Rev. Lou Sheldon of the California Traditional Values Coalition (CTVC) who later produced the anti-gay hate videos *The Gay Agenda* and *Gay Rights, Special Rights*. Its original target was a million signatures (New Zealand's total population was just over three million) in three months. When the target was not met, the time was extended, and eventually 850,000 signatures were claimed. When the claim was examined by the Justice and Law Reform Select Committee, it was exposed as a massive fraud and, after debate in Parliament, decisively rejected.

Support for the Bill was widespread.[14] An important early development was the formation of Heterosexuals Unafraid of Gays (HUG). HUG combined with Gay Task Force and Campaign for Homosexual Equality to form the Coalition on the Bill (COB). It was obvious that the campaign would be a long one and, as such, had to incorporate mass support. COB organized public meetings, marches, and other events, all designed to attract large numbers. These public activities were very important in the growth of public support. Similar groups sprouted in other New Zealand cities. The LGRRC became an increasingly vital asset: support service, research centre, creator, and producer of educational and publicity materials.

The anti-reform elements coalesced into an organization called the Coalition for Concerned Citizens, which produced a booklet full of homophobic nonsense.[15] At the height of the campaign, the booklet was sent to all New Zealand libraries, and yet the Gay Task Force rebuttal,[16] which thoroughly discredited it, is found in only a few libraries.[17] The main weapon of the anti-gay forces was, however, the petition, and its failure was an important blow to them.

It was evident from the very start of the campaign that AIDS would be used against the gay community and that, to keep control, public attention would have to be focussed on AIDS in a constructive way. We were in the fortunate position of being one of the last western countries to be infected, and to have a sufficiently coherent gay political movement and communication system to organize the start of a health camapaign in the gay community fully two years before officials of the Department of Health could come to grips with the problems. The AIDS crisis furnished another, urgent reason why law reform was needed at once.

After it passed its Second Reading late in 1985, the Bill went to the Committee stages. Interest still centred on the age of consent and the Human Rights Commission Act amendments. The numbers favouring an equal age of consent and the numbers rejecting the Bill as a whole were close. The small number of "moderates" who favoured a discriminatory age of consent (mostly eighteen) thought that tactical voting would secure the compromise they sought. An amendment to raise the age to twenty was easily defeated, as was the compromise of age eighteen because, ironically, it was voted against by both of the large blocks. If the opposing block had voted with the moderates on the compromise and effected a change in the age of consent, the gay movement was committed to sinking the Bill. When the crucial vote was taken on the age of sixteen, most of the moderates voted against it, but Fran Wilde had calculated the numbers very carefully, and the clause passed. The anti-discrimination provisions were lost altogether, and so it was a truncated, decriminalization measure that finally passed the Third Reading on July 9 1986. The news was immediately relayed to Copenhagen where our delegate at the International Lesbian and Gay Association, Miriam Saphira, was able to announce it. The Homosexual Law Reform Act came into effect on August 8, having received the seal of the Governor General on July 11.

FIRE! FIRE!

The night of September 11, 1986, barely two months after the successful culmination of the law reform campaign, brought two arsonists to Boulcott Street. The contents and the premises of the LGRRC went up in flames. Arson is ugly violence. This arson was especially shocking in the euphoria following reform. Worse, the LGRRC had been an integral part of two campaigns that had given the gay and lesbian community sustained public prominence and had engendered a strong positive sense of political identity. The fire evidenced a destructive desire to violate that identity.

Here is the administrator's description of that night as he reported it to the LGRRC trustees a few days after the fire:

I left the Centre at about 10:00 . . . . When the next door neighbour returned home about 11:00 the front door was shut, but the intruders may already have been in the building by then. The fire was noticed soon afterwards, when residents smelled smoke and the arsonists were seen in the building before they fled. There were two young men about 18–20 who looked "very straight" according to Carol, a resident who saw them. She said they looked "like christians." After the fire was located the residents fought it with buckets of water and a hose (which wasn't working) before the brigade arrived. The brigade did a very good job, using powder extinguishers and some water, and their efforts reduced the damage considerably. . . . I was called to the scene just after midnight by a friend who happened to be in town. When I arrived about 12:20 the fire was out. I made a preliminary statement to a policeman and a preliminary inspection to determine the damage.[18]

The intruders, who incidentally had defecated in the stackroom and daubed "FAG" on the floor in Twink (white correcting fluid), used some recent issues of *Campaign Australia*—and perhaps cleaning fluid as an accelerant—to start fires in half a dozen places. Most, fortunately, did not do much damage; the worst was the fire fuelled by the bean bags and armchair.

Much of the furniture was badly damaged by the fire itself as were ephemera and other materials stored in one corner. Outright losses were remarkably few; charred edges were most common, while soot and smoke damage was fairly widespread. The filing cabinets protected the archival papers well, though one collection of archival material relating to the involvement of Campaign for Homsexual Equality (CHE) in the recent law reform campaign was largely destroyed. Much vulnerable material (photos, cassettes, and the like) was stored well away from the seat of the fire. In addition, despite the best efforts of the Fire Service, parts of the collection got wet. Some of the damage was indelible and can be seen in and on papers, pamphlets, and so forth still in the archives, which acquired, in addition, a rather macabre exhibit as a consequence of the blaze. It is described thus in the report: "The heat from the fire above the stacks can be imagined from the fact that a plastic lampshade above the bookstack melted and enveloped two books below it like a large jellyfish. This has been collected as an artifact."

The Alexander Turnbull Library, which has traditionally helped libraries and archives that suffer fire or flood damage, provided space (and security) in its premises in Courtenay Place, in Wellington, which were being evacuated as a new building in Molesworth Street (as it happens, a mere stone's throw from Parliament Buildings) was occupied. As the National Librarian acknowledged in a letter of support:

Any action which aims to destroy collections of the national record is unjustifiable, more so when a small collection with unique material is involved. These small collections, such as the Centre's, are part of the wider collections of New Zealand's social, political and economic history. Because of the way material is acquired, frequently through donation, and the nature of items and content, often in manuscript form and confidential, such collections form a unique resource of value to contemporary and future researchers.[19]

A team of people evacuated filing cabinets and boxes of damaged material to that site where they were to remain for almost a year during the cleaning, drying, sorting, and re-organising that followed. Other, undamaged materials were stored in Roger Swanson's garage and in the suburb of Newtown at the Awhina Centre,[20] Wellington's HIV/AIDS counselling and information centre. The NZAF also assisted by making a staff member available to help with the cleanup. But it would be August 1987 before the collections were all re-assembled in one location.

THE LGRRC COLLECTIONS

What was imperiled by the arson?[21] Victoria University's Stout Research Centre, in a letter of support in the wake of the fire, described the LGRRC as holding "a significant place among the educational and archival centres both in Wellington and in the country as a whole." Since 1983, the LGRRC had been a member of the Archives and Records Association of New Zealand (ARANZ). It concurred, in another letter of support, that the collections comprised "a community-based archive of national importance."

Most of the records of lesbian and gay life in New Zealand before the 1960s have perished. No lesbian or gay organizations existed before 1963, and the community was largely invisible. Unpublished diaries and letters were suppressed or destroyed, undoubtedly to conceal gay identities. Unwritten gay folklore was lost as death diminished the community. Apart from a few figures in the arts and literature, most are invisible; and even known literary gays, such as Katherine Mansfield, Sir Hugh Walpole, Frank Sargeson, and James Francis Courage, are not widely known as gay writers. That the open acknowledgment of their sexuality is still controversial became apparent with the preparation of a substantial literary anthology on gay writing in New Zealand: "As late as 1995 Sargeson's homosexuality was coterie information, to be carefully screened from a public assumed to be ignorant and prejudiced. Charles Brasch's literary executor, Alan Roddick, denies hotly to this very day that Brasch's work can be read in a homosexual context. In fact he refused pointedly to allow Brasch's poetry to be included in this volume."[22] There remains a sense of indelicacy in presuming to discuss their sexual orientation in relation to their creative work. For more ordinary gay people, information is even more meagre, largely limited to the distortions of the newspaper press.

One antidote to the negative image presented in published material available to the general public, an image that nurtures and feeds off homophobia, was the growth through the 1970s and beyond of gay and lesbian commercial publications and communications networks. Another was for the community itself to present a fair account of gay and lesbian history and culture. That was why the LGRRC was necessary.

In the eight years leading up to the arson attack, the Centre collected on the principle that "if we do not get it now, we may not even get a second chance." As well as archives and personal papers, the LGRRC collected books, magazines and newspapers, photographs, memorabilia, and ephemera. Audiotapes include early meetings of the NZHLRS, and oral histories of gay people in New Zealand, delicate and sensitive work undertaken in cooperation with specialists in oral history.

Ephemera, often clandestinely produced, embrace posters, stickers, hand-outs, throwaways, banners, badges, cards, and other items not intended by their creators for long-term survival. They tell us much about social events and political concerns, as do the newsletters of the many short-lived political and social groups. Study of these newsletters over the years shows the changing concerns of groups and the communities they represent, the trend being away from the venting of political anger to promoting civil rights, counseling, and community welfare concerns.

The LGRRC fostered close links with *Pink Triangle*, the lesbian and gay community newspaper. The collection of magazines built up on exchange by *Pink Triangle* was deposited with the LGRRC and incorporated into the collection, along with review copies of books sent to the paper. At the time of the fire, some 500 magazine titles, ranging from odd solitary issues to sizable runs, were held along with numerous magazine articles and newspaper clippings.

The LGRRC collections included The Jack Goodwin Collection, a collection of some 1,300 books and pamphlets developed around a substantial donation of books from the estate of Jack Goodwin, long-time Secretary of the NZHLRS and indefatigable gay campaigner. Most of the books in the collections were of overseas origin, though New Zealanders were producing significant writing including a study of lesbian mothers,[23] of gay men who marry,[24] and a volume of short stories.[25] Bibliographic control of the printed collections presented unique problems because of the negative bias of conventional classification schemes and subject terminology. Consequently, like other lesbian and gay archives and libraries, we were obliged to devise something to suit our special character.[26]

One of the functions for which the LGRRC was originally set up was the organization and preservation of the archives of the NGRC and other groups. By 1986, it held the archival records of about eighty New Zealand organizations, many contained in a slim folder but a number of them very substantial indeed. They included those of the New Zealand Homosexual Law Reform Society, the National Gay Rights Coalition, the Gay Task Force, the Pink Triangle Publishing Collective, and the AIDS Support Network. Together these papers were contained in twenty-two filing cabinet drawers. Some 600 letters, personal archives of several individuals, and about 120 manuscripts were the remaining components of the collections.

THE AGREEMENT WITH THE ALEXANDER TURNBULL LIBRARY

The LGRRC trustees had always thought that finance and location were the two problems to be solved in finding a new home for the collections. The fire added security to the list in no uncertain terms. In practical terms, the issue was how to ensure that ownership and control of the collections could be preserved consistently with robust security in a location to which lesbians and gay men could have reasonably easy access for research and study. The solution the trustees eventually favoured was to establish a formal legal trust to provide for future secure ownership and responsibility for the collections, and to lodge them in the Alexander Turnbull Library.

Alexander Horsburgh Turnbull (1868–1918) was a nineteenth-century bachelor bibliophile.[27] A homosexual of means living in a colonial society in which an openly homosexual life was impossible, he poured his sexual energy—there is no trace anywhere that he ever had sex in his life—and, no doubt, paternal instinct into book collecting. At the time of his death his collection numbered some 55,000 books. In a codicil to his will signed just a few months before his death,[28] Turnbull bequeathed "to His Majesty the King all my Library comprising my printed books pamphlets engravings charts manuscripts sketches maps photographs plans and pictures as and to constitute a Reference Library in the City of Wellington for the use and reference of persons and students interested in the subjects specialised in the said Library"; he further stipulated that it must not be lent or divided but be kept together "as the nucleus of a New Zealand National Collection."

The Turnbull Library (it did not become the Alexander Turnbull Library until October 1921) was originally housed in his house on Bowen Street until 1972. The Library was incorporated into the National Library established under the National Library Act 1965, but preserved its own identity as a research library. By the mid-1980s, it was spread between seven different buildings; its holdings were reassembled, in 1987, in a modern National Library building in Thorndon.

Community support for the agreement was sought and forthcoming at the National Lesbian and Gay Conference held in Christchurch at Easter in 1988; the motion passed was:

THAT this conference supports the agreement in principle made between the Trustees of the Lesbian and Gay Rights Resource Centre and the Management of the Alexander Turnbull Library for the future accommodation of, and access to, the Lesbian and Gay Archives of New Zealand.

The agreement was duly signed on March 30 1988, and formally announced on April 5, the whole collection of materials which was the subject of the agreement having been renamed the Lesbian and Gay Archives of New Zealand (LAGANZ). Rachel Barrowman, in her history of the Turnbull, notes:

In 1988 the Lesbian and Gay Archives of New Zealand were established when the research collection of the Lesbian and Gay Rights Resource Centre, whose offices had been damaged in an arson attack two years before, were transferred to the Turnbull Library. Ownership and control over access to the collection remained with the resource centre trustees, while two Turnbull staff members were appointed its honorary curators.[29]

It was, however, to be many more months before the task of restoring the collections and getting them into a state that would permit regular access was complete.

In broad terms, the agreement was that the LAGANZ collection would be permanently housed in the Alexander Turnbull Library, would retain its integrity as an independent collection, would be cared for by curators appointed by the trustees, and would remain in the ownership of the LGRRC trust on behalf of the gay and lesbian communities. Sara Knox and Phil Parkinson were appointed the first Honorary Curators of the LAGANZ collections. They and their successors have, in accordance with the terms of the agreement, sole discretion over issues of access to the collections and are accountable to the trust in its exercise. The collections are accommodated at 13.5°C and 40% relative humidity in a monitored environment with swipe card access.

Sharon Dell, Turnbull's Keeper of Collections who signed the agreement on behalf of the library, commented in a press release on April 5: "These collections form a unique and valuable range of research materials on the lesbian and gay movement, and we are pleased to be able to help a significant social movement to preserve its records under conditions of access which protect the often sensitive personal information such records contain."

The terms of such an agreement obviously are crucial, because they define the safe harbour to which the LAGANZ collections were brought, so we have reproduced in full the document, as it currently applies, in an Appendix to this chapter. On September 3, 1992, a revised agreement with the Alexander Turnbull Library, confirming the substance of the very satisfactory arrangement that had been established four years earlier, was signed by a new trust, and we turn next to its genesis.

THE ESTABLISHMENT OF THE LAGANZ TRUST

The curators and trustees had begun what was to be the lengthy task of reconstructing the trust into a form appropriate to the collections' changed circumstances. Concensus eluded them, and so for about four years the LAGANZ collections continued to be the responsibility of the informal LGRRC trust. The shape of the new trust was finalized in 1992. The purpose and identity of the LAGANZ trust continued the spirit of its predecessor. The original objectives were amplified in the light of intervening experience and now read:

- The provision of an archival repository for the personal papers of lesbians and gay men, the archives of lesbian and gay organisations and for related documents of historical interest
- The provision of an advisory service to assist lesbian and gay organisations to preserve and organise their archives
- The active collection, preservation and making available for creative use of the historical and cultural records of lesbians and gay men
- The advancement of learning and research through the facilitation of access to historical, cultural and sociological documents on the subjects of human sexual orientation, behaviour and identity
- The promotion of a supportive social environment for lesbians, gay men and their families and the promotion of the health of lesbians and gay men
- The facilitation of public education to promote wider understanding of sexual orientation and identity, and in particular to combat prejudices against people stigmatised on account of their sexual orientation or identity

And so the remaining three LGRRC trustees, acting as settlors, transferred the LGRRC assets—the collections and some funds—to a new Lesbian and Gay Archives of New Zealand Trust which was created by deed on February 24 1992. Continuity between the original informal LGRRC trust and its formal successor was assured in that two of the settlors became members of the new trust board, while the third, initially Administrator of the NGRC Resource Centre, then LGRRC trustee and administrator of the LAGANZ collections before the establishment of the LAGANZ trust, was appointed Honorary Curator under the new trust board.

The frustrations of the preceding four years seemed to be over, but that proved to be not entirely so. In August 1992 the new trustees resumed application to the Inland Revenue Department (IRD) to grant the trust charitable status so that supporters have the option to claim the relevant benefits when filing their income tax returns. A draft set of rules for the proposed trust had been sent to the IRD as early as October 1989 and there filed in the mistaken belief that they were the actual rules; the application for charitable status was declined in March 1990. Further confusion in the correspondence with the IRD coupled with the inability of the LGRRC trustees to agree on a revised set of rules meant that no further action was taken until 1992.

A response to the August application did not come until April 1993, notwithstanding three followup letters. This response agreed that the objects of LAGANZ were indeed charitable in nature, but reiterated its previous comment that we did not meet the "public benefit test." The sticking point was the curatorial discretion, standard professional practice in dealing with archival documents, personal information, and fragile historical records, to approve or decline access to the collections. This was deemed an impediment to access, which precluded the "public" from benefit. Efforts were made, in an ongoing exchange of correspondence, to clarify the nature of curatorial authority, with the Acting Chief Librarian of the Alexander Turnbull Library writing to support our point that the matter was one of normal professional practice and no impediment to public access. Successive treasurers continued efforts into 1994, and it was not until July that the IRD's review of our application finally found favorable issue. Charitable status, for income tax purposes, had been granted.

A further confused situation had to be untangled when the trust faced up to its final legal commitment, that of registering the trust as a charitable trust, a legal process quite distinct from that of obtaining charitable trust status for the purposes of the Income Tax Act. Once again the Library provided positive support, this time in the form of the good offices of its solicitor, and the registration processes were completed in mid-1995.

HARBOUR VIEW

In Wellington, as in many towns and cities on New Zealand's seaboard, a harbour view is synonymous with having a highly prized location. LAGANZ has enjoyed just such a location since 1988, and has flourished. In the ten years that have elapsed since the arson,[30] the general picture is one of a threefold even fourfold growth in most areas of the collection. In 1996, the collections contain approximately 4,500 catalogued items. Perhaps one of the most heartening statistics is that we now have archival records from about 440 groups and organizations, some of which are very substantial. But the small folders are, in their own way, just as important, for they may be all that stands between a group and oblivion. The manuscript collection has grown to about 450, and the few dozen posters of a decade ago now number in excess of 450. The ephemera and memorabilia have increased in diversity as much as in quantity. Our video and audio recordings have been added to, including oral history tapes, and we also hold some film footage. This means that some of our collections are stored in a variety of ways over and above conventional shelving. Nonetheless, the LAGANZ collections now occupy some 247 metres of shelving. Full reprographic services are available through the National Library.

In 1993, the unfinished business of human rights protection was brought to a conclusion when the passage of the Human Rights Act 1993 conferred a substantial measure of statutory anti-discrimination protection, one of the objectives of the 1985 Bill and a principle of the gay movement since 1981. LAGANZ was crucially involved in that campaign just as the LGRRC had been with the campaign of 1985 and 1986.[31]

Our resources were drawn on for a celebratory purpose in 1996. The tenth anniversary of the passage of Fran Wilde's Homosexual Law Reform Bill was marked in Wellington by a fortnight of celebrations, coordinated through the Wellington Gay Task Force under the slogan "Ten Years Out." The fair included a concert and a HUG reunion, a video and drag show, a special church service, a conference for workers in education and a couple of panel discussions, a Magical History bus tour, a commemorative Gay BC radio program and a dinner to honour Fran Wilde (who has since left politics). The celebrations were officially opened by openly gay MP Chris Carter, who also hosted a reception for hundreds of lesbians and gay men and supporters from HUG and NZHLRS in Parliament itself.

The official opening of the "Ten Years Out" program took the form of an official opening of "Two Years of Fury: The Homosexual Law Reform Campaign 1984–1986," a public exhibition presented by LAGANZ in the Victoria University Law School. This was the first display we had mounted outside the National Library building, and the law school's exhibition area in the recently refurbished Old Government Buildings was attractive and readily accessible. Admiring comments were offered on the variety, extent, and interest of the exhibits, and on the professionalism of their immaculate presentation. This reflects great credit on our curators and their many helpers, who included more than a few members of the Library's staff with their specialist skills. The Honorary Curator compiled, initially in serial form through the pages of our newsletter,[32] and then as a stand-alone pamphlet at the exhibition,[33] a diary of significant events leading up to the reform. The exhibition was extended into a third week by demand, and provided a unique opportunity to increase awareness of the existence and value of our collections. Acknowledgement of a different kind came at the close of 1996 when Phil Parkinson was given the inaugural Gay Association of Professionals (GAP) Award. The award bears the citation: "Community Award in establishing and maintaining the Lesbian and Gay Archives of New Zealand over 15 years."

The trust board and the curators continue to meet challenges concerning the collections. It has taken time, with the inevitable resignations along the way as people's commitments change, to build up the board of trustees to its full complement of eight. The trustees are beginning to explore systematically how their role might best be developed. A more coordinated effort to publicize the archive and to attract deposits of material before they are lost is a priority. The trust is endeavouring to encourage and extend a national network of supporters, called Friends of LAGANZ, partly for financial security but also to cement close contact between the archive and the community it serves. With a current financial membership of fifty-five we have a long way to go to reach the 100 Friends we set our sights on. But none of these and other challenges originate out of the agreement or our wider relationship with the Alexander Turnbull Library. On the contrary, we are able to develop new plans and aspirations for the future from our safe harbour.

APPENDIX: THE AGREEMENT DOCUMENT

Agreement between the Lesbian and Gay Archives of New Zealand Trust Board (the Board) and the Alexander Turnbull Library (the Library) concerning the collection of materials known as the Lesbian and Gay Archives of New Zealand

1) This agreement supersedes the "Agreement between the Trust Board of the Lesbian and Gay Rights Resource Centre and the Alexander Turnbull Library" dated the 30th day of March, 1988 signed for the Trust by Phil Parkinson and for the Library by Sharon Dell.

2) The Board and the Library confirm that:

 (i) the collection of materials forming the collection known as "The Lesbian and Gay Archives of New Zealand" and comprising archives, personal papers, published books, serials and pamphlets, tape cassettes, ephemera, photographs and curios shall be permanently housed within the Alexander Turnbull Library under the care of an Honorary Curator appointed by the Board.

(ii) the Lesbian and Gay Archives of New Zealand remain the property of the Board.

(iii) the Board shall continue to be entirely responsible for the acquisition, processing, cataloguing and conservation of the collection. The Library will accept deposit of additions to the principal collection once processing is completed.

(iv) the Lesbian and Gay Archives of New Zealand will be maintained as a physically distinct collection or collections, not physically integrated with the collections of the Alexander Turnbull Library, but the precise location of the collection or its constituent parts within the building shall be subject to arrangements agreed from time to time between the Board and the Library.

(v) the Chief Librarian of the Alexander Turnbull Library, or the Chief Librarian's nominated representative, may attend meetings of the Board with the right to speak but not the right to vote, and the Board shall not hold itself as having the right to make any determination which binds the Library without the assent of the Chief Librarian or the Chief Librarian's nominated representative.

(vi) the Honorary Curator appointed by the Board shall have responsibility for maintenance of the collection and the provision of access thereto, including the retrieval and reshelving of materials from the collections and the provision of reference and research services to users of the collection upon the same terms as for other collections of the Alexander Turnbull Library and upon the same basis as other reader services provided by the Library.

(vii) the Honorary Curator shall have the sole discretion, exercised under the authority of the Board, to approve or to decline access by specific persons to specific documents in the collections consistent with the need to safeguard conditions of deposit agreed between depositors and the Board, and this discretion shall not be overruled by any discretion of the Chief Librarian or the Chief Librarian's representative.

(viii) use of materials in the collections for purposes of exhibition or loan shall be subject to the discretion of the Honorary Curator. The Library may provide advice concerning the exhibition or loan of items from the collection but shall not be held responsible for any loss or damage occurring to any items while off the Library's premises.

(ix) the Library shall provide reader accommodation for users of the collection during its normal opening hours in its Manuscripts and Archives Reading Room on the same basis as for other materials used in that reading room and subject to the Reading Room rules. The Honorary Curator shall maintain a readers register which every user of the collection shall be required to sign at each visit. The Library shall provide a workspace for the Honorary Curator to use while preparing material. The Library shall grant the Honorary Curator security access to stack areas in which the collections are housed.

(x) photocopying and photography of the materials in the collection shall be at the discretion of the Honorary Curator, and the reprographic service arrangements and charges of the Alexander Turnbull Library shall apply. Reproduction fees from photocopying or from photography shall accrue to the Alexander Turnbull Library unless prior alternative arrangements are agreed between the Honorary Curator and the Chief Librarian. Copying, in all cases, shall comply with the provisions of the Copyright Act and shall be subject to such provisions as are necessary in the view of the Honorary Curator to protect the material from physical damage in the copying process.

(xi) maintenance of the catalogues and other records of accessions and the preparation of inventories, indexes and other collection guides shall be the responsibility of the Honorary Curator and the catalogues and other collection guides shall be made available in the public area of the Manuscripts and Archives Section. Ownership and copyright in these collection guides remains with the Board.

(xii) any arrangements for the inclusion of bibliographic records or holdings records for the LAGANZ collections in the New Zealand Biliographic Network, in TAPUHI or other Alexander Turnbull Library databases, or in the National Register of Archives and Manuscripts shall be subject to explicit supplementary agreements made between the Board and the Library.

Signed in confirmation by:
Paul Raymond Smith,
Chairperson, LAGANZ Trust Board
Margart Calder,
Chief Librarian, Alexander Turnbull Library
Date: 3rd September 1992

NOTES

The authors acknowledge with appreciation the assistance and suggestions of Roger Swanson, one of the Curators of the LAGANZ collections.

1. Phil Nash, "Our place in history is assured," *Outfront* (Denver) 17 (February 1984).

2. It would take us too far afield to explore the development of the New Zealand AIDS Foundation, established in 1986. The interested reader is referred to Peter Davis (ed.), *Intimate details and vital statistics: AIDS, sexuality and the social order in New Zealand* (Auckland: Auckland University Press, 1996) especially Chapters 5 and 6, 84–119.

3. For further information on this and the next two sections, see: Phil Parkinson, "Strangers in paradise: God's own country and the situation for gay people in New Zealand," in *The second ILGA pink book: A global view of lesbian and gay liberation and oppression* (Utrecht series on gay and lesbian studies no. 12) 188, Utrecht, 163–74.

4. Minutes of the Annual Conference of the Methodist Church of New Zealand 1961, Christchurch, 94–96.

5. *Report of the Committee on Homosexual Offences and Prostitution* 1957, HMSO, Cmnd 247.

6. Arthur O'Halloran, "The law and homosexuality," *NZ Monthly Review* 4 (1964): 11–12.

7. "Homosexuality." Report of the Justice Committee, Auckland Branch, National Council of Women. *Woman's Viewpoint* 2, no. 4 (November 1963): 19, 35.

8. The Christchurch *Press* (12 May) and the *NZ Listener* (5 June) published editorials voicing disquiet; Gordon Troup made brief reference to the incident in his *Christchurch Star* column (May 21); Professor Ian Breward commented on the silence in the Presbyterian Church's *Outlook* (May 8, 1965) and reviewed the episode and its outcome in: "Hagley Park treatment," *Landfall* 74 (1965): 155–61; Phil Parkinson returned to the incident in: "The Hagley Park killing," *Pink Triangle* 51 (Summer 1984–85): 13.

9. The issues of a Wolfenden-style reform were traversed, inter alia, in Chris Parkin, "Limitations of criminal law," in R.S. Clark, ed., *Essays on New Zealand criminal law* (Wellington: Sweet & Maxwell, 1971), 28–46. It also lay behind a more popular essay: Chris Parkin, "The queer law," *Metropolis* 13 (June/July 1967), which was re-worked under the same title, *The Queer Law*, when published as the NZHLRS's first pamphlet in January 1968.

10. *Parliamentary Debates* 358 (1968) 2980–84; the report and its reception were reviewed by P. L. Reynolds, "Parliament and the law relating to homosexuality," *Comment* 11, no. 2 (November 1970): 12–16.

11. *NZHLRS Newsletter* 19 (September 1972) summarized events with extracts from the correspondence.

12. Chris Parkin, "Keeping the Wolfenden Report from the legislative door," *Landfall* 22, no. 2 (June 1978): 174–80.

13. Chris Parkin, "The Gay Rights Movement in New Zealand." A public lecture given at Victoria University on June 28, 1979 to mark the tenth anniversary of Stonewall, it was later published in *Salient*, the student newspaper, under the title "Worth Fighting For!" Part of the lecture gathered together samples of homophobia; at the time feeling was still running high over the New Zealand Government's willingness to offer public apology to Iran over an alleged death threat from New Zealand homosexuals. See: Chris Parkin, "Scapesheep?" *Comment* 8 (September 1979): 8–10.

14. Public opinion polls indicated that about 61 percent of the population favoured reform with about 37percent opposed. Most of the main churches supported reform, and there was a measure of support even within the ranks of the dissenters, the Roman Catholics, Salvation Army, and fundamentalists.

15. C. James Bacon (ed.), *The social effects of homosexuality in New Zealand* (Christchurch: Coalition of Concerned Citizens, 1985).

16. Gay Task Force (NZ), *Rebuttal of a handbook of homophobia* (Wellington: Gay Task Force, 1985).

17. Phil Parkinson, "Greater expectations: Services to lesbians and gay men," *New Zealand Libraries* 45, no. 5 (March 1987): 96.

18. Phil Parkinson, *Preliminary Report to the Trustees on the Arson Attack on the Centre,11 September 1986*, typescript, September 16, 1986.

19. Phil Parkinson," Greater expectations: Services to lesbians and gay men," *New Zea- land Libraries* 45, no. 5 (March 1987): 96.

20. Sadly, the Awhina Centre itself was damaged beyond repair by a fire on March 26, 1997. The building is to be demolished and the NZAF is looking for new premises.

21. An overview of the scope of the collections and of collecting activity before the fire is found in: Phil Parkinson, "Lesbian and gay archives in New Zealand: a minority gathers its own history," *Archifacts* (Bulletin of the Archives and Records Association of New Zealand) 4 (1984): 7–14.

22. Peter Wells and Rex Pilgrim (eds.), *Best Matse: Gay writing in Aotearoa New Zealand* (Auckland: Reed, 1997), 12; ironically, the anthology itself struck problems in securing permission from the Auckland Museum to reproduce, on the cover of the book, a historically valuable photograph, probably taken in the 1890s by pioneering photographer

Henry Winkelmann, of two men kissing. See Finlay MacDonald, "Stolen kisses," *Metro* (January 1997): 42–43.

23. Miriam Saphira, *Amazon Mothers* (Auckland: Papers Inc., 1984).

24. Michael W. Ross, *The homosexual married man* (London: Routledge & Kegan Paul, 1983).

25. Welby Ings, *Inside from the rain* (Auckland: Brookfield Press, 1983).

26. Phil Parkinson, ed., *Thesaurus of subject headings* (Wellington: LGRRC, 1984); Phil Parkinson, *GDC: Gay decimal classification—A classification scheme designed for use in a gay studies library* (Wellington: LGRRC, 1984).

27. In 1964 Eric McCormick was commissioned to write a biography of Turnbull to mark the Library's jubilee in 1970; it was not published until 1974: E. H. McCormick, *Alexander Turnbull: His life, his circle, his collections* (Wellington: Alexander Turnbull Library, 1974).

28. Rachel Barrowman, *The Turnbull: A library and its world* (Auckland: Auckland University Press, 1995) , 25; Barrowman cites the codicil, dated March 1, 1918, which is itself held in the Library's manuscripts and archives collection.

29. Rachel Barrowman, *The Turnbull: A library and its world* (Auckland: Auckland University Press, 1995), 195.

30. Chris Parkin, "Out of the ashes," *Friends of LAGANZ* (The Official Newsletter of the Lesbian and Gay Archives of New Zealand), 13 (December 1996) : 1, 3–6.

31. OUT LAW: *A legal guide for lesbians & gay men in New Zealand* (Auckland: Auckland Lesbian & Gay Lawyers Group, 1994).

32. Phil Parkinson, *Friends of LAGANZ* (The Official Newsletter of the Lesbian and Gay Archives of New Zealand) 8–11 (July 1995 – June 1996).

33. Phil Parkinson, *Reform retrospective: Key events in the homosexual law reform campaign and events leading up to the reform 1984–1986* (Wellington: Lesbian and Gay Archives of New Zealand, 1996).

Part Four

Owning Our Names: Gay Graduates

15

Destination Library

Donald H. Forbes

The *coda* precedes the body as I hurl myself into this profession. I cannot be associated with the next biological generation of librarians. I am middle-aged, a matured product of the rebellious, spoiled sixties. Preparing to enter the profession at a time when most have made their mark or have otherwise reconciled themselves, I bring with me overstuffed, antiquated luggage and a different perspective. My decision to become a librarian occurred serendipitously. It was based neither on plan, order, nor scholarship. The future has slapped me like the rebound of a rubber band upon the palm. It is far from what I had dreamed when, as a teenager who loved science fiction, I conjured aerodynamic, cylindrical air cars and other Walt Disney paraphernalia. I remember now that few had then thought of the social upheaval to come, only technological bliss. The nasty bedlam of the 1990s was impossible to imagine, then. And who cared? By the year 2000, I would have been a graying fifty-four.

LIKE A TRAIN

The sub-heading sounds like a bad song. I was born scared, my core composed and still laden today with the type of psychological baggage that Jung and Freud described. Recently I negotiated a long train trip. I boarded in the wee hours of the morning. The passengers were asleep. Scared, my heart was beating fast as though amphetamines thumped through my veins. Never having ridden a long-distance train, I knew nothing of train comportment or of the location of services. Could I smoke, and if so, where? How do the bathrooms work, and where are they? Where will I eat, and how will I obtain the food? Always the outsider, I found myself once again crouched up against a wall of new people; and as usual, I found apprehension to be more painful than the reality. This is exactly how I felt when I contemplated my future—full of fear and questions.

With cataloging class studies in satchel, I was reminded how one cannot smoke in libraries, either. Just read, I thought to myself, since you cannot smoke. Smokers are exiled, with no alternatives, to the out-of-doors, perhaps some anonymous entryway steps, or under side-door eaves. This is how morally liberal professionals like librarians treat those who do not match their utopian visions. Wonderful and blameless the public is, but please perform outside while we reform you. There are rules. I wonder how this could have happened, since rules were anathema to my generation.

When I boarded my train, lights were dimmed and I could not see well. A conductor, hushed and padding like a cat, led me to a seat beside a sleeping young lady and then vanished like a wraith. What now? This woman beside me was emitting visceral, frightful eructations of snorting. Worse, she had begun flailing her hands at some vision in her dreams.

I tried to read my cataloging material in the dark. I smiled: who in his right mind reads the *AACR2R* at all, like a novel, much less under these conditions? I was too hesitant to activate the little round overhead light for fear of awakening the entire car. Worse, what if I awakened this crumpled, uncomfortable woman beside me, who looked for all the world like a desiccated vulture, its talons flailing around its beak in the dark? I was on my own, wide awake in a dead world.

Just like my life, my ticket had been imprinted with my destination, but I could not interpret the computer-generated hieroglyphics. I had no assurance that I would arrive at the place I had aimed for. Were I lucky in that regard, how long would my journey really take? U.S. trains have terrible reputations, and the reservations desk had already informed me that the route would be circuitous. Just like interlibrary loan, I thought. I wondered if I was born to be a librarian. Who else would sit on a dark train thinking library thought to waylay fear? My mind wandering yet more, I decided that it had been far easier to reconcile with the outside world my life as a gay person than it had been to enroll in library school.

I myself did not wake the woman beside me. One of her own snorts did that. Before her eyes had opened, she fumbled for her purse and began shuffling through it for a cigarette. By using a little finesse, I thought I might be able to solve the smoking problem. "Where do you go to smoke those?" I asked. "Follow me," she cawed. And on the way to the lounge car, I saw the little closets trains use for bathrooms. Yet another problem had been solved. Somehow, I am reminded of those notorious municipal public library bathrooms that now house videotape monitors and toilets with no modesty panels in obeisance to family values if not slightly fascist views on sex. Flippantly, I imagine that sex in libraries might be good for the patron attitudes toward the library: at least sex makes the public think of libraries at all. I wonder if Pat Buchanan is aware of the large number of pornographic movies that contain scenes in libraries? There must be something sexy about libraries, a stereotype we librarians should nurture.

In the lounge car, I and my new friend smoked and talked. Did I exude gayness, or did my new vulture lady friend—just a nice bird, now—not care? For she spilled all. As casually as one might discuss a passion for chocolate, she told me about her breakup with her girlfriend, and how she was now on her way to Atlanta to start over. Having found that, occasionally, people east of the Mississippi find it interesting if one is from California, I told my new friend that I had lived in San Francisco. Alas, she was not impressed. She, too, had lived there, but rents were too high, she said, and she had left.

Scared people try to be autonomous, but another person had reassured me that I really existed in this place. This is how one wishes things could be, two strangers talking on a train. Why do both have to be alike for both to be comfortable? Studying for librarianship has given me a similar feeling. Once I was out to my classmates, the other men distanced themselves, though many of the women seemed not to care.

My new friend had inadvertently reassured me that I would, in fact, arrive in Alabama in one piece, sane. It would take too long, but I had ceased worrying about a diversion of the train. As a correlate, I also knew with certainty that I wanted to contribute to librarianship. My life could now remain on a branchless track, in contrast to my history of endless diversions. The anthropic principle behind my astrological chart had all along been ticking silently like a great brass machine. I remain on that train but now know that a penultimate stop will be at the library.

MY CHART

My astrologer had rotten bedside manners, exhibited by his delight in expressing to me how he had never seen such a tangled mess. A triumphant moment for the astrologer, his pronouncement threw me into a thick soup of depression lasting for months; but he was right. This chart was filled with tiny symbols, and this is supposed to be good. But these symbols were clotted together around a single point on the inside circumference of my life, like lymphocytes attacking a foreign cell. Each symbol, said the astrologer, represented a different talent. Your squares, said this self-styled mystic, were so crowded, one upon the other, that none could get enough breathing space to express itself. Mine was indeed a strong soul, he consoled, to have chosen such treacherous circumstances under which to apply an incarnation. Strong soul indeed! Since today I know that a wealth of little square talents serve a librarian quite handily. My chart had prepared me perfectly for cataloging, classifying, preserving, and otherwise providing access for those who have only a few strong expressible squares. Astrologers should be more imaginative, as I should have been myself.

A CONFUSED KID WHO THOUGHT HE WASN'T

Besides having been born scared, I had been born smart. From the age of four, I was to be a musician, although I probably could have been anything else except a practitioner in the hard sciences. I cannot think linearly (see discussion of planetary influences, above). Like many librarians, liberal arts were my forte.

My parents thought me to be a piano prodigy, and I agreed. They wanted me to be a great musician, because they thought the world was full of commonness and in need of their son. In my teenage years, when I discovered that I only liked to play the piano, not to practice it, I decided to be a great composer instead. I would be held in posterity by *New Grove's* and *Baker's* as one of the twentieth-century avant-garde leaders the likes of John Cage or Karlheinz Stockhausen. Those squares were acting up again. Who could have made a more practical decision?

We must now add shy to scared and smart. I know today that I had been using this weird modern music that I loved (and still do), because I knew everyone else hated it. The music represented the barrier between me and my social insecurities. Other boys did inconsequential boyish things while I, importantly, played the piano, wrote and taped my own weird music, and borrowed excessively from the excellent LP collection of the Pasadena Public Library.

Scared is the worst thing a composer can be. Composers must be politicians to become known, and in this I failed completely. A composer also needs to be an egoist, and in this, too, I floundered. Unconsciously attuned to multimedia, I also liked contemporary composers not only because they, too, were smart, but in addition to having often unpleasant personalities, the lot of them wrote about philosophy, art in general, and the society in which they lived. (These men and women had to write, since few could understand their music without verbal explanation). Multimedia was just beginning then, and my multimedia chart had already begun to affect my life. Since I had just boarded that dim train, I was unaware. I certainly was unaware of the multimedia nature of libraries, thinking them good mainly for borrowing recordings, though I could not help but to notice the book stacks and the quiet. Most people are unaware of it, but many music lovers, when otherwise engaged, like quiet. In those years, silence was enforced in the Pasadena Library, and today, despite new attitudes, libraries are still far quieter than the outside world. It is ironic indeed that, while a library is a bazaar of surprises, a simple, vocalized "Well, I'll be darned!" turns heads. We still produce a closeted environment.

COLLEGE

I made sure to reject or hide from my parents any acceptance letters from local schools. I intended to leave the plebeian Los Angeles suburbs for the Jerusalem of misfits, San Francisco. There was a small music conservatory there, and its only physical education requirement was a semester of Balkan folk dancing. San Francisco was a mistake but lots of fun. For two years after leaving home, I worked hard at being a genius, spilling Kerouakian tea that I drank from a glass upon my counterpoint assignments. My professors thought I was doing a good job of becoming a genius, too. (Today, I postulate that feel-good education had already started to develop). I made few friends during my five-year stay in San Francisco, save for two. Connie was a fellow composition student, an in-the-sanitorium-out-again schizophrenic lesbian ten years my senior whose singular qualities entranced me. Connie and I tried to make love once, because she perceived me to be small and thought perhaps with me she might like heterosexual sex. She therefore unwittingly helped me discover men in life outside of my imagination. The first was Mel, a magnetic, rather larcenous hippie. Upon meeting him, I jumped innocently and immediately into the fetid society of the Flower Children of Haight-Ashbury, their semi-acceptance of homosexuality, and the drug culture of both worlds. We stayed attached like mating barnacles for the next ten years. A metamorphosis had occurred, with the mad-contemporary-composer wall having been replaced by the crazy hippie wall. This was a natural transition; both allowed me to hide in rebellion.

I had a natural talent for getting high, and I quickly began to forget to make appearances at the Conservatory. A letter from the Director to my parents reminded me that I was supposed to be a college student, but efforts at reform from home were unsuccessful. I continued joyously to follow the instructions of Timothy Leary, The Jefferson Airplane, and The Doors. I dropped out and soon forgot to make appearances anywhere, including that train station check-in window where I should have obtained the ticket for my future. Such chores seemed so irrelevant at the time. It took me fifteen years to realize that my life needed rescue. It had become one of exceeding turmoil and confusion, relieved only by psychotropic drugs and booze.

BACK TO A CHART OF SORTS

The gears in that anthropic machine, slowed by the viscous inertia of my self, finally locked. My parents thought that my problems had been initiated by my hippie partner, whom they viewed as one of Satan's agents, embodied on the mundane plane to corrupt the innocent. Of course this was not the case. It was my fear that had been objectified. Who could know the cause? Upheavals continued, including a couple of blameless drug arrests. The coupling of myself and my hippie lover mercifully loosened over time, and I somehow managed to pick up two rather long-term accounting clerk jobs. Being smart, these were for me easy, boring daytime activities. Had I not drunk so much after five-o'clock, I would undoubtedly have become yet more insane. Worn out from being where I did not belong, I decided to resume my escape.

I took a job as a bartender in a sleazy gay beer bar on Colorado Boulevard in downtown Pasadena. The block of that street is one that TV viewers never see during the New Year's Day Rose Parade, when squishy, bland, sentimental announcers dressed in bulky headphones explicate from helicopters what viewers can plainly see for themselves. My new job supplied for three years an unbroken alcoholic haze punctuated by drugs. It led, quite literally, to eventual unemployment, abandonment, and homelessness. The Pasadena Public Library was two blocks down the street, but it now had a different significance. No longer was it the repository of all that music I had so loved. It was now the place where I sat in a reading area with a newspaper or magazine—anything I could obtain unobtrusively from the lobby—to escape the rain or to ease the agony of just being alive. Today, when discussions about public libraries and the homeless occur, I quite naturally sympathize with those who today are what I briefly once was.

SAVED BY A JOB HE LIKED

I began participating in a recovery program. I purged my corpus except for caffeine and cigarettes while coincidentally finding work I liked, manipulating bits and bytes for NASA's noted Jet Propulsion Laboratories (JPL), administrators of spacecraft probes like Voyager and Galileo. I have mentioned that I was smart, and I managed well despite my lack of formal computer education. The wall had now been replaced by work. Mine was a solitary job, ideal for the reflection needed for healing. It was thanks to the ensuing six years of work at JPL and associating with those stamped with formal education that I gained momentum to return to college and finish, of all things, that impractical music degree I had forsaken so long ago.

I recall a job posting for a librarian in one of NASA's special libraries. The minimum education requirement was an MLS. I wondered, Why on earth does it require a Master's degree just to be a librarian? And today I remember the Pasadena Library, its place in my life, and all the other libraries I have visited. Of course there was much more to librarianship than merely keeping things in order.

NOW THAT HE IS A GRADUATE . . .

We have seen what can happen when one cannot interpret a train ticket. I feel today that my once cavalier attitude about the future has all been to prepare me to be a librarian. Ultimately, all libraries are containers of life. The smallest of libraries are macrocosmic. I have accumulated personal experiences that could correspond to many classes of patrons. I have spent my private intellectual life in the humanities and fine arts, worked in business accounting, served and assuaged the multifarious, seedier side of the walk-in public, and serendipitously gathered computer knowledge and a smattering of science from the public sector. I recently received employment in a local community college library, with its wide range of patron types. I feel that my life corresponds to the reality my interviewers sensed when they chose me instead of another to be their reference assistant.

I hope to bring into the profession some of my own broad, hard-won liberal attitudes. Public service is my preference—to be out there in the fray of the living, to help. I feel that public and academic libraries must preserve history and fight for funds to continue collecting not only computer systems but the tangible representations of the output of all human endeavor that libraries have traditionally collected. It would be tragic indeed were published print to be treated in some nightmare future as realia. I feel that libraries can contribute to stabilizing a society that seems to be gagging on a continuous stream of vivisected sound bites. It seems to be swimming upstream to state the obvious palliative to information-age oversell: books can transmit connection just by feeling the grain of their pages. When members of a society are able to see that humanity can and has been just about anything imaginable, that makes its members tolerant of those who differ from them. A gay person like myself has a personal stake in this. Computer displays and printouts are miraculous tools for locating and transmitting information, but they are far from the ideal medium for producing the kind of nurturing environment we all would like. As Marshall you-know-who wrote long ago, "The medium is the message." To continue quoting, Jeffrey Hart, in the September 30, 1996, issue of *National Review*, remembered one of my college professors, who said, "History . . . is to a civilization what memory is to an individual, an irreducible part of identity."

Our health depends upon our diversity— "e pluribus unum," and all that. Today more than ever, there is a leaden mass hunkering on the "e pluribus" end of the lever of balance. While I realize that my effort can be only microscopic, I hope to help slide that weight just a little more toward the fulcrum of "unum."

Librarians are important. Robert Heinlein, that Mozart of science fiction, once postulated that librarians of the future would become the most essential people in the galaxy, for only they, because of their special skills, would have the ability to gather, organize, and provide access to the infinitely scattered keys to wisdom.

16

Social Responsibility and Acceptable Prejudice

Richard L. Huffine

Social responsibility and a sense of ethics are cornerstones of most professions and they have been mainstays of librarianship through perilous times. From the opening of social libraries in the eighteenth century to the conflict over intellectual freedom during the McCarthy era, librarians have been concerned with issues of access and freedom of thought. The advent of the electronic age, with its attendant litigious and complex social context, brings with it more subtle but no less challenging problems of interpretation. The current atmosphere of minority sensitivities and simplistic morality is not conducive to gay outreach or specialized lesbigay library services, yet from a professional point of view, it has never been more tantamount that public libraries do exactly that.

Now that the world of ideas is available from a desktop via the Internet, it appears possible to circumvent the librarian altogether. This technological development is especially attractive to individuals seeking information without the traditional human interaction that normally accompanies the provision of information. Easier, quicker access has its risks, however: information without context, and the lack of the librarian's leading hand toward appropriate levels of information. These are issues that the library profession, and particularly, the upcoming generation of librarians, will have to deal with as technology becomes even more pliable and tailored to individual tastes.

Lesbian and gay people are at least a part of that population seeking information without human interaction, or, if past attitudes are any guide, the possibility of social confrontation, and they may be best suited as a population to best benefit from the relative privacy afforded by technological advances in information delivery. For too long, the issue of how to provide information for lesbigays in the public library context without compromising dominant social mores has remained unasked and unanswered mainly because lesbigays themselves felt stifled and paralyzed, and did not demand it. It is always uncomfortable to approach someone different from oneself in some sensitive fundamental way (say, sexual orientation, but also race, or gender, or even sociopolitical orientation) for help, and this is especially true in libraries. Imagine the similar issues for a black or Hispanic patron who may fear librarians because of language differences, or the marked lack of these minorities at the reference desk.

I approach my career with the premise that lesbian and gay people exist, and their presence in society demands a presence in libraries. It is not so much that libraries need an advocate for each and every social concern so much as it needs validation for each person within its service community. The library profession can institutionalize this validation by reinforcing the principles behind access and freedom, and drawing a strong symbolic line between personal beliefs and public freedoms. Between a library's open shelves and the wealth of materials now being produced by and for lesbigay people, a comfortable balance between freedom and responsibility should be possible in every community.

I have gained these views from my education in library and information studies and from my personal life within libraries; not from courses in ethics and professional issues per se, but from open dialogue with future professionals of every type, from every conceivable social background. I have been the gay person in many people's lives, and that fact has allowed me to see my responsibility clearly. I see that my presence must be footnoted with the fact that I am gay. At times, this reality strikes fear in my heart. Since I was young, I have imagined myself being killed because of my sexuality. The image of my dead, beaten body is in my mind every time I come out to someone. It would be useful if librarians could imagine this scenario every time someone has the courage to ask for material on homosexuality in the library.

The first lesbigay issues paper presented within my library science curriculum was a presentation of the *Daddy's Roommate* controversy by a straight woman who simply could not believe the stir over the title. That student had no ideological axe to grind. Her perspective was one of a concerned citizen, not a person with any kind of personal agenda to forward. Librarians can reject any agenda from the left or right, but they find it impossible to reject dispassionate interests. Similarly, librarians find it difficult at best to reject co-workers who simply happen to be gay or lesbian. To see "my issue" explored in a library education class from a purely academic perspective opened my eyes to how anyone can serve a gay or lesbian community objectively.

Librarians approach the profession from both their personal perspectives and from the collective experience of their forbears. It is that collective voice that must be presented in the education of librarians, the voice that demands open dialogue and "liberal" policies. That voice can offer solutions to the current round of struggles over electronic property and privacy rights, electronic censorship, and unparalleled open access on the Internet.

The current era has already brought perspectives to bear on the access debate that will ultimately greatly change librarians' view of their work. The fact that librarianship is now a second or third career option for many professionals means that the workforce is becoming more mature in years. I have been greatly enriched by the views of my colleagues who represent the generation that matured in the 1960s and 1970s. By the same token, my eyes have been opened to the mysteries of Generation X. Having been reared in the rhetoric of Reaganomics, the social Darwinism of Wall Street, and the Me Generation, I see the evolution of information as a natural consequence of market forces rather than a mutant beast.

I have a real concern for what libraries will look like and whom they will serve in the new information age. If the idea of an "acceptable prejudice" against lesbigays in particular is allowed to persist in librarianship, as one library media pundit would have it, the future client base of libraries will surely dwindle; certainly the richness of the lesbigay perspective will be missing on the shelves, and the cultural heritage available in libraries will be impoverished by just that much. If lesbigay information is not available on the shelves, gays and lesbians will find or create a site where it will be accessible. I don't want public libraries of the future to be beset by the inadequacies of today's public health system, or stigmatized as serving only the lowest common denominator of sanitized customers. Libraries already face competition from retail vendors that are supplanting their venerable, expensive, and once-irreplaceable reference tomes with bits and bytes of coded information that can be downloaded in the home as stock quotes or gardening guides. The user-friendliness of this digital information often surpasses the approachability and retrieval speed of reference staff. As this information is further disseminated into deeper levels of the culture, librarianship will find itself less concerned with the identity (including potential sexual orientation) of their client base, and may find itself scrambling for new recruits as well. America Online has found a way to serve lesbigays, and so should libraries of all types.

A call from the library profession should be forthcoming to include open dialogue on any subject. The profession should send a resounding message that this profession values access to information more than it fears potential trouble. Whether our over-institutionalized library education system will ever adopt such an unequivocal stance again is doubtful, but I do believe it is possible to instill such a value without necessarily naming a course after it.

Lesbigay issues call our foundations into question, as does the changing face of the library profession, the emergence of new technology, and the continuing debates over funding. Finding a unified voice that tolerates diversity on each of these issues can only establish the profession more firmly in the future.

17

Out Publicly:
The Professional and Personal
of Gay Public Librarianship

John A. Barnett

Library school seemed like gay intellectual paradise to me. After years of unsplitting infinitives and feng shui-ing misplaced modifiers, I sheathed my editor's blue pencil and prepared to sharpen my mind. The decision to return to school as an adult had not come easily or quickly. After taking the age-old questions of "Who am I?" and "What am I going to do with my life?" to new depths of excessive rumination and discussion, I had very little confidence in my intellectual abilities. I wasn't even sure library work suited me—in fact, during the early stages of applying for library school, I also was applying to graduate history programs. With all the information gathering I'd done through the years as a newspaper reporter, however, as an editorial assistant at the Smithsonian Visitor Information Center, as a compiler of directories at the American Historical Association, and as an information specialist at the National HIV/AIDS Hotline, plus my natural bent toward intellectual eclecticism, librarianship seemed the best fit. From a gay perspective, libraries seemed to be nonthreatening, even inviting places—comfortable, uncompetitive, quiet. I was sure all librarians were devoted to intellectual pursuits, and devoid of corporate avarice, rampant egos, hypocrisy, and bureaucratic protocols.

In the midst of all this, surprising to me, I fell in love. I was a veteran of the Love Wars and the Sex Wars of the 1980s. I came out in 1980, so I had seen the glamour of gayness only briefly, watching it explode like the Hindenburg over the New Jersey of AIDS, fear, and hatred. I thought I was walking wounded, maybe even walking dead, at least emotionally. Up until the time I met my then-current lover, I didn't think I had any feeling left in me, above or below the neck. Now I rediscovered my ability to give love and found that I could receive it as well. Therefore, the stars in my favor, in library school I could be as out and open as I wanted to be about my sexual/affectional orientation. I didn't have to make a point about it, I didn't have anything to prove, and I didn't need to attract anyone's attention with it. In other words, for the first time in my adult gay life, I wasn't looking for anything or anyone special: I was just looking for me. I felt as though I was starting to become comfortable with myself. I could relax, at least in that part of my life. It was an incredibly stable period of my life, one that gave me the confidence to study, work, love, live, and excel.

Figuring out who I am has been a lifelong endeavor. So getting to a point where my homosexuality was manageable, where my life felt settled, and I was sure of who I was and what the expectations were, at least for a moment in time, was a sublime discovery. I'd found Shangri-La in my own little way. That's not to say my homosexuality didn't come up from time to time in graduate school, but it came up on my terms. I could write on gay topics and indirectly encourage others to do the same. I could bring up gay issues in discussions of evaluating reference works or providing public service. I could discuss my experience as an HIV/AIDS information specialist, make valid comparisons to librarianship, and not feel shunned or dismissed. I felt as though I didn't have to hide my mind and my thoughts.

However, none of my success and acceptance would have been possible without the example set by the faculty, who readily accepted my ideas, both gay and non-gay, for projects and papers. They encouraged me to see my ideas differently by relating their professional and personal experiences. My research methods instructor in particular guided me through statistics and helped me to develop a workable approach to surveying the lesbigay college student population. I owe my biggest debt of gratitude, however, to my departmental adviser and mentor, a gay man who had recruited me for a diversity scholarship based on my background statement. But more than that, he listened to me and heard me. The scholarship was more than financial reward; it was a symbol of the offer of a safe place to do the research and learning I had longed to do but had never found the encouragement or guidance to carry out.

For me the ultimate moment of this acceptance came not with the receipt of my first semester's grades, but with a thank-you from a fellow classmate. The woman, in her forties, always the well-dressed North Carolina suburbanite, seemed to have little in common with me. Yet after I presented my master's project in my research methods class, she pulled me aside to compliment me on the work I had done and the chances I had taken. "You did something special," she said. That meant more to me than she'll probably ever know. It represented for me personal and professional success, not in conventional terms, but in the truest form: satisfaction and acceptance.

Graduating from my library program and "suddenly" being faced with the desperate reality of unemployment changed my outlook, although I wasn't sure for a while just how. As I had tried to be during the application process for graduate school, I was as open as I dared to be about "my little secret"—a phrase indicative of my mood and perception of my status as a gay man in the working world. I stated on my resume and in my letter of application that I was interested in diversity issues and that this had included working on an HIV/AIDS service agency library project and on a research study on lesbigay college students. If the search committees who reviewed my papers didn't read "gay" there, then they just weren't paying attention. I was hoping they were paying attention and that they did care, but that they wouldn't count my homosexuality against me. I and classmates at six sites throughout North Carolina and Virginia had been assured by a library director of a well-known religious university that sexual orientation would not affect employment in an academic environment—a lofty but wishful sentiment, I later decided.

My experiences in interviewing at colleges and universities were overwhelmingly negative, cynical, and demoralizing events, like three-ring circus acts where I was the doped-up horse being made to jump through flaming hoops. No one seemed interested in me, my work, and my interests, which is what I had expected of the free environment of liberal education. Instead, repeatedly for entry-level positions I was told I didn't have enough experience or didn't have the right kind of experience.

My homosexuality came up once directly in an interview with a college president when he asked me the subject of my graduate research project. Despite my positive experience with the library director and the library staff, I never heard from the school again. Another interview with a university in the Deep South was a sham and downright hostile. Told that the interview would be informal, I was met by five staff members, two of whom seemed disinterested in me, and the other two of whom seemed to spend their time smirking at or challenging every comment I made. I fatally erred in the interview when I lightly said that the Internet was a "fun" research and educational tool for librarians and students, a medium for instruction and education that librarians shouldn't shy away from. It did not matter that I had proven my facility in cyberspace by constructing an elaborately linked Internet resource guide on endangered marine mammals, something that none of the practicing librarians at that table had even contemplated doing. My comments about the need for librarians to be cyber-literate were ignored. Instead, I was met with an incredulous "Fun?!" by the library director, who shortly thereafter left the interview.

Whatever the reason—and, granted, there's no way to say that my sexual orientation played any part in their hiring approach—it was obvious that standing out in any way was a bad idea. My impression—and one that has been reconfirmed by academic colleagues—is that the best interview strategy in an interview for an academic position is to blend in and to give the impression that one is not so creative as to rock any boats, all the while discussing "innovations" in a dry and pedantic tone. I've never managed to fade to gray convincingly and probably never will. For better or for worse, I have the kind of personality that attracts attention even when I'm being quiet.

In startling and inviting contrast, my experiences interviewing with public libraries were completely the opposite of those with academic institutions. I met more openly gay librarians, for one thing. I received congratulations for what I knew and encouragement for what I didn't know but was willing to learn. My homosexuality never felt like an issue in the interviewing and hiring process of public librarianship, although it didn't necessarily come up either. Still, I could tell during my interviews that those interviewing me had read my resume carefully. They must have known. And if they didn't, I was happy to help them along: I hesitated accepting the job I eventually took with San Antonio Public Library (SAPL), stating that I needed to consult with "my partner" first.

I'd like to claim that mentioning my partner was a bold political statement for me, but it wasn't in the least. More than anything, I brought him up out of true consideration and a tad of passive-aggressiveness. Having passed the two-year mark in our relationship, traits had turned into habits and eventually transformed into patterns. Both of us were changing and neither of us was willing or able to make the effort that enduring love requires. My partner was making key decisions about his life and not involving me, although they affected me. I could do the same, but I wanted to make a point. I made the effort to consult him, found out what I needed to know, and started packing up my life to move to a state that had only recently been featured on a network news magazine for its extreme anti-gay male violence. San Antonio, Texas, wasn't gay soul death, however, but what it was going to be, I could not tell. A year-and-a-half later, I would still feel befuddled by the town, especially in terms of its gay ethos. It looked like a big Sunbelt city—freeways, the requisite tall buildings, and strip development. But where was its spiritual-social nexus? What was its zeitgeist? And where were the other people like me, gay and otherwise? The two trips out for interviews and apartment hunting had yielded little information. I had taken the Gay Yellow Pages with me and hunted down some of the clubs and organizations listed. Everything seemed very scattered and no one at the gay switchboard returned my requests for information. There was no gay bookstore at that time, although there was possibly a feminist one that could lead the way. I reread the chapter on San Antonio in Neil Miller's *In Search of Gay America* and could only deduce that if I wasn't a Latina lesbian or didn't hang out in the parks, I would lead a pretty dull existence.

Then, during my second week there, I was surprised to discover during lunch that one of my colleagues was lesbian. I was taken aback that I could miss something so significant without her help. By week's end she had introduced me to another out lesbian, and the two then treated me to drinks at my first gay bar in San Antonio. While I was glad for the guidance, this bar didn't do much for my impression of gay life in the Alamo City. The meeting place looked like a modified doublewide mobile home, the same doublewide any honest southerner will admit to knowing all too well. One entered the bar through sliding glass doors and adjusted one's eyes to a dim, low-ceilinged room inhabited by one's older, country relatives, except that all of one's relatives seemed to have changed their gender roles: the men seemed more feminine, the women definitely more masculine.

Although I never quite bonded with these two lesbians, they were a godsend and soon had introduced me to other staff of our same persuasion at the library. The women, for the most part, seemed out and open. The men, on the flip side, were not open about or comfortable with their homosexuality, at least not with me. Then as well as now, a year-and-a-half later, only two male staff members have ever acknowledged officially to me their sexual orientation. This reticence on the part of the men to come out made me hesitate, too, and still does somewhat. The women, for a change, seem to have had it easier. There are more women first of all, and more lesbians among them, and these lesbians seem to have found a healthy way to be out even among their straight female colleagues, who seem equally accepting and comfortable with their lesbian colleagues. The men, however—gay or otherwise— are few and far between, and mostly older. A different generation perhaps, but this "standing in the shadows of love" seems, at times, to be bigger than all of us.

On the other hand, unlike earlier moments in life, this shadowland didn't spark panic attacks, staggering long-distance phone bills, or weekly therapy visits. I was too busy and the sun shined too brightly, naturally balancing my serotonin levels for the first time ever. I didn't have time to think about homosexuality, mine or anyone else's, personally or professionally. At this point in my life, I wasn't even sure how I felt about the contemporary expression of gayness, at least as it was being played out in the urban landscape of Washington, D.C., through which I had previously traveled.

I no longer was certain of what being gay meant, or, rather, I knew it did not mean to me what I was being told it should mean to me. I no longer wanted to receive my social validation by reading *The Advocate* and learning that Madonna or Elizabeth Montgomery thought it was OK for me to be gay. I no longer wanted to pretend to fathom "man-boy love" as a natural extension of the gay rights movement or sex with an assembly line of unremembered slabs of meat as a viable expression of my sexuality. I no longer desired to care about the music of the Gay Men's Chorus, comprehend the humor of Donelan, honor the endless requests for money for causes and candidates I had barely heard of, or pursue the hot man who couldn't talk about anything other than his gym routine, his disdain for effeminate men, and his sexual prowess.

I especially could not call myself queer, the mot du jour in politically correct labeling: no matter how one intellectually twisted that term, it was still understood by most people—including me—as an insult. I wasn't even sure I could call myself "gay"; it sounded so fluff-laden—the perfect accompaniment for the word "lifestyle," an equally silly-sounding term—and precisely what I was escaping from. Ill feelings had built up within me in Washington, enough to make me leave that life behind, in North Carolina and now in Texas. These feelings were strong enough to formulate into rejection of what I was being told was "my culture." If all this junk was how I should define myself, if this was what being gay meant, then I was ready to go back to being called homosexual. I wasn't about to start to look for a "gay cure," but I was willing to decline any alleged privileges of participation in what I perceived as an increasingly elitist, insignificant cultural identity.

Maybe my sense of taciturnity was caused by settling down in suburbia and midlife—and the feeling definitely grew stronger the longer I stayed in North Carolina and away from the major cities. Yet as I get older, I think a key component of figuring out one's homosexuality—or one's personal identity, period—is the act of throwing off the old lies and misconceptions we have about ourselves, handed down and slapped on us by unlearned others with no vested

interests in the outcome. Thus, for me the next step in dealing with my identity, gay
or otherwise, would involve throwing off everything that didn't fit, including the
doubtful gifts proffered to me so readily by those who claimed to understand me
and have my best interests at heart.

   Fortunately, I didn't have much time in San Antonio to ponder this philosophical abyss: we had a library to build from the ground up. I arrived soon after the
opening of the new Central Library, one of a flock of new librarians who responded
to the call for gainful employment in a state with moderate wages but no income
tax. We all were dazzled by the enchilada red architecture and lured by the siren
song of an opportunity to prove ourselves in the newly reorganized and automated
municipal library system.

   There was truly too much to do. The new building, designed by Ricardo
Legorreta, had sparked massive local, even national, attention, but the collections,
the services, and the automation weren't up to any of the staff's or public's
expectations. Local community groups and individuals were clamoring for a more
significant Latino representation in the collections of the library, when the reference
area—my department—didn't even have basic tools such as current business or
medical reference sources or online newspaper abstracts. The need for résumé
books and career guides was—and is—a bottomless pit in a city used to stable
civilian employment with five military bases, and suddenly faced with federal base
closings. People wanted Internet access and CD-ROMs providing advanced
business data and graphing capabilities. We the staff were trying to learn to crawl
while the public was ready for us to enter a marathon.

   I worked impossible, illegal schedules, eight, nine, ten days straight, spending
eight hours on the desk, learning to be a reference librarian on the job with only a
three-hour tour of the building separating chaos and me. Then at the end of the day,
I would drive eight miles out into the Great White North of San Antonio, to my
little apartment in the suburbs. From there I would stumble out on a hike in the Hill
Country, always trying to break my personal best of spotting more than five (live)
armadillos in a day. On brutally hot days—basically anytime from May through
September in South Texas—I'd thread my way through traffic to the malls, a
coffeehouse, or the movies, some place nice and safe and cool, where I was unlikely
to be asked for change (our copy machine wasn't operational yet) or for information
from some source that I remembered from library school but that we didn't own.
Sometimes I'd stay indoors and zone out to endless reruns of "Absolutely Fabulous"
on Comedy Central, lapsing into a temporary funk over my unglamourous and
drug-free lifestyle. That was the best I could do—survive. This wasn't librarianship, gay or otherwise: this was fast-food restaurant service with information on the
menu always in too-small or just-ran-out portions.

   Things settled down only with the hiring of a manager for our department. He
channeled the energy in all of us as best as possible. He gave us opportunity and
structure where before we only had confusion and tension, and he did so in the most
positive and supportive of ways. Within a matter of weeks, he enlisted the aid of the
staff to formulate workable schedules, he articulated a manifest destiny to weed the
collection and order new titles with relevance to our population's needs, and for

myself, he presented the perfect challenge: adult collection development for the library's new Latino Collection.

The Latino Collection has come to occupy more and more of my time as a librarian at San Antonio Public, and rightly so, as it has the potential to become an important cultural and educational resource for San Antonio and Bexar County's majority population. It has given me an intellectual focus and a purpose in librarianship. My original sense of purpose in library school had seen trammeling in job interviews and the first weeks of my job. Building the Latino Collection has offered me an opportunity to develop an important, precious resource from the ground up, to piece it together, book-by-book and policy-by-policy, and to make it balance healthily between reflecting our community's broad cultural interests and specific, nuanced information needs. It hits at the heart of what I wanted to accomplish as a librarian and in my life, providing useful services and relevant collections that accurately and joyously reflect human diversity. Plus—dare I say it?—it's been fun.

Despite living in one of America's most Latino cities, I was something of an aberration at San Antonio Public: a librarian with a knowledge of Spanish and an interest in the culture of Mexico and Mexican Americans. While I am no expert, I do have knowledge, especially about Mexico, and, more importantly, I have an interest in and a sensitivity to the issues. This is what I should do as a librarian, however—be interested in the interests of others, select materials to meet these interests, and help customers find their way to them.

But what can an Anglo gay man possibly understand about Mexican-American culture and experience? Quite a lot, I think, although there may seem to be several strikes against me: I'm not Latino, I'm not Roman Catholic, and I'm a gay man operating in what is perceived as a hyper-macho, anti-gay culture. In fact, I believe my homosexuality makes me, in many ways, an excellent librarian for the job. I would argue that my understanding of and sensitivity to Latino issues is directly born out of my homosexuality. Many people may not understand this connection, but I do: I know what it's like to have people dismiss and dislike me for the way I talk, look, and act, for what I believe in, how I live my life, and with whom I associate. That doesn't mean the two are completely interchangeable: I've had to abandon expectations and prejudices as I did when I acknowledged my homosexuality. I have learned to question myself and what I take for granted, and to build upon my insights to make this collection a source of education, information, entertainment, and pride for San Antonians.

Eleven months after I began my new duties as collection manager in this area, the Latino Collection officially opened with approximately 1,000 titles on the shelves, another 500 or so on order, an exhaustive collection development statement, and a funding level that had been tripled for the next fiscal year. This is not to imply that all has been light and breezy. It hasn't. Not everyone has been thrilled seeing an Anglo oversee the development of this collection, nor have they seen the natural parallel between gay oppression and Latino oppression. Still, I think many customers are just happy to see somebody in the library doing *something relevant for a change.*

In the middle of getting the Latino Collection under way, however, if anyone had asked me what gay librarianship meant, I couldn't have answered. In fact, I probably would have stared blankly and mumbled, "How I would I know? There are no gay people in San Antonio." Latino librarianship—yes; gay librarianship—apparently not. The gay in librarianship began to reveal itself only a year into my professional career. It did so with several rolling jolts, not unlike seismic shockwaves. Except that the plates slip-sliding against one another were the concepts and expectations I had acquired on my job and taken as gospel so quickly.

Of all people, I shouldn't have been so woefully ignorant, but I just had not been confronted with any real examples of the need for a gay understanding in public librarianship. Cal Gough discussed this in his seminal essay on gay collection development. Among the many salient points he made, he maintained that librarians who fail to buy gay books because they don't see a need in their community for them just aren't looking hard enough. I wasn't looking hard enough or just wasn't looking at the right time or in the right places. I can now make quite valid excuses for my ignorance—gay identity in San Antonio, for example, while not of the pre-Stonewall variety once perceived, is somewhat hidden. It's definitely hidden out in the suburban wilds beyond Loop 410, San Antonio's inner beltway, where I spent my first year. I didn't see a tell-tale rainbow flag on a car bumper until I moved into the gay-friendly Olmos Park area just north of downtown. There was, as I first perceived, no gay bookstore in San Antonio (although we were home to Shocking Gray, the gay and lesbian mail-order company) until about a year after I moved to town. I had tracked down the location of a few of the clubs but usually only went there if a gay friend was visiting from out-of-town. The only local gay media representations were of those men unfortunate enough to be caught on camera while giving each other head in public rest rooms, a feature on which local station KENS-TV seemed to be fond of focusing.

I could also plead pragmatism: how attuned is any librarian to a subject matter about which they are rarely asked? Gough asserts, however, that just because questions about gays and lesbians and homosexuality aren't being asked doesn't mean they're not on the minds of the customers. In one respect, at least, I was failing a basic tenet of librarianship: I was failing to perceive the real questions behind the questions being asked.

Moreover, I was still trying to figure out what a gay librarian should be. I had no role models on the job, other than the few out lesbians at work, none of whom I worked with directly and rarely saw in our massive, six-floor building. Was there going to be a stigma by being out at work? Was it even necessary? And what was my reason for wanting to be gay at work? Was it just so I could be in people's faces or was their a true relationship between homosexuality and librarianship?

I didn't want to be perceived as playing favorites either. Within my first few months of working at SAPL, the library had its first gay controversy. A local group wanting to develop a gay community center in town asked for and received meeting space at the library. The community center organizers advertised the upcoming meeting in the local daily. Soon the Central Library's Telephone Reference Department was being inundated with calls in protest of the meeting. Our library system director, June Garcia, and Central Library manager, Craig Zapatos, didn't back down, however. There were protests the day of the meeting along with a full complement of reporters and camera crews, but the meeting took place without further incident.

At least I finally had some evidence of gay life in this town, albeit clouded in controversy. I wasn't sure what to do next. If I took up the gay cause at work, what would be the repercussions for myself and for the library? I didn't want to be perceived as manipulating the collection for personal reasons. Wasn't there something in collection development class about this? Our library already seemed to have experienced that problem in the past as the collections were chock-a-block with specialized academic texts (a bibliography on the Ethiopian Coptic Church, for example) and too few hands-on, real-world, how-to-do-it books. While there were examples of texts on medieval music, a customer couldn't find out how to build or buy a house. The last thing this library needed, I told myself, was more irrelevance to community information needs. I concentrated on the Latino Collection and ducked my head back into my shell, but I soon changed.

Soon after the meeting held at the library regarding the gay community center, a friend, colleague, and fellow UNCG alum called me from the Telephone Reference Department. "There's a man on the phone by the name of Greg Tidwell. He wants to ask some questions about establishing a library at the gay community center. He started off by asking for a list of who all was gay at the library. I couldn't give him that, of course, but I remembered your interests from grad school and thought you could help. Would you mind talking with him?"

Greg was an intense, slow-talking, soft-spoken Tennessean who was very determined to have a library resource available at the new community center. He thought it would be very beneficial to those coming-out or trying to deal with their gayness to have a comfortable, safe place to look into books and other materials on homosexuality. During our conversation and at later meetings, he told me that he had felt a need for such a resource in San Antonio for some time, all the more so for his own deprivations growing up in small-town Tennessee.

Although he never said so directly, Greg obviously didn't think that our new and improved San Antonio Public Library was going to offer that comfortable, gay-friendly place. By not countering his underlying argument, I tacitly agreed. I had to admit that, at least as far as complete anonymity and a freedom from gawkers was concerned, a community center would reach the target population better than a massive public library would. Otherwise, we had a pleasant enough chat during which I outed myself and told him I would be interested in hearing more about his ideas for a library in the gay community center. I agreed to meet with him and another librarian from the University of Texas at San Antonio (UTSA) who also was interested in the community center library idea.

At that meeting held a couple of weeks later, I met my first gay librarian in San Antonio—finally, a role model. Stephen Sorensen was head of cataloging at the UTSA. He had moved to Texas after spending his life in the San Francisco Bay Area. He had the unmistakable look and appeal of Castro Street, a handsome man who was highly intelligent, funny, friendly, and extremely loquacious. At our first meeting, I was barely prepared for the volume or depth of questions he asked me about the library, my job, reference work, San Antonio, North Carolina, graduate school, my colleagues, the Latino Collection, everything. I knew we were going to be friends.

I now was becoming part of a circle in San Antonio, a circle that would introduce me to gay men, lesbians, and others interested in books, librarianship, and community development. I didn't know where it would lead, but I finally felt as though I was rooting myself to a community here. North Carolina seemed very far away and no longer that interesting. My relationship with my former partner was over; it was time to define myself, here and now. Other incidents helped me to understand gay librarianship. When a weeding project took me out from behind the desk and into the stacks, I learned a lot about the library's collection of gay and lesbian materials and its use by the public. The library actually had done a fair job over the years of collecting gay and lesbian nonfiction literature with what appeared to be a good balance between gay male and lesbian titles, and an emphasis on popular, rather than academic works. The only problem was finding some of the titles. Many of the titles listed on my shelf-list print-out were no longer on the shelves. I discovered books on gay and lesbian themes hidden in the stacks in other Dewey ranges or behind other books; I found the books among the piles of recently-circulated books awaiting reshelving; and some books had been stolen. Many of the gay and lesbian books had very high circulation or at least very high use, as evidenced by their tattered and torn condition. I was wrong: There was a community in San Antonio, and, despite the lack of questions, its members did want information from the public library.

In other words, gay and lesbian books were being used—and used a lot. Nobody was asking for them per se, but people were finding them, reading them, hiding them, checking them out, returning them, or keeping them. Perhaps, as Gough had suggested, I'd read the signals wrong. Perhaps in a city without a gay social or cultural center, a gay bookstore, or a vocal gay community, there was even more need for a strong gay and lesbian book collection. If I wasn't sure of this point, it was driven home to me near the end of my weeding tenure when a very angry young college student approached me with a complaint. She couldn't find any of the titles she wanted, all on the Nazi persecution of homosexuals. I wasn't surprised given our shelving situation. I tried to come up with alternate suggestions, even offering to bring her books from my personal collection. She was appeased by my attentiveness but still empty-handed and unrepentant. "It seems librarians are just really conservative and don't want these books in their collections," she said. Her taunt stuck and prompted my further examination of our gay and lesbian book collection over the next several weeks. In addition, it provoked me to question my perceptions of the San Antonio gay and lesbian community's information needs.

I compiled my findings in my weeding report, giving both factual and anecdotal evidence of what I had discovered, took a step out of my self-imposed closet, and handed the report in along with a stack of order slips for gay and lesbian books. My boss was more than happy that I wanted to order the titles; his only restrictions (which were more like instructions) were that I choose titles that would be useful to the public and avoided overly academic texts. The gay and lesbian issue didn't end there, however. Although the Latino Collection increasingly demands my time, I've taken it as a personal challenge to find materials on lesbian and gay Latinos for this special collection, as well as for our circulating collections. I am also trying to build for our library a collection of lesbian and gay reference resources, with the hope that customers will see these, use these, and feel comfortable enough to ask for more.

A small backlash, nonetheless real, perhaps inevitably occurred. It began in a completely different area of the collection—books on abortion. We had plenty of books on abortion, but according to one very persistent Sister at one of the city's many convents, not enough that discussed the opposing side of the abortion argument— abortion-as-murder. I didn't even know what we did have; again, my other professional demands hadn't allowed me to ponder the balance of the collection. This nun was going to make me deal with it now. Fine, I would examine the collection and buy more books to reflect all viewpoints on the issue. Abortion was an easy topic to objectify, since I had no personal investment in the issue.

But the rational high road was more elusive with regards to the gay issue. Soon after the abortion issue came to my attention, so did the gay issue. A man called my supervisor one day and offered to give him some books on homosexuality. As is our policy, my boss said he would be happy to receive them and leave the collection development decision to the librarian in charge of that area. He turned the volumes over to me, which consisted of two titles on saving oneself from homosexuality through belief in God, psychotherapy techniques, and group support such as that offered by Awakenings and other gay cure programs. This was a much thornier professional issue for me to handle than the previous one.

After I'd examined the titles, my first professional move to problem solving was to put them on my desk among the stacks of other books I had to process. I let them sit there for a week until I could face them a bit more objectively. I picked them up again and realized the relatively simple task was going to take more than a week. I let them sit there for another week, repeated the procedure, and realized that I could never be objective about these books and that I needed to make a decision.

I invited a colleague to examine the books; she was more matter-of-fact but shocked by the subject matter nonetheless. She suggested keeping one and getting rid of the other because someone had gone through the text to underline passages they felt made a particularly strong point against homosexuality. It was simple to her, much the way it had been for me on the abortion decision.

Later, I felt that I had passed on my professional responsibilities to someone else. How could I make up my own mind, and not let others do it for me, when the issues hit a sensitive area of my own life?

My boss must have sensed some hesitation and conflict on my part because he asked me how the books had been handled. He always trusts the staff's judgment on collection development matters unless we seek out his advice. "The guy who donated the books called. He wants to know if we're going to add them to the collection. Can you call him back?" I told him why I was hesitating, what the

books were like, and that as a gay man, I found them offensive and full of lies. I'd
hemmed and hawed about my homosexuality and never discussed it openly. He
looked at me sympathetically, "I can only imagine how difficult this is for you," he
said. "I know I would find it hard to make this decision if I were in your place. Just
do your best and call him back at some point."

From that point on, the issue has caused me no further distress. All it took was
understanding. Here was a man with a wife and two children who didn't flinch at
my homosexuality, who was willing to make the effort to understand how painful
a decision this was going to be for me, and yet who still trusted my judgment
enough to let me make the decision myself. Later that day, I reported back to him.
"I kept both of the books. One had markings in it, but so do a lot of our books.
One even had the organization's telephone number in it, but I didn't mark it out.
I figured I wouldn't mark out the number of an organization I agreed with, why
should I mark this out? Besides, if someone asked me for the number at a service
desk, I'd find it for them without any argument. 'Save the time of the reader.'
Ranganathan's law." "Good decision," he said.

Would other gay or lesbian collection managers have done the same?
Regardless, it's what I chose to do, and I think it was the right decision. In fact, it
was the ultimate professional challenge for me, to get beyond my own very strong
personal feelings and make a decision to support a community information need.
Whether I like it or not, there are people out there who don't want me to be gay.
On the other hand, I have spent so much of my life marking my time by someone
else's schedule. I have listened to so many opinions about who I should be, and
have become who I am anyway. So in all honesty, how could I ever stand in anyone
else's path to self-determination?

Beyond this fundamental lesson, gay librarianship came to have a much deeper
meaning in my life. As I mentioned earlier, I became involved in the library
committee for San Antonio's gay and lesbian community center. I met regularly
with Greg Tidwell, Steve Sorensen, and others and discussed what would be
visionary and what would be practical in such a library. We all agreed a li-
brary-type resource center would be beneficial to the community; we weren't sure
what would be the best form for this library to take, but we agreed that, in time, we
would be able to present a cogent proposal to the community center board.

The committee's work went on, much of the time without me because as a
public librarian, I had the most unmatchable schedule of all. I kept in touch through
e-mail with Steve Sorensen, who gradually became a friend. The fun was starting
to come back into my gayness without the attitude and pressure. It's the kind of fun
and satisfaction that comes with growing up. I'd aged five-plus years since I had
left Washington.

Steve directly and indirectly prompted me to get out of my house more and
explore San Antonio. The more I did get outside my house and outside the library,
the more I liked where I was, and who I was. I began making road trips to Austin
and Houston; I began thinking about and making plans for the next step in my
professional career and education; I began making friends, both gay and straight,
in and outside the library. I even began to get over my old relationship and start a

new one with a beautiful, caring man from Mexico, now a resident in the United States. Was this all Steve's doing? Who can say for sure? It may have all come about eventually anyway. Nevertheless, Steve triggered memories of the past—what I had, what I lost, what I wanted—and inspired me to slowly accept back into my life some of the happier aspects of gay living, which I had vanquished from memory since I left Washington. As the demands of the Latino Collection loomed, it was harder to keep in touch with Steve. He had encouraged me to get out, but I was unable, for whatever reason, to do the same for him. He seemed to resort to homebodiness. I wasn't doing much with the library committee either. I saw Greg with an acquaintance at brunch one Sunday, and he didn't speak to me or even seem to see me. It was an odd moment, but then Greg was an odd person. I knew he and Steve had had some sort of relationship—the nature of which I was never sure—and that it was now over. Was Greg aware of my friendship with Steve? Did it bother him? I never knew.

Steve told me one day that he had had a fight with Greg, not an argument, but an actual physical confrontation. After his work on the library committee, Steve had become a member of the gay and lesbian community center's board. Steve had never much cared for San Antonio and missed his old life back in the Bay Area; he thought though that his work with the community center was a sign that he should stay, and that he had a purpose here. Apparently, however, Greg had wanted to be nominated to the center board as well, and Steve failed to do so, for whatever reason. According to Steve and others, Greg slapped Steve at a board meeting and stormed out. Later, Steve resigned from the board and vowed that he was never going to have anything to do with Greg again. Although I heard these events recounted over the phone by Steve, I didn't pay much attention. It didn't seem of significance to Steve and smacked of the pettiness of gay community politics I had known all too well in Washington.

Steve's communications became scarcer. Again, I didn't think much of it because Steve was hard to pin down. He had health problems (diabetes) and had lived a hard, fast life in California from which he was still recovering emotionally. I didn't push too much. I was disappointed, but I was busy, so I did my best to check in—leave a message, drop an e-mail—to let him know I was available. I once told him I had been in his neighborhood and thought I would drop by unannounced to see him. He was very clear that I shouldn't do that, that he would rather I call first, and that I should never surprise him.

Soon after that, he sent me an e-mail relating how Greg had broken into his home recently, held him at knife-point with a butcher knife and scissors, beat him up, and threatened to kill him. Steve had managed to lock himself in his bedroom and call the police. Greg had been arrested and would have his day in court soon. The matter was settled, as far as Steve was concerned. Steve had a restraining order out against Greg; he wouldn't be bothered anymore. I was shocked by the news and concerned for Steve's well-being, but I took him at his word that he was safe. Two weeks later I was watching the 9 o'clock news and as soon as I heard that two people had been killed in the UTSA library, I knew what had happened. I didn't even need to know their sexes, names, or ages: I knew. Why I or Steve or anyone else hadn't suspected as much would happen beforehand, I don't know. But when it was revealed that Greg had walked into Steve's office at 4:30 p.m. on Monday, August 26, 1996, the day before his court date, shut the door behind him, fired four shots into Steve's chest and head with a five-chamber, snub nose .38-caliber revolver and then another into himself, it all made perfectly horrible sense to me.

It took me a few weeks to get over the restless sleep and bad dreams, none of which I could ever remember clearly after I woke up. I spent a month or two battling this irrational fear that Greg was going to come after me next because I was friends with Steve. I had to remind myself that Greg was dead. And so was Steve. I still feel a little unnerved when I go into a restaurant and realize I was last here with Steve, or when I see the gay community center advertise for volunteers on the public access channel, or when I pull Steve's business card out of my wallet, instead of my own, to give to a library customer.

But whenever I doubt the effect that books, information, libraries, or professional librarianship can have on people's lives, I think about Steve and Greg. Steve felt cataloging was his life's calling; he made it an exciting, intellectual enterprise. He believed cataloging provided a conduit for him to provide access to all the books librarians bought for the public. Greg had a vision of library access, as well, to make relevant library materials available on gay and lesbian subjects to those who most needed them, where they most needed them, in a comfortable, safe place. Greg lacked the librarian's professional body of knowledge, but he certainly possessed the librarian's sense of mission.

I wonder how differently Greg's and Steve's lives would have turned out if only Greg had had access to the materials he needed growing up that would have helped him cope more effectively with his homosexuality. While I don't subscribe totally to the belief that librarians are social workers, I do believe that, at least in public libraries, we are social service providers. Librarians need to divine what the community's information needs are, for even if they are never expressed, they are there. Librarians also need to remember what it's like to be human and desperately seeking something that will help us make sense of our lives. Families and friends can potentially provide some direction to those already able to articulate those needs, but lacking self-knowledge and confirmation, books and service-oriented librarians can help in the articulation and discovery process.

I am guilty of forgetting the librarian's spiritual and social mission all too often, being by nature a bit too fact-oriented for my own good. Information becomes a commodity all too easily, something given out to appease one person so that one can move on to deal with the next. It's hard for me to remember the potential of the library and information profession on a day cluttered with mundane inanities. It's especially hard to have any concept of the meaning or significance of gay librarianship or even gay life, after a day of invisibility in the non-profit closet, an evening of negative media portrayals of gays and lesbians, or the unwitting mimickry of the worst stereotypes in some of our "social" behavior.

I still can't claim to agree with much of the contemporary expression of gay and lesbian identity. I support any lesbigay person's right to choose what's best for him or her, but I continue to question the wisdom behind conventional urban gay culture and politics. Nevertheless, despite my kvetching, it is important to remember that lives are at stake. Literally. One book available at the age of six, twelve, or twenty-four may not have stopped Greg Tidwell from murdering Steve Sorensen or from killing himself. But then again, who's to say that a book placed in the right hand, a helpful attitude conveyed, or a few accurately placed subject headings wouldn't have stopped the pain and confusion and opened up a world of understanding and acceptance for Greg or countless others? I'd like to think so. Such thoughts keep me running and remind me that the work I do does have significance. I am not just a man in a paper hat taking orders for information. As a gay man, I have an important place in this culture; as a librarian, I have a career; as a gay librarian, I have a mission—to provide access to gay and lesbian materials that I hope will satisfy customers' needs, informational or otherwise.

Index

About the Editor and Contributors

JOHN A. BARNETT is reference librarian at the downtown campus of the University of Texas at San Antonio. He graduated from the Department of Library and Information Studies, the University of North Carolina at Greensboro in 1995, and served as a reference librarian at the San Antonio Public Library from 1995 to 1997.

JUDY BRADFORD is Director of the Survey Research Laboratory, Center for Public Policy, Virginia Commonwealth University. She has conducted many studies on sexual orientation, AIDS, and AIDS-related issues.

JAMES V. CARMICHAEL, JR. is an Associate Professor in the Department of Library and Information Studies at The University of North Carolina at Greensboro. Since joining the faculty in 1989, he has taught Information Sources and Services, The Academic Library, Humanities and Social Sciences Bibliography, Advanced Information Sources and Services, and Special Collections and Archives. He received his education at Emory University (B.A., French, 1969; M.Ln., 1977) and the University of North Carolina at Chapel Hill (Ph.D., 1988). Before 1977, he was a bank assistant. He has written extensively in the field of southern library history, gender issues, southern female library biography, and in the past several years has addressed the lesbigay and gender image problems of librarianship through several exploratory studies. He served as Chair of the Library History Round Table of the American Library Association in 1994-1995.

JANET COOPER was a founding member of the American Library Association's Task Force on Gay Liberation. She received an ALA-accredited library degree from Simmons College in 1965, and worked both as a practicing librarian and library educator. Since 1978, she has earned her living as a cab driver in Boston.

ISRAEL D. FISHMAN was the founder of the American Library Associations Task Force on Gay Liberation. After receiving his Master's degree from Columbia University, Fishman worked for several years as a Public Services Librarian in a university library. Since he left librarianship in 1974, Fishman has lived in Brooklyn with his lover, Carl Navarro. Since 1974, Fishman has worked as a masseur, a tour guide of historic Brooklyn, and in various forms of therapeutic and holistic healing. He currently operates (with Navarro) a printing business out of their apartment.

DONALD H. FORBES received his Master's degree from the Department of Library and Information Studies at the University of North Carolina at Greensboro in 1997. He is a musician and composer and worked for the Jet Propulsion Laboratory in California for many years. He is currently employed at Guilford Technical and Community College (Jamestown, NC) as a librarian/instructor.

BARBARA GITTINGS has been a well-known activist for gay liberation most of her life, and with her partner, Kay Lahusen, has supported herself by a variety of means so that she could participate fully in the struggle for gay equality. She was coordinator of the American Library Association's Task Force for Gay Liberation (now called the Gay, Lesbian, and Bisexual Task Force) from 1971 to 1986. She has received awards from nearly every national gay organization indicating long and sustained service as a gay activist: Integrity (1976), National Gay Health Coalition (1979), Gay Academic Union (1979), Lambda Legal Defense and Education Fund (1983), the Hetrick-Martin Institute (1989), Human Rights Campaign Fund (1992), Uncommon Legacy Foundation (1994), Association of Lesbian and Gay Psychiatrists (1994), and the Gay, Lesbian and Bisexual Task Force of the American Library Association (1995), plus many other recognitions for outstanding service at the regional and local level. She founded the first East Coast Chapter of the Daughters of Bilitis in 1958, and edited the first national lesbian magazine *The Ladder*, from 1963 to 1966. She is a charter member of the Boards of Directors of both the National Gay Task Force (since 1973) and the Gay Rights National Lobby (since 1976).

MARGARET ROSE GLADNEY is an Associate Professor of American Studies at the University of Alabama. Her collection of correspondence from Civil Rights activist, playwright, and author Lillian Smith was published in 1993 by the University of North Carolina Press under the title *How Am I to Be Heard? Letters of Lillian Smith*.

CAL GOUGH is Adult Materials Selection Specialist in the Collection Management Unit of the Atlanta-Fulton Public Library. He has served in a variety of capacities with the Gay, Lesbian and Bisexual Task Force of the American Library Association in the past fifteen years. He is perhaps best known for co-editing with Ellen Greenblatt *Gay and Lesbian Library Service*, now under revision for a second edition.

RICHARD L. HUFFINE received his Masters degree in Library and Information Studies from the University of North Carolina at Greensboro. He is currently an Internet services librarian for Garcia Consulting Incorporated.

JIM KEPNER (1923–1997) was the founder of the International Gay and Lesbian Archives now housed at The University of Southern California, and one of the early actvists, writers, and instructors in ONE, Inc., publisher of one of the earliest gay magazines, *ONE*. (He sometimes wrote under pseudonyms, not for reasons of anonymity, but so readers would think the ONE staff was larger than it was.) A volume of his groundbreaking editorials, *Rough News, Daring Views: 1950s Pioneer Gay Press Journalism*, was published in 1998 by Harrington Park Press.

NORMAN G. KESTER, a professional librarian and social sciences selector at the Mississauga Library System in Ontario, Canada, is editor of *Liberating Minds: The Stories and Professional Lives of Gay, Lesbian, and Bisexual Librarians and Their Advocates*. He is also a contributor to the forthcoming *Civil Rights, Libraries, and Black Librarianship* edited by John Mark Tucker and is a columnist with the national library press of the Canadian Library Association *Feliciter*. "Queer Histories/Queer Librarians" was originally presented at the seventh annual queer conference, "Forms of Desire," sponsored by the Center for Lesbian and Gay Studies (CLAGS), City University of New York, April 1997. His work in progress includes *I, Moffie: A South African-Canadian Queer Memoir of Loss, Madness, Love and Desire.*

KAY TOBIN LAHUSEN was a research assistant in the reference library of *The Christian Science Monitor* from 1956 to 1961. In 1961, she met Barabara Gittings at a regional meeting of the Daughters of Bilitis, and they have been together ever since. Through the years, Lahusen has engaged in a variety of work ranging from editing and free-lance photography to selling real estate, all so that she and Gittings could devote more time to gay activism. At the meetings of the ALA's Task Force for Gay Liberation from 1970 to 1986, Lahusen was nearly always present with her camera—an unofficial chronicler of Task Force history. She and Gittings now live in semi-retirement in Wilmington, Delaware.

BRENDA J. MARSTON went to Kalamazoo College in Michigan, studied at the University of Dakkar in Senegal for a year, and earned masters degrees in U. S. Women's History and Library and Information Science at the University of Wisconsin-Madison. She worked at the State Historical Society of Wisconsin and in 1989 moved to Ithaca, NY, where she is the Curator of the Human Sexuality Collection and Women's Studies Selector at Cornell University Library.

CHRIS PARKIN is a professional philosopher with special interests in ethics, politics, and law and feminist theory. He taught for over thirty years at the Victoria University in Wellington, and currently teaches medical ethics at the Wellington School of Medicine. In the late 1950s and early 1960s he was involved in law reform initiatives in the UK. A founder-member of the New Zealand Homosexual Law Reform Society, he was its president for a number of years. He has undertaken educational work about sexuality and sexual orientation with campus and adult education groups, church committees and marriage guidance counselors, and teacher and police training colleges, among others. He was an active supporter of the active gay rights coalition, with an early involvement in its resource centre. He joined HUG (Heterosexuals Unafraid of Gays) in its infancy—he is a straight man—and worked for the successful passage of the New Zealand sexual orientation anti-discrimination law through HUG as well as within, both as a supporter and a trustee, the Lesbian and Gay Rights Centre. He was one of the founding trustees of the Lesbian and Gay Archives of New Zealand Trust, and is currently chair of the trust board. He finds relaxation with his harp, his cats, his CD collection, and his running shoes.

PHIL PARKINSON is Senior Librarian, Early Maori Imprints Project, in the Alexander Turnbull Library, a research library within the National Library of New Zealand, Wellington, New Zealand, and has been Honorary Curator of the Lesbian and Gay Archives of New Zealand (LAGANZ) since its creation in 1988. From 1981 until the creation of LAGANZ, he was the Administrator of the Lesbian and Gay Rights Resource Centre. He was actively involved in the gay movement through the Gay Task Force (1984–1988), the Pink Triangle Publishing Collective (1981–1989), the New Zealand AIDS Foundation (1983–1995), the National Council on AIDS (1988–1994), the Gay Broadcasting Collective, and several other groups. His major current work is a critical bibliography of works in and about the Maori language from 1815 to 1900, and he is also preparing a thesis on the history of the printing activities of the New Zealand mission of the Church Missionary Society from 1807 to 1870.

LOUISE S. ROBBINS is Associate Professor and Director of the School of Library and Information Studies at the University of Wisconsin-Madison, where she has been a faculty member since 1991. A Ph.D. graduate of the Texas Women's University, her research interests center on libraries and the library profession as part of the social matrix, especially during the McCarthy period. Her explorations both reflect on and inform her long-standing interest and participation in politics. The first woman to run for the Ada, Oklahoma, City Council, Robbins was, in addition, the first woman to serve as mayor. She and her husband, Orville, were active in groups promoting civil rights and women's rights during their years in Ada. Her most recent work centers on the intersections of race, gender, and politics in a 1950 censorship case. The "Indiscreet" Miss Brown and the Bartlesfield Public Library: Racism and Censorship in Cold War Oklahoma (working title) has been accepted for publication by the University of Oklahoma Press. Robbins is active in ALA's Library History Round Table, serving as 1997–1998 Chair. She currently teaches Government Information Sources, User Education, and a doctoral seminar on Library and Information Science Education.

CAITLIN RYAN has worked in lesbian and gay health issues for more than twenty years. She conducts research on sex orientation and health. Her latest book is *Gay and Lesbian Youth: Care and Counseling*.

POLLY J. THISTLETHWAITE volunteered at the Lesbian Herstory Archives from 1986 until 1996 while employed by day as a librarian at New York University (1986-1990) and Hunter College (1990-1997). She now lives in Denver, Colorado and works at the Colorado State University Morgan Library in Fort Collins. During the late 1980s and 1990s she was a member of the Women's Caucus of ACTUP/New York, which produced *Women, AIDS and Activism*. Other publications include *Not Just Passing Through*, a 53-minute documentary about lesbian history and activism . She also wrote the entry "Lesbian and Gay Library History" for *The Encyclopedia of Library History* and co-authored with Daniel Tsang the entry for "Lesbian, Gay, Bisexual and Transgender Entries" for the eighth edition of *Magazines for Libraries*.

CHRISTINE L. WILLIAMS is Associate Professor of Sociology at the University of Texas, Austin. She is the author of *Gender Differences at Work: Men and Women in Nontraditional Occupations* and *Still a Man's World: Men Who Do "Women's Work."* She is currently working on a study of sexuality and sexual harassment in the workplace.

Lightning Source UK Ltd.
Milton Keynes UK
UKOW02n1453241115

263413UK00007BA/87/P